Warfare Witness

'*Warfare Witness* offers sane biblical guidance for Christian engagement in the invisible war that rages between God and the Devil. In contrast to many misguided strategies for spiritual warfare-one thinks of spiritual mapping, words of knowledge, binding demons, and the like-Stan Gale shows what the Bible really teaches about the attacks of Satan and defending against them. His approach to spiritual warfare is centered on Christ, rooted in church history, and focused on the ordinary means of grace that the Holy Spirit uses to save people in Christ: prayer and the ministry of God's Word.'

Philip Graham Ryken
Senior Minister, Tenth Presbyterian Church, Philadelphia
Bible Teacher, Alliance of Confessing Evangelicals

'Stan Gale reminds us that the Gospel of Jesus Christ is not a Gospel of peace and joy only, but of the Kingdom of God, and power for living, and an advancing reign of righteousness, peace, and joy which we are privileged to enter and to proclaim. Here are the believer's marching-orders in the spiritual warfare. This book will shake up your understanding of the Christian life and point you toward an exhilarating mission of seeing God work in you in ever-new and ever more surprising ways. Read this book; but don't just read it: take up the challenge Dr Gale holds out to us. As he assures us from the Word of God, the adversary, though formidable, is bound, and all his house is open for the plundering.'

T. M. Moore
Pastor of Teaching Ministry,
Cedar Springs Presbyterian Church, Knoxville

Warfare Witness

Contending with Spiritual Opposition
in Everyday Evangelism

Stanley D. Gale

CHRISTIAN FOCUS

Copyright © Stanley D. Gale 2005

ISBN 1-84550-079-2

10 9 8 7 6 5 4 3 2 1

This edition published in 2005
by
Christian Focus Publications Ltd.,
Geanies House, Fearn,
Ross-shire, IV20 1TW, Scotland

www.christianfocus.com

Cover design by Alister MacInnes

Printed and bound by
CPD, Wales

Contents

I Enlistment

II Equipment

III Engagement

Stanley D. Gale has been married to his wife, Linda, since 1975. They have four children. He holds Bachelor of Arts and Master of Education degrees from the University of Delaware, a Master of Divinity degree from Westminster Theological Seminary in Philadelphia, and a Doctor of Ministry degree from Covenant Theological Seminary in St. Louis. He is an ordained minister in the Presbyterian Church in America and has served his current charge in West Chester, Pennsylvania since 1988. He has written a number of articles and taught in the area of practical theology. In 2002 he launched a ministry of prayer-based outreach called Community Houses of Prayer with the publication of *Community Houses of Prayer Ministry Manual: Reaching Others for Christ through Strategic Prayer* (Deo Volente Publications). The following year he developed a website (www.CHOPministry.net) to provide support for those starting and leading that ministry in their local settings.

To my children,
Samantha, Luke, Sarah and Nathan,
whom God has used to keep me on my toes
and on my knees.

Acknowledgements

I owe special thanks to Phil Douglass for his turning my attention to the subject of spiritual warfare in evangelism, to T. M. Moore for his godly example and instruction, and to Archie Parrish for teaching me much about prayer and spiritual opposition. I am especially indebted to my congregation for supporting me in the writing of this book. I have greatly appreciated Larry Woodruff for his continual encouragement to bring this book to print. I am grateful to Don Nicholson for his provision of a place conducive to writing and for his living illustration of kingdom kindness.

Finally, I would like to express my indebtedness to Willie MacKenzie and Christian Focus Publications for their investment in this work, and especially to Philip Ross for his helpful suggestions and patient editorial work that made for a much improved book.

Foreword

As this fine book was in preparation, Stanley Gale's country and her allies were at war in Iraq. The critical early days of that war, like other recent conflicts, appeared nightly on the television screens of virtually every home in the western world and beyond. Yet it is only when we pass through extra security measures at an airport, pay more to fill up the fuel tank in the car, or—most poignantly of all—watch the flag-draped coffin of a young man being borne to its resting place by his comrades, that we feel the war encroaches on life in the homeland. The daily routine for most of us seems largely the same. The war is on, but it is 'somewhere out there'. Such is the reality of our times.

But these events serve as an allegory for the church. We are at war, engaged in a mighty spiritual battle. But this war, as Stanley Gale reminds us, is being fought in the homeland. Indeed, it seems a latter day Trojan horse is already within the gates. Enemy activity is already present within the city of God. Meanwhile many of us sleep unaware or heedless of the call to wrestle with principalities and powers, the forces of spiritual darkness in the heavenly realm. For Christ is building his church in territory occupied by forces antagonistic to his kingdom. We are confident they will not prevail. Yet if we are to remain standing against their onslaughts and ultimately share in Christ's victory, we must learn—as Paul encourages us—that our weapons are not material but spiritual.

It is just here that Stanley Gale provides us with wise counsel, well rooted in Scripture and dispensed from a concerned pastoral heart. He helps us to think about our Christian witness in the world; he underlines the importance of our fellowship in the church. He calls us to recognize the importance of prayer. In doing so, he 'scratches where we itch'. More than that, he painfully exposes a festering wound in the life of many churches where gatherings for corporate prayer, if they even take place, are often the most sparsely attended. Without realizing what has happened, we have been disarmed and, indeed, deeply wounded. And perhaps the most severe blow of all is that the weapon John Bunyan (using Paul's language) called 'All-prayer' has been snatched from our grasp without us feeling the loss.

We need someone with a concern for the church and a pastor's love for it to speak to us about these things. This is exactly what Stanley Gale does. In addition to giving helpful counsel on such themes as personal witness, the life of fellowship, prayer, and other vital themes, he sounds the reveille in our ears to awaken us to serve with renewed vigour in the King's army.

I hope that his counsel will be a significant help to many and that all will heed his call.

Sinclair B Ferguson
Westminster Theological Seminary
Dallas, Texas

Preface

Though this world with devils filled,
should threaten to undo us.
Were not the right man on our side,
the man of God's own choosing.
For still our ancient foe,
doth seek to work us woe;
his craft and power are great,
and armed with cruel hate.

Those are words from Martin Luther's sixteenth century hymn, 'A Mighty Fortress.' They speak of a worldview, a perspective on life that knows of a spiritual dimension, fraught with danger—a world in which we live, grow, and serve.

In this world, as children of God and soldiers of the cross, we face opposition, both in our growth in spiritual maturity and our work for the cause of Christ. Satan desires our demise. He seeks to thwart us at every turn, standing against us because we stand with Christ.

Not only do we find in these words a worldview with a spiritual realm and a theology of spiritual conflict, we discover a theology of victory. We are reminded where our victory is found. Jesus Christ came into this world to destroy the works of the devil. The Son of God became incarnate as a human being to deliver us from evil and to usher us into his eternal kingdom of righteousness, joy, and peace.

Yet our enemy, the devil, continues to this day to oppose us. We are no match for him. Our strength is in the Lord and his mighty power. Satan, the prince of this age, cannot depose him who sits on the throne, alive, as one crucified. Neither angels nor demons can ultimately harm us who repose in him. Yet while we are in this world, we experience and encounter him whose craft and power are great, and fueled by cruel hate for Christ and for us who know and serve him.

But what does it mean that devils oppose us? What do they look like? What are their tactics to oppose us? How do we deal with them?

God has not left us without instruction on the subject of the spiritual opposition we face and how we are to wage spiritual warfare. In fact, the Bible is full of the counsel of God to equip us for the task. Spiritual conflict forms the backdrop against which we understand life, the work of Christ, and our work of ministry in this present age.

When we open God's Word in the beginning, we find ourselves stationed at the tree of the knowledge of good and evil, looking on to witness the encounter of the serpent with Adam and Eve. There we witness his tactics. His counsel betrays his intentions. We are granted access that Job himself did not enjoy into the throne room of the Sovereign Lord Almighty, where we are privy to the celestial conversation of Satan seeking the permission of God for his nefarious intent. We may be surprised to see that God grants that permission! At the same time we wonder at the relationship of the holy and all-good God to a fallen angelic being known as the evil one. In the book of Zechariah we are shown Joshua the high priest standing before the throne of God. Our gaze is directed to God's right hand where we see Satan leveling accusations against Joshua. Clearly, our God wants us take note of something, both about Satan and about God himself who acts for his own.

It is for good reason we are informed that 'our enemy the devil prowls around like a roaring lion looking for someone to devour.' Our alertness heightens as we realize that prowling ground is where we live. We shift nervously as our Lord Jesus makes us aware that 'Satan has asked' to sift Peter as wheat. But Peter finds protection in the intercession assured him by Christ. Does that apply to us as well? It is not without purpose that Jesus identifies Satan as the culprit, the thief of the seed of the gospel sown in the hearts of those hearing. How do we deal with his thievery, knowing that the seed of the gospel is spread from our hand?

In these and a multitude of other scenarios and explanations, God is giving us a profile of our enemy and a feel for life in his shadow. In so doing, his intention is not to create intrigue or to satisfy morbid curiosity. Rather, God is equipping us for kingdom living and service in 'this world with devils filled'. In our spiritual growth and in our kingdom work we will face a foe. We will have to contend with his opposition. But what does that opposition look like and how do we deal with it?

Pick up a popular book on the subject and you will get answers to these questions, answers that claim to reflect God's teaching in his holy Word. More than likely you will be instructed to bind the devil and how to go about it. You may be armed with figurative spectacles of faith by which you can detect the enemy, just as infrared goggles allow soldiers to see the enemy through the veil of darkness. Fascinating stories may be told and Scripture brought to bear in support of the stories' messages.

The question is, do these popular writings accurately reflect the perspective God gives us on the subject? Do these popular writings fit us with God's plan and provisions for addressing the spiritual opposition to which he alerts us? Or, like Saul putting his adult armor on the boy David, are we provided with the way that seems right, but it will not profit us for engagement with the enemy in God's way?

Spiritual warfare is a popular topic. No shortage of books address the subject. Most, however, seem to approach the topic from a perspective that steps over the boundaries of biblical precept. Often, Scripture is brought to serve fanciful ideas of demonic hierarchy, devilish monikers, and spiritual assault. Rather than developing the important topic of spiritual warfare from a biblically-founded, biblically-balanced view, it is drawn from extra-biblical ideas, with God's Word brought to the service of human notions.

While most popular literature on the subject tends to excess, the Reformed camp has tended to neglect. The former rightly lays hold of the reality and activity of spiritual opposition to the work of evangelism, but carries it to biblically unwarranted extremes. The latter also recognizes the legitimacy of spiritual opposition to the evangelistic endeavor, but then for all practical purposes ignores it. The sobriety and biblical studiousness of such seventeenth century Puritan works as William Gurnall's *The Christian in Complete Armour*, Thomas Brooks' *Precious Remedies Against Satan's Devices*, Isaac Ambrose's *The Christian*

Warrior, and John Bunyan's *The Holy War* has been conspicuously missing in our day.

This book seeks to understand and address the spiritual opposition believers face in reaching others for Christ with data and direction drawn from God's Word rather than brought to it. Specifically, we will address spiritual opposition for the work of gospel witness to which our Lord Jesus Christ calls us. There will be overlap in understanding and dealing with spiritual opposition in our sanctification. The enemy we face in our growth in Christ is the same enemy we face in our service to Christ. His goals and tactics are similar. But our concern will be to address spiritual warfare in our every day encounters with others for the sake of the gospel. As is the case with the popular literature, so is the case here: what is presented should be held up to the plumb line of God's Word. Only that which survives biblical scrutiny is worthy of embrace and provides firm ground on which to gain solid footing for spiritual battle.

> Did we in our own strength confide,
> Our striving would be losing;
> Were not the right Man on our side,
> The Man of God's own choosing;
> Dost ask who that may be?
> Christ Jesus, it is He;
> Lord Sabaoth, his name,
> From age to age the same,
> And he must win the battle.

Jesus has won the war, as only he could. There remains, however, a battle afoot. It involves us. It qualifies our life and mission. It directs our efforts and maps out our plan of attack. Let us seek to understand it that we might give glory to the incarnate Lord of Hosts as we serve under the banner of his victorious and eternal kingdom.

Introduction

'Well, I think God helps those who help themselves. On top of that, God is full of love and compassion. He will surely smile on people as long as they make a sincere effort.' Across the table from you sits Betty, your next-door neighbor. For months you have been working to build a relationship with her so that you can share your faith in Jesus Christ. You've had conversations before, but now your discussion seems to be moving to a whole new level. It's taken some time, but Betty is sharing her deep faith convictions. How do you respond to her, preserving your relationship yet correcting her error? Do you just let loose and lay it on the line? Where does she get these ideas anyway? Exactly what are you up against as you enter her world to speak of salvation in Christ? How can you possibly be an influence for Christ in her life? What tactics and resources has God put at your disposal?

Your church has adopted a mission statement that targets a particular geographic region for outreach with the gospel of life in Jesus Christ. God's Word informs you that the congregation will face spiritual opposition as they seek to reach the area for Christ. There are demons present, demons intent on thwarting your efforts, demons opposing you because they oppose Christ. How do you deal with this spiritual opposition? Do you offer a Sunday School class on exorcism? What strategy do you use? What battle plan do you put to work? What sort of power is involved?

Scripture leaves us with no doubt about the spiritual conflict inherent in evangelism. The description the Apostle Paul gives us clearly characterizes the work of witness as contending with spiritual opposition.

> For our struggle is not against flesh and blood, but against
> the rulers, against the authorities, against the powers of
> this dark world and against the spiritual forces of evil in
> the heavenly realms. Therefore put on the full armor of
> God, so that when the day of evil comes, you may be able
> to stand your ground, and after you have done everything,
> to stand. Stand firm then, with the belt of truth buckled
> around your waist, with the breastplate of righteousness
> in place, and with your feet fitted with the readiness that
> comes from the gospel of peace. In addition to all this, take
> up the shield of faith, with which you can extinguish all
> the flaming arrows of the evil one. Take the helmet of
> salvation and the sword of the Spirit, which is the word
> of God. And pray in the Spirit on all occasions with all
> kinds of prayers and requests. With this in mind, be alert
> and always keep on praying for all the saints. Pray also for
> me, that whenever I open my mouth, words may be given
> me so that I will fearlessly make known the mystery of the
> gospel, for which I am an ambassador in chains. Pray that
> I may declare it fearlessly, as I should.
>
> Eph. 6: 12–20

Paul's mission takes place in the same plane as does ours, on this side of the fall, on this side of the cross, on the same field of battle. The enemy is the same. The nature of the conflict is the same. The goal is the same. Our God outfits us with the same weapons.

Clearly, there is spiritual opposition with which we have to deal as we reach out to Betty and as the church ventures into its targeted mission field. The question is, how do we understand that opposition and how do we engage it for the cause of Christ?

A large body of literature on the subject would have us adopt a particular tact for our work of witness. Allow me to sketch it out in a broad way.[1] First, these writers want us to recognize an army of evil forces, organized in a chain of command. One author puts it this way:

> The only way I can imagine that Satan can effectively
> blind 3 billion minds is to delegate the responsibility. He
> maintains a hierarchy of demonic forces to carry out his
> purposes. Exactly what that hierarchy is we may never
> know, but we do have some general indications. Perhaps
> our clearest hint is found in Ephesians 6: 12 where we are

told we wrestle not against flesh and blood, but against (1) principalities, (2) powers, (3) rulers of the darkness of this age, and (4) spiritual hosts of wickedness in the heavenly places.[2]

The importance of understanding this chain of command, we are told, is so that we deal more effectively with demons in their areas of control. Presumably, the higher the rank, the greater the territory, the bigger the catch.

This literature contends that each area is presided over by a territorial demon[3], one who has claim to a locality and reigns over it. It is his turf. He has hung out his sign. Spiritual warfare is typically conducted through spiritual mapping, divinely aided spiritual reconnaissance that identifies the demons in charge and traces out their formations and strongholds. Such mapping compares to calculating exact coordinates for the laser-guided precision of our spiritual weapons, so that smart bombs of binding can be launched. One writer suggests 'we need the highest precision of aim to hit the enemy at his most vulnerable point. Wisdom in battle is to win the victory without wasting ammunition.'[4]

This spiritual mapping is pursued through corporate prayer. The idea is that once we have a divinely dispensed 'word from God,' we can then bind the enemy and loose the occupied territory. Leverage is gained over the territorial demons by naming them. In binding them, we are freed to enter the region with the gospel. The model of Jesus is held up for us to follow. In Luke 8: 26ff., Jesus asked the demon its name. The answer was 'Legion.' Just as Jesus bound the strongman (Matt. 12: 26ff.) so that his territory could be looted, so are we to go and do likewise. Our binding and loosing are accomplished through agreement in prayer (Matt. 18: 18ff.).

In this approach, the Bible is appealed to, but are the conclusions the Bible's? While doing the church great service in sounding the battle cry for spiritual warfare in evangelism, some of these writers have overstepped the bounds drawn for them by Scripture. In some cases, seeds of biblical truth have been developed to grow up into plants of a different species. In other cases, the wheat of valid, biblically-founded points is intermingled, and even overgrown, with the weeds of unbiblical error or caricature. At least three overlapping reasons make the conclusions suspect and raise considerable cause for caution, all of which are pathways leading away from the firm foundation of God's written revelation into the quicksand of fanciful imaginations and machinations.

First is the tendency on the part of some writers to look for understanding and direction beyond the pages of Holy Scripture, which God himself assures us is sufficient for all of doctrine and life. One way this tendency is expressed is to give experiential anecdote authoritative legitimacy with biblical revelation. What that means is, if we see it happen, that must be the way it works. The literature abounds with personal stories used to establish, buttress or validate concepts. Instead of interpreting experience by biblical precept, it is often given equal (or even more real and relevant) footing as the traditions of men over the Word of God.

Another way extra-biblical revelation is seen is in the frequent use the literature makes of phrases like 'God told me.' Immediate revelations from God and 'words of knowledge' are common elements in gaining spiritual discernment for conducting spiritual warfare. Fresh revelation provides ability to spiritually canvas a city or region and determine the spirits at work. Or, it may be that direct revelation from God allows us entrance into a person's life. We find examples of evangelists remarkably learning something hidden in a person's heart, exposing it in his or her hearing, with the result of that person professing faith—a profession even without benefit of the presentation of the gospel, but on the sheer glamour of revelation of the once-hidden secret. The result is some sort of faith, but faith in what?

The second pitfall is method of interpretation. In some cases a whole theology seems to be built on the use of a single term or on some inherent mysticization of Greek, the original language of the New Testament scriptures. Is it true that the Greek word for 'wilderness' is known as territory of Satan, into whose turf Jesus moved for spiritual warfare? Are the semantic domains of certain words such that we are justified in using interchangeably the terms 'overcome,' 'conquer,' or 'bind' when we describe our activity in taking the offense against the enemy in spiritual warfare? Do words mean all things they could in all cases, regardless of context?[5] Is one of the key texts for understanding the 'territoriality of spirit beings' founded on a Dead Sea scroll discovered in Cave 4 at Qumran, where we really learn that Deuteronomy 32: 8 speaks of God setting the boundaries of the peoples according to the number of the angels of God rather than the children of Israel? Does the Greek word *kairos* mean a 'divinely appointed time' that intercessors must seek to discern rather than simply 'time?' Is the Greek word *rhema* to be regarded as 'a more immediate word from God which we do not find in the 66 books of the Bible.'[6]

Furthermore, we find interpretive gymnastics in the practice of uttering biblical words as magical incantations or using words or phrases in a superstitious way because of their indefiniteness.

> One minute past midnight…we started our prayer actions near KGB headquarters. We had received two words of knowledge from an Israeli intercessor and from a sister in Scotland, both saying that they saw us praying in a tunnel. In front of the KGB headquarters is an underground station with a walking tunnel under the square…We entered the tunnel, and no one else walked through the entire time we prayed. Here we proclaimed the Mene, Mene, Tekel Upharsin, the handwriting on the wall that had announced the downfall of the Babylonian Empire. We prayed, 'in the name of Jesus we bind you, power of Pharaoh, you controlling power of Assur and we lay you under the feet of Jesus. We proclaim that your grave has been prepared. We cut your influence from the root.'[7]

Sound principles of biblical interpretation that recognize the context and the propositional[8] nature of God's revelation are often ignored, leading to a distortion of the text and unwarranted approaches to spiritual warfare in evangelism.

The third way in which the inspired text is compromised relates to the second, but warrants separate mention. Sometimes a point will be supported with reference to those portions of Scripture that are not prescriptive but descriptive. The most serious of these sorts of support are found in the call to emulate Christ in his encounters with demons. As we will explore later, WWJD ('What Would Jesus Do') is a worthy question to ask for the conduct of the Christian life. However, it is unwarranted and inappropriate to presume that we are to follow in the steps of Christ in those areas where he alone was qualified and called to tread. For example, when Jesus was led by the Spirit, following his baptism at the Jordan River, into the wilderness to do battle with Satan, he stood alone as the second Adam. He acted as the representative of his people in confrontation with the tempter. Though we learn of our enemy's tactics and how we might stand against them from Jesus' example, we do not accomplish what he did by our actions. The same is true of Christ's binding the strongman. His work is not our example but our confidence in the work of witness. We may be called to take up our cross as did Christ, but our cross is not substitutionary or redemptive as was His.

If this popular approach does deviate from God's revealed battle plan and does pervert the approach God lays out for dealing with the spiritual opposition we surely face in evangelism, then what can we safely conclude from God's Word? That question captures our challenge in the pages ahead. We will examine three primary areas: enlistment, equipping, and engaging. Enlistment calls us to the field of battle in sober awareness of our enemy for the task of evangelism. Equipping arms us with the weapons God give us for the task and instructs us in their use. Engaging takes us to the field of battle of our everyday lives in reaching others with the gospel of life in Jesus Christ.

Some might not feel comfortable with the military concept and terminology. Yet, as will become increasingly evident, this is exactly the way our King and Commander would have us understand the nature of evangelism and approach to the work of witness, whether that witness is to Betty or to Baltimore. It involves warfare, spiritual warfare. All of us enfolded into the kingdom of God, as children of God and heirs of life, are servants of the Most High and soldiers of the cross. Together we face a common foe, for a common cause. And our Lord has not left us unaware or ill prepared.

I

ENLISTMENT

1

Commissioned for Service

Twenty-five. That was the magic number. American presence in Vietnam was in its final days. President Johnson had issued an order to bring the troops home. The deployed troops were thinning. As a result the military draft was not as comprehensive as it had been. When the time came for me to enter the draft, each date of birth was assigned a number and a lottery was held to determine which numbers would be conscripted into military service in an unstable world situation. The cut off that year was twenty-five. My number was 193.

Since that time, America's standing army has been all volunteer. Young people today must still register for selective service, but there is no draft as there had been from 1948 to 1973. People now enter the military as a matter of personal choice.

Nonetheless, in America and around the world there remains a draft, a required participation in military service. The ranks of these soldiers cut across national borders, across political boundaries, across ethnic and racial lines. God describes these military personnel as citizens of heaven, forming a holy nation, subjects of a kingdom, and soldiers of the cross. If you have confessed Jesus Christ as your Lord, then you have been conscripted into his service. Your term of service is the term of your life in the world as his disciple.

COMMISSIONED

Where do we find our papers to report for service in Christ's army? Perhaps our most direct orders, carrying the official seal of our Lord, are contained in what is often called 'the Great Commission.' After his successful mission of salvation, Jesus spoke to his followers:

> Then the eleven disciples went to Galilee, to the mountain where Jesus had told them to go. When they saw him, they worshiped him; but some doubted. Then Jesus came to them and said, 'All authority in heaven and on earth has been given to me. Therefore go and make disciples of all nations, baptizing them in the name of the Father and of the Son and of the Holy Spirit, and teaching them to obey everything I have commanded you. And surely I am with you always, to the very end of the age.'
>
> Matt. 28: 16–20 [9]

On the basis of newly received authority,[10] Jesus Christ, the risen Lord, turns to those who have aligned themselves with him and gives them a parting command, marching orders for those who count themselves his disciples.

Such commissions are not new for God's servants. Jeremiah, the prophet of the Lord around the time of the fall of Jerusalem in 586 BC, received a commission from the Lord.

> The word of the LORD came to me, saying,
>> 'Before I formed you in the womb I knew you,
>> before you were born I set you apart;
>> I appointed you as a prophet to the nations.'
>
> 'Ah, Sovereign Lord,' I said, 'I do not know how to speak; I am only a child.' But the LORD said to me,
>> 'Do not say, 'I am only a child.' You must go
>> to everyone I send you to and say whatever I
>> command you. Do not be afraid of them, for I am
>> with you and will rescue you,' declares the LORD.
>
> Then the LORD reached out his hand and touched my mouth and said to me,
>> 'Now, I have put my words in your mouth. See,
>> today I appoint you over nations and kingdoms to
>> uproot and tear down, to destroy and overthrow, to
>> build and to plant.'
>
> Jeremiah 1:4-10

Our commission as ambassadors of Christ follows much the same pattern. God comes to give Jeremiah a mission; Christ came to the disciples in Galilee. Jeremiah protests; some doubted Jesus. God asserts his authority; 'All authority in heaven and earth has been given to Me,' Jesus said. God commands Jeremiah to go to the nations; 'Go and make disciples of all nations.' God promises his presence and power for the duration of Jeremiah's mission; 'I am with you always, to the very end of the age.'

We stand in the prophetic line, proclaiming the message of God with which we have been entrusted. Not that we are vehicles of new revelation, but we are ambassadors of Christ, carrying his message, under his auspices and with his authority. We are called to venture out into an inhospitable, even hostile environment. Our Lord assures us of his presence. He also reminds us that he will use our message to achieve his purposes in the lives of those to whom we carry that word.

Every one who has come to know and follow Jesus Christ is given the responsibility to 'make disciples of all nations.' The line dividing Christ's corps is not nation, but salvation. Peter describes us as a 'holy nation.' Paul says our 'citizenship is in heaven.' We belong to God, having been purchased for him by the blood of his Son. Our job is to go with the comprehensive, redemptive authority of our Lord to reach the entire world with the good news of his victory and deliverance.

God gives us a picture of the end result of Christ's goal through us. He shows us a people from diverse backgrounds, believing Jew and Gentile alike, gathered around the throne of him who reigns, raising one voice:

> And they sang a new song:
> > 'You are worthy to take the scroll
> > > and to open its seals,
> > because you were slain, and with your blood
> > > you purchased men for God
> > from every tribe and language
> > > and people and nation.
> > You have made them to be a kingdom
> > > and priests to serve our God,
> > and they will reign on the earth.'
> > > > Rev. 5:9-10

We are now to be engaged in that work, seeking worshippers of God in Spirit and truth, who give him glory both in this life and the life to come. God is at work through us forming the heavenly chorus of his kingdom. In its richest expression, evangelism is gathering worshipers for the heavenly chorus, where God's people will sing the new song of life and hope in Christ with hearts tuned by his Spirit.

The command of Matthew 28 is aptly named a 'commission.' Our Lord is giving his disciples marching orders. He has conferred upon each of us who bear his name the authority and responsibility to carry the message of life, liberty, and the pursuit of true happiness to those still held hostage in the bonds of sin. The task given to us by Jesus is nothing less than a search and rescue mission. Our mission is not search and recovery that gathers dead bodies to bury. We deal in life, looking to bring from death to life.

I don't intend to rehash the responsibility of the church to evangelize. That's not news to most of us. The mandate to witness to others fits in the category of knowing we need to eat healthier or to pray more. We know it, but how seriously do we go about it? I don't want to *rehash* our responsibility to bear witness to Christ, but to *recast* that mission in a military model. Seeing Christ's command as a military commission is not only warranted by Scripture, it also provides a framework that captures the nature of the mission and cultivates what is necessary to carry it out.

A MILITARY MODEL

Your approach to something makes all the difference in the world in how you carry it out. Right now my children and their friends are entering a new phase of life. They're graduating from college and entering the work force, or at least working at it. They are moving from being recipients of parental support to being co-laborers in society.

That transition is rough. It requires a whole different attitude, a new approach to life. It's now that the umbilical chord is ultimately severed. With their newfound status comes newly gained responsibility to lead productive lives. It's one thing to enter a business establishment as a carefree consumer. It's quite another to be employed at the business as a conscientious worker. Loyalties, use of time, frame of mind all change.

How much more true is that of disciples of Jesus Christ? His lordship over us stretches beyond forty hours a week and stretches us in our priorities and goals. As his followers, we need to see ourselves in the light of this relationship and to conduct our lives in its redemptive reality. God's work of redemption radically changes us, giving us meaning, purpose, and identity in communion with him.

God presents the work of redemption in decidedly militaristic terms, in the work of Christ to bring it about, of the church to carry it out, and of individual Christians to live it out. We'll touch on each of these aspects here, although the entire book draws from Scripture to give shape to this model that frames our new lives in Jesus Christ.

Christ's Mission. Christ's work of salvation is painted in military terms, from anticipation to accomplishment to application. God's promise of a Savior, on the heels of the fall in Genesis 3, is couched in terms of combat: 'And I will put enmity between you and the woman, and between your offspring and hers; he will crush your head, and you will strike his heel' (Gen. 3: 15). This seed of the woman would 'crush' the head of the serpent. That's warfare talk. Two combatants are identified, one would inflict harm, the other would defeat.

As we look ahead to the fulfillment of this promise in the fullness of time, we see Jesus Christ, the seed of the woman, coming into this world for battle.[11] He came to destroy the one who holds the power of death—the devil. He was incarnate to destroy the devil's work. His ministry was full of encounters and conflict with enemy opposition. The culmination of his saving work is displayed in the Book of Revelation in terms of warfare, conquest and banishment.

> And I saw an angel coming down out of heaven, having the key to the Abyss and holding in his hand a great chain. He seized the dragon, that ancient serpent, who is the devil, or Satan, and bound him for a thousand years.
>
> When the thousand years are over, Satan will be released from his prison and will go out to deceive the nations in the four corners of the earth—Gog and Magog—to gather them for battle. In number they are like the sand on the seashore. They marched across the breadth of the earth and surrounded the camp of God's people, the city he loves.

> But fire came down from heaven and devoured them. And
> the devil, who deceived them, was thrown into the lake of
> burning sulfur, where the beast and the false prophet had
> been thrown. They will be tormented day and night for
> ever and ever.
>
> Rev. 20: 1–2, 7–10

Jesus came to wage war. His redemptive work is portrayed
in military terms. The picture of the consummation of that
work given to us in Revelation carries the image to its cosmic
conclusion.

In all this we see the Lord Jesus not fighting for personal
victory, but for the redemptive rescue of those held in the grip
of sin's power and condemnation.

> When you were dead in your sins and in the uncircumcision
> of your sinful nature, God made you alive with Christ. He
> forgave us all our sins, having canceled the written code,
> with its regulations, that was against us and that stood
> opposed to us; he took it away, nailing it to the cross. And
> having disarmed the powers and authorities, he made
> a public spectacle of them, triumphing over them by the
> cross.
>
> Colossians 2:13-15

Our salvation is the result of military intervention by our Lord.
He subdued us to himself. He leads us in triumphal procession,
captives of his grace, in the bonds of his love. When he says that
he came to seek and to save those who are lost, he is referring
to a military mission of mercy and meekness as the promised
Messiah of God.

The Church's Mission. Not only is the work of Christ cast in
military terms, the church and its work are as well. We lay siege
to the gates of hell. Jesus says that he will build his church. That
building is set against the backdrop of spiritual opposition that
seeks to overcome. The church operates in enemy territory and
contends with enemy opposition. The mission of the church is
decidedly militaristic.

Bob Hope recently died at the ripe age of 100. Not only was
he renowned the world over as a comedian, he was noted for
his many trips overseas to entertain the troops. He logged many
hours and many miles to lift the spirits of the men and women

on the field of battle, both by his presence and his humor. Bob Hope no doubt did wonders for morale. But as important and noble as that was, his work was mainly entertainment and not military. He provided a welcome diversion from the struggle, but his efforts were divergent from the military operation.

Morale of the troops is important. It helps to motivate us for the mission, not by serving as a diversion from the work, but by showcasing the grace that makes us part of it. While morale is important, it is not the mission. The church is not the USO,[12] with a mission of hospitality and recreation. The church is the army on a mission of kingdom advancement. Not only do we need the proper model for service, we need to remember our role in it.

The church in this world is to be seen, and to understand itself, as the church militant, marching out to war. We are the church triumphant in that we fight in victory, not for victory. We are to savor now that triumph by Christ over sin, death, and the grave; yet the church triumphant looks to the church in heaven, removed from the field of battle in this world, in glory, at rest, fully and eternally enjoying the victory of our Lord.

Nowadays, we are an invading church as well as an inviting church. The covenant community of the Old Testament stood as a light to the nations. The true and living God was present there, dwelling with his people in mercy and grace. The temple attested to the presence and prominence of this God. It also spoke to the character of the nation itself as it followed his holy laws, both attracting the attention of the surrounding idolatrous nations, and serving as a welcoming beacon of light to the hope of salvation.

The new covenant community is still an inviting church and in much the same way. But to our mode of inviting, God has added the mandate of invading. The 'go' of our Lord's Great Commission is the go of invasion. It is not the 'go' of a casual stroll or pointless wandering, but the go of military mission. We go to the nations not as tourists or as terrorists, but as ambassadors of life and hope. The church is not merely situated in the world; it is stationed here at the placement of our King with his orders in hand.

To 'make disciples of all nations' is a military mandate that casts the church in a military mode that sets the stage for a military offensive to rescue. Also in our Lord's commission is a note of recruitment. Those enslaved to Christ are enfolded in the covenant community, the church, and so enlisted for the military service of the cross. When Jesus says in Matthew 28 that disciples are to be baptized in the name of the triune God, he is pointing to the building of the church—growth in the active forces of his army. Baptism is the sign of initiation into God's covenant community, expressing alliance with the true God and agreement with his covenant promises. This means that taking vows of membership in Christ's church carries the weight of being sworn in to his service.

The Christian's Identity. Every local church has been established by her Lord as an outpost of his kingdom, the congregation his army, the members his soldiers. Paul calls those laboring with him for the sake of the gospel 'fellow soldiers' (Phil. 2: 25; Philem. 2). He urges Timothy to be a 'good soldier of Christ Jesus' (2 Tim. 2: 3). Soldiers are identified through military paraphernalia.

When we are drafted into Christ's army we are issued a uniform. It's rather strange at first. The typical uniform for a soldier on a field of battle is some sort of camouflage that blends in with the terrain. It would not be the brightest of ideas to wear a florescent orange uniform in combat. That would be like setting yourself up as a target for the enemy's attention. However, our uniform is strange in that it runs counter to conventional wisdom. Our battle garb is white. If we were deployed in the Siberian winter wilderness that might be fine. We'd blend in like a polar bear in a snowstorm. But we are deployed in the darkness. Our uniform is the robe of Christ's righteousness. Not only does that uniform make us stand out, it is designed to make us stand out. It carries the designer label of God's wisdom. Our conspicuousness is actually part of our combat.

Our work is described as 'waging war.' Just as our uniform is issued at God's design, so are the tools for the task. We are outfitted with weapons suitable for the nature of the combat we are called to undertake. Our tactics reflect military strategy, conducted in the wisdom of God. We stand on the truth against the assault of error. We pray against the opposition we face in mission. The model prayer of our Lord in Matthew 6 instructs us to pray 'Your kingdom come,' reminding us of our ultimate allegiance, our Lord's militaristic means of its growth and our role in it as soldiers of the cross. Everything about us and our service is couched in militaristic terms.

RETURN TO ACTIVE DUTY

My brother-in-law is a colonel in the US Army. I should say, 'was' a colonel. He retired a few years ago and now receives his pension. When he was on active duty his life was consumed with the military. He was stationed at various bases throughout the world. Orders from his commanders directed his steps and dictated his address. He had people under him; people over him. Certain privileges and responsibilities belonged to him when he was on active duty.

But when he retired and entered civilian life, things changed dramatically. He became his own boss. He decided how he would spend his time and invest his life. The structure and demands no longer dictated his steps. While his military training no doubt stayed with him, shaping his outlook and way of doing things, all that became optional, dispensable.

Many in the church have fallen into the same mentality. With the downplaying of the military model given by our Lord for the work of the church and the role of believers, we have lost the edge of active duty. Evangelism and involvement have been reduced to options and confined to periodic participation in programs.

A major part of the indifference and malaise lies in the loss of the military framework resident in the church's identity and the consequent distancing of the work of evangelism from the orders of our King. Evangelism has to be reclaimed from the list of offerings in the church's assortment of programs for its members to choose or not. It has to be retrieved from the pastor's desk where it has been dumped or from the mass evangelist where it has been outsourced. The mission given to his church by her Lord has to be recast as a commission in more than name only and reinstated as the marching orders for his spiritual army, of which every disciple is a soldier. Can you imagine an army at war ignoring the air raid sirens because they don't want to tear themselves away from the latest episode of M★A★S★H, entertained by war instead of engaged in it? What would it be like for an army to march only in good weather or only if it were in the mood, to be willing servants only during commercial breaks? This sort of mentality can prevail because the military model is not prevalent in the mindset and ministry of the church, at least not in practical terms.

MODEL SOLDIERS

The military model offers an array of benefits for the preservation of what our Lord calls us to do. First, it reminds us who we are. We are ones rescued and called to join the cause of liberation from the tyranny of the devil. We see ourselves in a particular light. If we see ourselves as soldiers, then we will understand our role. If we know we are on active duty, we will direct our steps accordingly.

Who are you? When asked that question, people usually respond by roles. They are fathers or mothers or engineers or students. Who you are is a question of identity. Identity directs activity. A mother mothers. A student studies. When our Lord appeared to his disciples in the book of Acts, he invests them with an identity. 'You are My witnesses,' he asserted (Acts 1: 8). In the Great Commission and elsewhere disciples are called to 'bear witness.' These two aspects serve as an important reminder for us. We must see witness first as a noun, then as a verb. It is who we are, from which flows what we do. As Paul informs us, we are light; therefore we are to be light (Eph. 5: 8). The indicative grounds and mandates the imperative. Identity directs activity and gives responsibility. Responsibility emerges from a sense of identity. If we see ourselves as customers then we will saunter in to be served. If we see ourselves as soldiers then we will report to serve.

Second, the military model reminds us what we are to be doing. If I am an engineer, I am not to be spending my time on the job in the accounting department. The primary use for my office computer is not playing solitaire or participating in on-line auctions. To follow Christ as Lord means that we do what he says. The Great Commission is a command. He has given us a mission to accomplish. Our lives are devoted to him and our goals defined by him.

Third, the military model speaks to motivation. We obey our Lord because we love him. We are indebted to him. We owe our lives and liberty to him. When Paul tells Timothy to 'endure hardship with us like a good soldier of Christ Jesus,' he explains the degree of commitment and reason for it: 'No one serving as a soldier gets involved in civilian affairs—he wants to please his commanding officer.' How much more should we seek to please him who loved us and gave himself for us?

We engage in search and rescue because we love our neighbor. We've been in their situation. Christ came to us through his instruments with the message of life. Now the message is in our hands as his instruments, with orders to deliver it.

Love, biblical love, will sacrifice. It will set aside self for the good of the other. Isn't that just what a soldier does? A soldier sets aside his rights and whims and comforts for the good of the whole, for the sake of the mission, for the cause of the kingdom, and for obedience to his commander.

Fourth, the military model presents us with a method, a way of going about the mission our Lord has given us to carry out. We fight in his way. We look at the weapons differently. As impressive as Satan's resources and tactics are, God's will prevail.

I remember watching one of the Indiana Jones movies. Harrison Ford was confronted with an opponent well skilled with the sword. Several frames were devoted to watching this guy twirl and manipulate his sword, showing how adroit and formidable he was as an opponent. I was mesmerized as I watched and started fearing for the hero's life. The hypnotic spell was broken when Indiana Jones heaved a big sigh, took his pistol from the waistband of his pants and shot the guy. End of battle.

The military model reminds us we fight. More than that, we fight with God's weapons, in God's way. As we will see, his weapons and ways carry his wisdom to demolish strongholds and defend against the skilled opponent we encounter in keeping with the nature of the mission.

Fifth, the military model reminds us that we have a mandate. The church today is more like a mall and the people consumers. The people are part of a church for what they can get, for what Jesus can do for them. Conversely, the church feels an obligation to provide the services and programs to meet those desires. The mandate of the mall is catering to customers.

Its commission and conflict, which are always contemporary with the age, cast the mandate of the church. The church is a military unit, an outpost of the kingdom of God. Opposition and engagement for the cause of Christ qualify our life in this world as Christ's disciples. We are at war. Archie Parrish stresses the point that 'all Christians must recognize that the Church is not a peace-time business to be managed but a war-time army engaged in spiritual combat.'[13] He quotes John Piper:

> The crying need of the hour is to put the churches on a war time footing. Mission leaders are crying out. 'Where is the church's concept of militancy, of a mighty army willing to suffer, moving ahead with exultant determination to take the world by storm? Where is the risk taking, the launching out on God alone? The answer is that it has been swallowed up in a peace-time mentality.'

John Bunyan, in *The Holy War*, anticipated this tactic of Satan to distract the church from the mission mandated by her Lord. This tactic not only displaced the church from her service of witness, it replaced that commission with a mission to serve another king and seek another kingdom, ourselves and our own. I think we can get the gist of Bunyan's allegorical characters and can painfully recognize the truth of the picture he presents for our day.

> [Lucifer's strategy] Mr. Sweet-world and Mr. Present-good are two men of civility and cunning. Let those engaged in this business for us, and let Mansoul be taken with much business, and if possible with much pleasure and this is the way to get ground of them. Let us but cumber and occupy and amuse Mansoul sufficiently, and they will make their castle a warehouse for goods instead of a garrison for men of war.

The military model even affects the leadership of the church. The leaders are to be officers more in the sense of engaging the people in the mission rather than administrators to manage the organization. In God's organizational flow, he establishes leaders to care for and to prepare the troops for service. The book of Ephesians has much to say about the power and effectiveness of the church. Notice the flow of ministry instituted by God for that effectiveness.

> It was he who gave some to be apostles, some to be prophets, some to be evangelists, and some to be pastors and teachers, to prepare God's people for works of service, so that the

body of Christ may be built up until we all reach unity in the faith and in the knowledge of the Son of God and become mature, attaining to the whole measure of the fullness of Christ. Then we will no longer be infants, tossed back and forth by the waves, and blown here and there by every wind of teaching and by the cunning and craftiness of men in their deceitful scheming. Instead, speaking the truth in love, we will in all things grow up into him who is the Head, that is, Christ. From him the whole body, joined and held together by every supporting ligament, grows and builds itself up in love, as each part does its work.

Ephesians 4: 11–16

The officers are not the only doers of ministry. They are gifted and trained and installed to lead the troops in the ministry. We can represent it in this way:

The boxes represent the nouns, the lines the verbs. The result of unimpeded flow and function is unity, maturity and growth in Christ—a well-oiled military unit. Engaging is implied in that the equipping or preparing is for a functional purpose.

Each part is to do its work. The picture is not of the officers charging into battle, while the troops cheer them on. The officers equip the troops for engagement, all in keeping with the direction and provision of the Commanding King under whom they serve. I once heard someone saying in reference to Jesus' assertion, 'the harvest is plentiful but the workers are few' (Luke 10: 2), that the workers are in our seminaries. The workers are not in the seminaries. They are in the pews. The equippers are in the seminaries.

Notice God provides this design for the protection of the troops and work of the kingdom. Cunning, craftiness, and deceitfulness are hallmarks of the Satanic opposition that characterize the enemy and the environment in which we do battle.

And as for those workers, the gathering for worship on a weekly basis is not the sum of our involvement in the service of our Lord Jesus Christ. Rather, corporate worship serves as a time for refocus, refreshment, and recommitment for our lives and mission to him whom we worship through the service of our lives.

FRONT AND CENTER

There is an old joke about a sergeant barking out a command to the soldiers lined up in formation for all interested in a mission to step forward. Those selected stepped forward only because everyone else took a step back. That's not particularly funny when it rings true in respect to the church, its mission and its members' commission. Actually, it's tragic and borders on insubordination.

In Christ's kingdom there can be no conscientious objectors. In Christ's church, there is no inactive duty. To be a disciple is to be a soldier of the cross. We'll see how there are varying degrees of giftedness, but no one is exempt from military service for the cause of the kingdom. The term of enlistment is a lifetime, beginning with conversion, ending with the discharge papers of transfer to the church triumphant in heavenly rest, where we are eager to hear the words, 'Well done, good and faithful servant.'

We've talked a lot about warfare in surveying our involvement. The whole notion begs all sorts of questions. Where is this enemy territory? Under what banner do we march? Just who is the enemy? How do we go about warfare? What battle plan do we follow? What weapons are provided for us? Our understanding begins with a look at daily life.

2

This Present, Evil Age

If I told you that a treasure of great value was at a particular place and that treasure was yours for the taking, I'd probably catch your attention. But there's a catch. Aha, you knew it was too good to be true! No, the only catch is that to get the treasure you have to contend with vermin. The place where the treasure lies is crawling with rats. To gain the treasure, you have to deal with the rats. What will you do? Although the idea of mingling with large rodents might make your skin crawl, you would probably be undeterred. You're going to get that treasure, rats or no rats.

However, knowing that you'd have to fend off rats would undoubtedly make a huge difference in the approach you take to lay hold of the treasure. You probably wouldn't wear shorts and sandals. You might wear gloves. You'd want to take some sort of weapon with you. You would venture in with expectation, but also with considerable caution. Knowledge of the presence of the rats and what rats are like would have a marked influence for your treasure-hunting mission.

Now imagine your Lord Jesus has given you a mission. He wants you to reach those around you with the gospel of life. He wants you to venture in to the lives of others with the goal of laying up treasure in heaven. But, he warns you of an enemy with whom you will have to deal. He informs you about this enemy—his character, his tactics, his intentions, his power. This enemy is strong, relentless, crafty and resourceful. He opposes you and wants to thwart you every step of the way. And you thought rats were bad!

Can you imagine listening to your Lord's warning of the enemy, even studying the profile given to you of that enemy, then nonchalantly venturing out into his stomping grounds with no regard for what you've been told? You're not on your guard. You make no preparations. You gather up none of the provisions your Lord supplied. You take along some repellant only later to read the label to discover it has no effect on your adversary. What you may take up from God's arsenal, you don't really know how to use. You just saunter out with little attention to the spiritual threat, conflict and opposition you will face.[13] Strange but true. That's exactly what we often do when it comes to the spiritual opposition inherent in the work of evangelism.

AN INHOSPITABLE HABITAT

As believers, we've seen we do have a mission. Orders from our Commander-in-chief are in hand. We'll look at that commission in a personal way a little later. First, we need to survey the setting and the situation into which we are sent.

In presenting ourselves to our Lord for the work of witness, we need to get a good feel for the reality of the environment into which he sends us. Understanding that environment alerts us to the danger that goes along with it and puts us in tune with the nature of our mission. In this section we want to get our bearings for the territory in which we live and labor for the cause of Christ. We begin by knowing the times, what the Apostle Paul calls 'this present, evil age' (Gal. 1: 4).

We begin at the beginning. Life was good. The eternal God had spoken creation into being by the word of his power. The sky and seas were clean. The garden in which God had placed them was beautiful, filled with all sorts of foliage, colored with a multitude of fruits and varieties of vegetables. On top of that, the garden's caretakers enjoyed intimate communion with God. He had made Adam and Eve in his image, capable of knowing and enjoying him, called to glorify and honor him. Those walks in the cool of the day through the Garden of Eden must have been a delight. Man, male and female, fellowshipping with their Creator. Care of the garden was a labor of love, not onerous in the least.

God had given his image-bearers but one command—not to eat of the tree of the knowledge of good and evil. In so doing, they would surely die. The issue wasn't the fruit. It was all about obedience. The death brought about by the eating of the forbidden fruit would not be like the physical death resulting from eating the poisonous fruit of fairy tales. No, this death would be far more devastating. It would be physical—eventually. But the most severe impact would be spiritual and eternal. Adam and Eve had been commanded and they had been warned. The rest of the vast garden of delights lay before them for their enjoyment.

'Did God really say?' Enter the serpent, with his lies, deceptions, false promises, and competing counsel. Our first parents took the bait and took a bite. The hook sunk deep. And they found themselves exiled from paradise. Not only had they been affected by their sinful rebellion, the entire created order had been subjected to the disintegrating, degenerating effects of sin by that act of disobedience. On top of that, not only had the present been afflicted, the future would be as well. Sin was around to stay. Sin would leave its mark on everything. All those descending from Adam by ordinary means would be physically alive, but dead in sin. Alienation would be the norm: man with God, man with man, man with his world, man in his very personhood.

Let's take a step back for a wider view. God had created from nothing. He had made everything good. By Adam's disobedience, the moral evil of sin had intruded to contaminate and pollute everything about God's created order. God could have brought an end to things right then and there. He would have been perfectly just to do so. But in his graciousness, God promised deliverance. The seed of the woman would come to crush the head of the serpent. God allowed history to continue, history that would become the womb for the birth of that unexpected, undeserved, and unmerited promise of salvation. The question is, what would that post-fall history look like?

We leave the backdrop of Genesis 1–3 and turn to Genesis 4, the story of Cain and Abel. Here we find an historical account that amounts to a case study of what life would look like in a fallen world. We see man in worship. No surprise there. That's how God hard-wired those created in his image. Both sons of Adam and Eve bring offerings to present to their Creator, each in keeping with his occupation. Cain brings fruit of the ground; Abel takes from his flock. The text draws attention to the disparity between the two offerings. The significant contrast is not made so much in terms of what, but why. Abel brings his best, the fat portions from the firstborn of his flock. The qualification of silence leads us to believe that Cain did not bring his best. The New Testament explains that Abel's best is the fruit of faith. That was the substantial contrast between the two offerings, one was of faith, the other not. It's worthy of note to see God was already at work in hearts, claiming a people for his own possession, working to counter the sin that reigned in the heart.

Going on with our post-fall overview: God is pleased with Abel's offering. He rejects Cain's. Cain is furious. God tenderly and graciously speaks to Cain to warn him and call him to repent. Cain's prideful anger hardens his heart and sets him on a course to disaster. He had better turn from it. Cain rejects the counsel of God. The fruit of that rebellion is the murder of his brother.

Such is life in a post-fall world. Sin intrudes on man's relationship with God and with his fellow man, reaching even to the nuclear family. We see the character and capability of sin resident in the heart of fallen human beings, and it's not a pretty sight. We also get a surprising glimpse of sin's assault even on those whose faith is in God.

But the nature of life in a fallen world receives an even more ominous tone with the counsel God gives to Cain, which he rejected: 'If you do what is right, will you not be accepted? But if you do not do what is right, sin is crouching at your door; it desires to have you, but you must master it' (Gen. 4: 7). What a frightening portrayal of post-fall life! At the same time, however, it is illuminating. Personified sin lies in wait and with bad intentions. It means to do harm. It crouches like a wild animal ready to pounce and devour. Can you imagine having a thief or a murderer camped outside the front door of your home, ready to do you harm every time you gave him a foot in the door? That's exactly what life is like in this world corrupted by sin—opposition, injury, assault. Spiritual conflict characterizes the day. Evil is in the air.

We live on the same side of the fall as did Cain and Abel. We face the same danger and struggles. The challenge of spiritual battle is ours as well. Sin will either master us or we will master it. Sin lurks with a desire to sift us as wheat, to do us spiritual harm. God's counsel gives warning and instructs us that only righteousness, doing what is right, will overcome the power and condemnation of sin.

We live and walk in the valley of the shadow of death. When we read the twenty-third psalm and hear of God's presence with his sheep, so that we need fear no evil when we walk through the valley of the shadow of death, our hearts are warmed. God's hand will hold us and guide through the tunnel of our life's end in a world that has been infected with death. But that shadow of death is not merely the waning moments of life. It is descriptive of life in a fallen world. We live in death's shadow. It casts its pale over our existence. Each day is a step toward physical death on the individualized path set before us by our sovereign God.

It is into this domain and dominion of death that the light of God's promise in Genesis 3 dawns. Zechariah, the father of John the Baptist, speaks of God's realization of God's promises for deliverance from death's dominion in these terms:

> And you, my child, will be called a prophet of the Most High; for you will go on before the Lord to prepare the way for him, to give his people the knowledge of salvation through the forgiveness of their sins, because of the tender mercy of our God, by which the rising sun will come to us from heaven to shine on those living in darkness and in the shadow of death, to guide our feet into the path of peace.
>
> Luke 1: 76–9

The light from heaven bursts forth in promised brilliance to bring salvation and peace. Matthew in his gospel account, quotes the same passage from the prophet Isaiah to identify that light as Jesus Christ.[15]

Into this environment, this present, evil age, came the seed of the woman. When the time had fully come, God sent his Son, born of a woman, born under law, to redeem us from under law (Gal. 4: 4–5). God did for us what we could not do for ourselves. Jesus comes in respect to sin and to do battle with him who holds the power of death—the devil (Heb. 2: 14–15). He grants us a righteousness we could not earn. He brings us to a position of privilege we had no right to claim. Jesus delivers us from the bondage of an evil environment in which we were perfectly at home, blissfully ignorant of the iceberg that lurked in the darkness ahead. Listen to how Paul frames Christ's work on our behalf:

'Grace and peace to you from God our Father and the Lord Jesus Christ, who gave himself for our sins to rescue us from the present evil age, according to the will of our God and Father, to whom be glory for ever and ever. Amen' (Gal. 1: 3–5).

That mastery of sin God said was required in Genesis 4, he himself provided in Jesus Christ. In Chapter 5 we'll explore in greater detail just what Jesus did to accomplish this. But for now we want to take note of the environment into which our Lord Jesus came to us, the nature of his work on our behalf, and the setting in which he has left us and called us to mission. It all has to do with a present, evil age.

EVIL ENVIRONS

What exactly does it mean to live in an 'evil' age? We've already answered that to some degree by noting the presence and perversity of sin that contaminates all of life this side of the fall.

In what way is the world in which we live 'evil'? Certainly, we see evidence of evil. All we need to do is scan the daily paper for proof of that—rapes, murders, scams—at home and around the globe. We can look at our own hearts and see lust, greed, and pride. Telescopically and microscopically, evil is everywhere.

A quick inventory of life will show us effects of the fall. With wholeness, there is decay. With plants, there are weeds. With health, there is sickness. With pleasure, there is suffering. With peace, there is pain. With life, there is death. All these are symptoms of the present, evil age. We can't get away from it. It is where we as descendents of Adam live and move and have our being.

Nothing remains untouched by the contamination from sin. That does not mean that the world is as bad as it could be or that everyone is a Hitler. It just means sin's fingerprints are everywhere. A friend of mine and his wife had what we might call a catastrophic incident that serves as a good illustration. They were sitting in their living room one evening reading and relaxing. They looked up to see their gray cat walk across the room in front of them. The problem was their cat was supposed to be white. They looked around the room and noticed their curtains were discolored. It turns out their home's central heating system had malfunctioned and emitted a soot that adhered to everything. Nothing was left unaffected. That soot even managed to find its way inside the cabinets and drawers to coat everything from Tupperware to silverware to underwear.

That's the way it is in a fallen world. Nothing is left untouched, uncontaminated by the ravages of sin. Sin affects our relationships. It works its way in to pollute our hearts. It taints the best of motives. The Bible describes people as 'dead' in sin. That's language to describe the spiritual effect of the fall in rendering the age in which we live 'evil.' It highlights that the prevalent evil is a moral evil. People are bound by their fallen nature so that none are righteous, none will seek God.

That's really the crux of the evil in this present age. We live in a dysfunctional world. Sin has seeped in to pervert what God has made good. The most severe of these manifestations of dysfunction is a humanity that is alienated from God, at odds with the One whom they were created to glorify and enjoy. The image of God in which we were made remains, but it is now a marred image.

It is in this sense of a world distorted, perverted, and corrupted from God's pristine design that the day in which we live, and every day this side of the fall, is considered evil. Darkness, decay and disintegration appropriately describe the state of the world. When the Bible speaks of 'darkness,' it refers to the moral morass that grips the world and shrouds it in the blindness of unbelief. The evil of this present age particularly refers to the moral evil of sin, its consequences, its capabilities, and its incapacities.

Getting back to where we started this discussion, this present, evil age is not just where we as believers live. It's where our Lord Jesus sends us, orders in hand. The character of this age, the world in its fallen state, tells us that this mission will be no picnic. We can expect rejection, persecution, hardship, and suffering as we live and operate in this world.

We look forward to the day when this present, evil age will become the past, evil age. That will happen when Jesus comes in glory. The book of Revelation speaks of God ushering in a new heaven and a new earth. The newness is the newness of a creation uncorrupted by the effects of sin—renewal unchanging and unending. God will dry the tears of his redeemed from their years of living in the present, evil age. And 'there will be no more death or mourning or crying or pain, for the old order of things will have passed away' (Rev. 21: 4).

Won't that day be great? But we have to wake up from our daydreaming about the wonderful blessings God has in store for us. That's all part of the age to come. We need to get back to the reality of life today, of a world where we as children of God are not at home, where sin and Satan oppress us. This world is where we set up camp for mission in service to our Lord.

SPIRITUAL TERRITORY OR TERRITORIAL SPIRITS

With this background, we can see how the 'evil one' finds a home in the fallen world. Like the sewer as a habitat for rats, the present, evil age seems the appropriate setting for the presence of the evil one. The world in which we live is Satan's stomping grounds. He fits right in. He is well suited for leadership. That's why titles such as 'prince of this world' and 'god of this age' are ascribed to him. John goes so far as to say that 'the whole world is under the control of the evil one' (1 John 5: 19).

But while God characterizes this present, evil age as Satan's territory, does that mean there are territorial spirits with whom we have to contend in mission, demonic landlords over regions or persons? If there are minions of Satan assigned to certain localities, Scripture doesn't emphasize it and certainly does not employ that concept for the spiritual conflict inherent in evangelism. Nowhere are we taught the necessity of identifying a territorial spirit in evangelistic outreach.

We do contend, however, with a demonic adversary as we would seek to penetrate the darkness of sin with the light of life. We don't want to minimize or overlook that spiritual reality for the spiritual work given to us. This age presents us with powerful, oppressive, spiritual opposition as we move out in gospel mission. But God's Word does not pin that demonic opposition down for us in any greater detail. The concern to which God alerts us deals more with the spirit of this age rather than spirits to be singled out. Suffice it to say, spiritual forces oppose us.

BE OF GOOD COURAGE

A little intimidating? Unnerving? Disheartening? Lest we become discouraged or frozen in fear, we want to remember that we serve in this fallen world as those rescued and cared for by him who gave his life for us. We rivet our gaze on the One who reigns in victory for us. We consider him who endured opposition and persecution at the hands of the present, evil age so that we do not grow weary and lose heart (Heb. 12: 1–3). God tells us this because he knows we need to hear it. He knows the terrain into which he sends us. Suffering is the road to glory, taken by One in whose steps we are to follow.

Our Lord knows full well what we face in this world. Suffering should not surprise us. Persecution for righteousness' sake should not offend us. It's all part of life with and for Christ. Jesus gives us warning and encouragement, with a dose of expectation: 'I have told you these things, so that in me you may have peace. In this world you will have trouble. But take heart! I have overcome the world' (John 16: 33).

The work of Jesus Christ on our behalf has freed us from the power of sin. Our Lord Jesus has rescued us from this age so that we no longer fit in. He has transferred us from the realm of darkness to the dominion of light. We have a new home—heaven, where, Peter assures us, our inheritance is kept for us and we for it, by the preserving grace of God (1 Pet. 1: 3–5). But for now, though we are no longer of the world, we continue in it, and not merely to endure, but to engage it for Christ.

Our God comforts us through Paul's first letter to the Thessalonians. Notice the post-fall language and themes used to describe the inevitable tension of life that we experience as those in the world but not of it.

> But you, brothers, are not in darkness so that this day should surprise you like a thief. You are all sons of the light and sons of the day. We do not belong to the night or to the darkness. So then, let us not be like others, who are asleep, but let us be alert and self-controlled. For those who sleep, sleep at night, and those who get drunk, get drunk at night. But since we belong to the day, let us be self-controlled, putting on faith and love as a breastplate, and the hope of salvation as a helmet. For God did not appoint us to suffer wrath but to receive salvation through our Lord Jesus Christ.
>
> 1 Thess. 5: 4–9

We desperately need to hear those words and to be reminded of life's realities, finding our bearings in the framework of God's grace. Otherwise, we will be discouraged in the struggle and disenfranchised from service.

We live as light in the dark. Our struggles are made worse by the sin that remains within us. It's like our enemy the devil having an ally on the inside. While sin no longer controls us, it continues to exert influence. We thought it was bad living in a sin-steeped world. How much more difficult living in such a world now as sons of light rather than children of darkness! We're fish out of water. Struggles abound. Suffering is the norm. But hope shines bright as he who began a good work in us will see it to completion. God is not merely waiting to welcome us into heavenly glory. He is with us each step of the way to guide and provide, direct and protect.

Listen to our Lord's prayer for us while we are on duty in this world:

> I pray for them. I am not praying for the world, but for those you have given me, for they are yours....I have given them your word and the world has hated them, for they are not of the world any more than I am of the world. My prayer is not that you take them out of the world but that you protect them from the evil one. They are not of the world, even as I am not of it. Sanctify them by the truth; your word is truth. As you sent me into the world, I have sent them into the world.
>
> John 17: 9, 14–18

By 'world' Jesus speaks of those who are still in bondage to the present, evil age, those 'sons of darkness' to which Paul referred. His prayer of protection and provision is for us who labor in his name in an unfriendly and inhospitable environment. Our Lord's prayer presents us with a reminder that those the Father had given him, those for whom he died, have been strategically positioned by our God for his purposes. We are 'sent' into a world that is no friend to Christ or to us, but at the same time he who sends us protects us.

The good news is that Jesus Christ, the eternal Son of God, came into this sin-steeped world to bring resolution and restoration. His redemptive work encompassed not only people; it embraced a whole new created order, liberated from the ravages of sin. The Apostle Paul describes it this way:

> The creation waits in eager expectation for the sons of God to be revealed. For the creation was subjected to frustration, not by its own choice, but by the will of the one who subjected it, in hope that the creation itself will be liberated from its bondage to decay and brought into the glorious freedom of the children of God. We know that the whole creation has been groaning as in the pains of childbirth right up to the present time. Not only so, but we ourselves, who have the firstfruits of the Spirit, groan inwardly as we wait eagerly for our adoption as sons, the redemption of our bodies.
>
> Rom. 8: 19–24

Contrary to these circumstances that challenge our faith, Paul gives us the hope[16] of a home that is ours in Christ: 'I consider that our present sufferings are not worth comparing with the glory that will be revealed in us' (Rom. 8: 18). That means though we groan under the weight of sin and in tension with our newness in Christ, we groan toward glory. Though we may live and work in this age, it is only temporary. In the big picture we will suffer in our life and labors in this age, but it is only for a 'little while' (1 Pet. 1: 6).

ON SITE

My first pastorate was only about nine miles from my home, but the commute was a challenge. Even though I got an early start, I found that everyone else in the Washington, DC suburb did as well. The traffic was a nightmare. It could take me 45 minutes to cover those nine miles, barring any encounter with accidents. My present pastorate requires only about a ten-minute drive, for which I am thankful.

A commute provides the boundary of time and space between home and work. When you're at home, you're not at work. Life in the two locales takes on a different complexion. Some people work at home or bring work to do at home, but even there exists a boundary that separates two aspects of life with divergent goals and agendas.

When it comes to entering enemy territory for the work our Lord Jesus gives us to do, we do not need to commute. This territory of the present, evil age is where we live. We do not need to travel to the footprint where the towers of World Trade Center once stood to witness the ravages of evil. It is within our neighborhood, within our doors, and even within our hearts. We address the evil of our hearts through God's means of grace in the work of sanctification, dying more and more to sin, growing more and more in righteousness, knowledge, and holiness. In the environment external to us in which we labor for Christ, we address the evil in other ways, through suitable weapons that we will explore later.

Not commuting to our spiritual labor relates both to where and to when. Since we live in the environment in which our Lord has stationed us, that means we are always on duty and continually to be on guard. The entirety of our life is qualified by our Lord's call as sons and servants, daughters and disciples.

In God's infinite wisdom he has not whisked us up to heavenly glory in a chariot of fire at the moment of our salvation. In the wake of his redeeming grace, our God leaves us behind, not by way of abandonment, but by way of deployment. He stations us in enemy territory, for his service.

We cannot escape the present, evil age until our Lord frees us from the confines of this world. Though in Christ we have been liberated by the work of his power and grace, are heirs of heavenly glory with the certain promise of eternal emancipation from all that characterizes a fallen world, still this world provides our work environment until our Lord grants us papers of discharge to the celestial city. May those discharge papers be honorable, inscribed with the words, 'good and faithful servant.'

PRESENT IN AN EVIL AGE

When I walk out the front door of my home I am greeted by a garden patch planted where we had a dead tree cut down several years ago. It's a pleasant little plot, with plants of various sorts adding color and beauty to our property. Yet it seems that no matter how much my wife tries to stay on top of things in its care, the flowers of that little garden patch share the soil with unwelcome and uninvited weeds. As undesirable as those weeds are, they do serve a useful function for me. They are inescapable reminders of the world in which I live and into which I am heading out my front door. They declare the reality of the curse of Genesis 3: 18, a post-fall world fallen under the dominion of sin. Those weeds testify to the struggles inherent in life—struggles that day I will experience in my own heart, in my encounters with others on the roadway, and in the office.

Those weeds also serve as reminders of another biblical image, one that conveys the extraordinary mission to which our Lord calls each of us who bear his name. One day, at the end of this present age, the Son of Man will send out his angels to gather the weeds and the wheat from the field of this world (Matt. 13: 36–43). He will separate the children of the kingdom from the sons of the evil one for their place in the age to come. But today, as long as it is called *today*, as long as the Lord tarries, Jesus is in the business of transforming weeds into wheat, by his Spirit. And he designs to use the likes of us in that enterprise.

In some armed forces a cluster of wheat forms part of the insignia of a military rank. Perhaps our insignia as soldiers of the cross, engaged for the occupation of hearts, should be a cluster of weeds. For such were we apart from Christ, when we were without God and without hope in the world, enslaved by sin, subject to the ruler of this age, at home in the darkness of this present, evil age, awaiting the judgment and fate of all therein. And to such we go, that they may be transformed by the redemptive purpose and power of God.

But from where does the power for such a mission come? What authority do we have to engage those of this world for the cause of Christ? What makes it worth the effort to risk the rats in pursuit of treasure? It is to these questions we turn as we explore the essential nature of evangelism as kingdoms in conflict.

3

Kingdom Conflict

God provided a wonderful place for the writing of this book, quiet, away from the distractions of office and home, about a 25-minute drive from my home. Monday morning and I was eager to start writing the chapter you are reading. About 6:30 a.m. I pulled in to the great bagel place I had discovered, where I bought my daily coffee for now and cinnamon raisin bagel for lunch later. Pleased with my purchase and ready to go the remaining mile of my trip, I got into my car, turned the key in the ignition and nothing. All I got was a buzz. It turned out the battery was dead. Almost four hours later, fitted with a new battery and a newly charged credit card, I made it to my fortress of solitude to finally start chapter three.

I share this exasperating event not for sympathy, but for illustration, timely supplied by God's providence. The problem with my car was power. My battery's get up and go had got up and gone. A simple recharge of the battery wouldn't do. It had to be replaced.

That incident serves as an apt illustration for the power necessary to carry out the mission our Lord has given us to be his witnesses in this present, evil age. This age does not have the power to change lives. In fact, it is dead, devoid of life. The power of reigning sin only drains. Just as my battery was impotent to start my car, so the battery of this present age is incapable of reversing the effects of a world held in bondage to sin and people held in captivity to Satan.

Reformation is not the answer. My battery was dead. It would not and could not hold a charge. In the same way, this present age cannot be recharged with life. It cannot be fixed. We can't bring in a crew to clean up the evil that touches and infects everything. The encrusted terminals of the battery of this age cannot be cleared of corrosion to allow the functioning of the battery the way it was before the fall of creation through the disobedience of Adam and Eve. A whole new battery is required to give power to bring life, change, and proper function. The Bible speaks of that power in terms of the kingdom of God.

In this chapter we're going to see how the kingdom of God supplies the power necessary for the transforming work of evangelism. Also evident in our mission is the spiritual opposition we face, reflected in terms of a clash of kingdoms. Our study will by no means be in exhaustive detail.[16] We just want to marvel and gain our confidence in what God has done to provide the power we need for the work he gives us to do, especially against the opposition we face in that work.

THE KINGDOM OF GOD

What exactly is the 'kingdom of God?' The kingdom of God is the redemptive reign of Jesus Christ. The kingdom looks to the sovereign, saving, subduing work of Jesus as the Messiah of God.

The prophets of old anticipated this kingdom. Nebuchadnezzar, sixth century BC king of Babylon, had a dream. All of us have dreams. Some of them can seem quite real. We may wake up in a cold sweat from a particularly vivid dream, and breathe a sigh of relief when we discover it was only a dream. Nebuchadnezzar was certainly shaken by his dream. The difference between this particular dream of his and the ones we have is that ours do not communicate a prophetic word from God, while his did.

No one was found capable of telling the king what his dream meant. Here is his dream as Daniel recounts it for him. See if you can analyze it:

> You looked, O king, and there before you stood a large statue—an enormous, dazzling statue, awesome in appearance. The head of the statue was made of pure gold, its chest and arms of silver, its belly and thighs of bronze,

its legs of iron, its feet partly of iron and partly of baked clay. While you were watching, a rock was cut out, but not by human hands. It struck the statue on its feet of iron and clay and smashed them. Then the iron, the clay, the bronze, the silver and the gold were broken to pieces at the same time and became like chaff on a threshing floor in the summer. The wind swept them away without leaving a trace. But the rock that struck the statue became a huge mountain and filled the whole earth.

Dan. 2: 31–5

Daniel, as a prophet of the true God, explains the dream as a series of kingdoms along with a sense of the character of each. What is of interest to us is that striking rock. What do you notice about it? It's separate from the statue, succeeding it, but not part of it. It's different from the other kingdoms in its power and longevity. The rock subdues the kingdoms represented by the various metals of the statue. Then, the rock grows. It fills the whole earth.

What is this rock the king sees? Daniel interprets it for us:

> In the time of those kings, the God of heaven will set up a kingdom that will never be destroyed, nor will it be left to another people. It will crush all those kingdoms and bring them to an end, but it will itself endure forever. This is the meaning of the vision of the rock cut out of a mountain, but not by human hands—a rock that broke the iron, the bronze, the clay, the silver and the gold to pieces. The great God has shown the king what will take place in the future. The dream is true and the interpretation is trustworthy.

Dan. 2: 44–5

That rock is a prophetic metaphor for the kingdom of God. Daniel related to Nebuchadnezzar, to the readers of his day, and to us that God himself would work in history to establish his kingdom. His kingdom would be an everlasting kingdom, a subduing kingdom.

The dominant theme of the New Testament gospels centers around the kingdom of God, its presence and character. Have you noticed how much they speak of the kingdom of God? The bulk of Jesus' parables open with these words: 'the kingdom of God (or heaven) is like.'[18] For example, notice the parable of the mustard seed, and parallel it with Daniel's growing rock.

> Again he said, 'What shall we say the kingdom of God is
> like, or what parable shall we use to describe it? It is like
> a mustard seed, which is the smallest seed you plant in
> the ground. Yet when planted, it grows and becomes the
> largest of all garden plants, with such big branches that the
> birds of the air can perch in its shade.'
>
> Mark 4: 30–2; cf. Matt. 13: 31–2

The thrust of Jesus' teaching was that the kingdom of God had
arrived. It was present because he was present as the coming
king, the anointed one of God. John the Baptist, the forerunner
of God's Messiah, announced that the kingdom of God was
at hand (Matt. 3: 2). Jesus preached the same thing, 'Repent,
for the kingdom of heaven is near' (Matt. 4: 17). He explained
that his kingdom was not of this world, something entirely
different from the kingdoms that marked human history or
that were depicted in dreams of statues (John 18:36f.).

John, in the Book of Revelation, understood that what
Daniel saw in the future, he saw happening in his day.[19] The
book of Revelation opens acknowledging Jesus as 'ruler of
the kings of the earth,' who has 'made us to be a kingdom of
priests.' This kingdom involves 'freeing us from our sins by
his blood.' When John turns to the apocalyptic section of the
book, he metaphorically escorts us to the control center of the
universe. There we see Jesus, sitting on the throne, reigning for
his church. Feel the power of this picture John paints for us:

> Then one of the elders said to me, 'Do not weep! See, the
> Lion of the tribe of Judah, the Root of David, has triumphed.
> He is able to open the scroll and its seven seals.' Then I saw
> a Lamb, looking as if it had been slain, standing in the center
> of the throne, encircled by the four living creatures and the
> elders. He had seven horns and seven eyes, which are the
> seven spirits of God sent out into all the earth.
>
> Rev. 5: 4–5

Jesus reigns as one living having been slain.[20] His kingdom rule
is comprehensive, resting on his saving work as the Lamb of
God, in fulfillment of prophetic promise. Jesus is the ultimate
Son of David to whom the promised eternal kingdom would
be given by virtue of his obedience. That is precisely why he
came, exactly what was expected of God's promised Messianic
King, as the angelic messenger of God informed Mary:

You will be with child and give birth to a son, and you are to give him the name Jesus. He will be great and will be called the Son of the Most High. The Lord God will give him the throne of his father David, and he will reign over the house of Jacob forever; his kingdom will never end.

Luke 1: 31–3

COUNTER-KINGDOM

Not surprisingly, the kingdom of God in the gospels is portrayed as a counter-kingdom to Satan's and as a combative kingdom to his rule over the hearts of his subjects. Jesus shows dominion over the evil one, his minions, and his rule as the prince of this world. This conflict reaches to the heart of Christ's coming and the essence of his saving work. Jesus explains his kingdom works of power and sway over Satan as evidence of the present presence of his kingdom.

Then they brought him a demon-possessed man who was blind and mute, and Jesus healed him, so that he could talk and see. All the people were astonished and said, 'Could this be the Son of David?' But when the Pharisees heard this, they said, 'It is only by Beelzebub, the prince of demons, that this fellow drives out demons.' Jesus knew their thoughts and said to them, 'Every kingdom divided against itself will be ruined, and every city or household divided against itself will not stand. If Satan drives out Satan, he is divided against himself. How then can his kingdom stand? And if I drive out demons by Beelzebub, by whom do your people drive them out? So then, they will be your judges. But if I drive out demons by the Spirit of God, then the kingdom of God has come upon you.

Matt. 12: 22–8

Jesus' parables showed this kingdom in conflict. Satan is identified as the opponent. He snatched the seed of the gospel sown. He sowed the tares among the wheat.

Rule over hearts is at stake. The kingdom of God advances at the expense of the kingdom of Satan.

RIGHTEOUS RULE

Hasn't God always been king? Yes. And no. God has always been king in that he has been, is, and always will be the sovereign

Lord over all that comes to pass. God's sovereignty speaks to his absolute, abiding and unaffected rule. He is the God who does as he pleases. Nothing can stand against him (Job 42: 2). All that comes to pass is governed by him and serves his sovereign rule, from the luck of the dice (Prov. 16: 33), to the elements of nature (Jonah 1: 4) and its creatures (Jonah 1: 17), to the stars in the universe (Ps. 147: 4), to the responsible decisions of people (Gen. 50: 20; Acts 2: 23). God is personally and purposefully involved in all things.

But there is a sense in which Jesus began to rule as king in a way he had not previously as eternal God. A point came when he was inaugurated as king. Christ rules now not only in the sense of creation, but of redemption. Just as Christ has always been God, but not man, so he has always been creative king, but not redemptive king, not Messianic king. Jesus became man at his incarnation. He added full and undefiled humanity to his deity. 'Immanuel' (God with us) became 'Jesus' (the Lord saves). The former speaks to his person, the latter to his mission (Matt. 1: 21–3). The eternal Son of God entered the world to be Messianic King for his people.

In the accomplishment of his saving work, Jesus was given rule. A king has subjects. Jesus reigns for his church.

> …his incomparably great power for us who believe. That power is like the working of his mighty strength, which he exerted in Christ when he raised him from the dead and seated him at his right hand in the heavenly realms, far above all rule and authority, power and dominion, and every title that can be given, not only in the present age but also in the one to come. And God placed all things under his feet and appointed him to be head over everything for the church.
>
> Eph. 1: 19–22

The church is where the invisible kingdom of God is most visible, through its community and character of righteousness, joy and peace (Rom. 14: 17). The church is the agent of the kingdom of God, charged with proclaiming Christ's redemptive rule. The message of Acts was that this Jesus was 'Lord.' Salvation is seen in terms of authority, kingdom authority.[21]

The kingdom of God is the promised, redemptive kingdom of God and his Christ, which was inaugurated at Christ's first coming and which will be consummated at his second. Through his Messianic mission, Jesus established the kingdom of righteousness, joy, and peace. That kingdom grows in the subduing of his subjects to himself as it fills the whole earth, embracing people from every nation, tongue, and tribe. It will continue to grow until all those purchased at the cross are procured by the Spirit, at which time the present age will be done away with and the kingdom of God ushered in in fullness.

KINGDOM AND AGE

What does all this have to do with the present, evil age and the power to transform? At the center of this present age dominated by the fall of sin stands the kingdom of Satan. Presiding over and empowering this present evil age is the dominion of darkness.

Jesus in his kingdom ushers in a new rule, a new authority, a new power. His kingdom looks to nothing less than the dawning of a new age that has been liberated from the effects of the fall of man. Christ's kingdom is expressive of the age to come. It speaks of deliverance from this present, evil age. Paul expresses that deliverance as a transfer of kingdoms.

> ...giving thanks to the Father, who has qualified you to share in the inheritance of the saints in the kingdom of light. For he has rescued us from the dominion of darkness and brought us into the kingdom of the Son he loves, in whom we have redemption, the forgiveness of sins.
>
> Col. 1: 12–14

As ones rescued from the power of this age and brought into the kingdom of life and light, we are no longer in bondage to sin's power and guilt, its mastery and condemnation. We have been emancipated, liberated.

Another passage of Paul's letter to the Colossians is instructive to us here. It reminds us that Christ, our King's disarmament of the power over us, accomplishes our deliverance.

> When you were dead in your sins and in the uncircumcision of your sinful nature, God made you alive with Christ. He forgave us all our sins, having canceled the written code, with its regulations, that was against us and that stood opposed

to us; he took it away, nailing it to the cross. And having disarmed the powers and authorities, he made a public spectacle of them, triumphing over them by the cross.

Col. 2: 13–15

The power that defined and dominated us has been broken. The power of the present age is expressed in terms of the prince and principalities that prevail in the present age. From this power and grip we have been liberated.

THIS PRESENT POWER

What exactly is that power of the kingdom of God? Again, we turn to the Apostle Paul, who pinpoints that power necessary for a new kingdom and age, capable of liberating us.

> For this reason, ever since I heard about your faith in the Lord Jesus and your love for all the saints, I have not stopped giving thanks for you, remembering you in my prayers. I keep asking that the God of our Lord Jesus Christ, the glorious Father, may give you the Spirit of wisdom and revelation, so that you may know him better. I pray also that the eyes of your heart may be enlightened in order that you may know the hope to which he has called you, the riches of his glorious inheritance in the saints, and his incomparably great power for us who believe. That power is like the working of his mighty strength, which he exerted in Christ when he raised him from the dead and seated him at his right hand in the heavenly realms, far above all rule and authority, power and dominion, and every title that can be given, not only in the present age but also in the one to come.
>
> Ephesians 1:15-21

Kingdom power resides in the resurrection of Jesus Christ. It is the power of the age to come, a power that enlivens, invigorates, and enervates us. Christ has subdued us. He has taken us captive in his train (Eph. 4: 8). As conquering King, he leads us in triumphal procession where we are fragrant to the world (2 Cor 2: 14–16). That aroma is the smell of life to some, the stench of death to others. The Spirit has caused us to be born again, qualifying us for kingdom habitation and inheritance. All this revolves around the resurrection of Jesus Christ, giving us strength for today and bright hope for tomorrow.

The miracles of Jesus gave testimony to the beginning of the final chapter in God's history of redemption. They provided evidence of the reversal of the effects of the fall and the establishment of a new order. Sin brought death; Jesus raised Lazarus to life from the dead. Sin brought grief; Jesus dried the tears of the widow of Nain by returning her dead son to her. Sin brought disease and disfigurement of that which God had created good; Jesus made the blind to see, the lame to walk. These mighty works showed not just power, but redemptive power, restorative power, validating Jesus' claims and verifying the presence of the kingdom of God.[22]

What this means is that evangelism is by its very nature power evangelism. But that which will convince someone of the reality of the kingdom of God will not be a demonstration of power by way of signs, wonders and works to the spiritually blind, but the work of kingdom power by the Spirit of God to give spiritual sight. The power of the Spirit of the risen Christ is at work as an expression of the saving rule of Jesus Christ in opposition to the kingdom of this world and the opposing forces of spiritual darkness.

THE GOSPEL AND THE KINGDOM

The gospel is kingdom-qualified. To preach the kingdom of God is to preach the gospel of salvation in the King, Jesus Christ (Matt. 24: 14). Jesus explained his mission and message in these terms: 'I must preach the good news of the kingdom of God to the other towns also, because that is why I was sent' (Luke 4: 43). When we look up all those reasons Jesus 'came' or 'was sent' in the New Testament, we find they all fit under the umbrella of the establishment of the kingdom of God.

The gospel is the gospel of the kingdom, meaning it points to what God has done in Christ and it carries God's power for his saving purposes. The gospel does not look to what we did, do, or could do (Rom. 1: 16–17). The gospel rises from the ashes of the fall in Genesis 3: 15 and reaches to the person and work of Jesus Christ, who is the subject of the entirety of the Bible in the redemptive kingdom he would establish and its message of hope to the fallen world, as Jesus explained to the disciples after his resurrection.

> He said to them, 'This is what I told you while I was still
> with you: Everything must be fulfilled that is written about
> me in the Law of Moses, the Prophets and the Psalms.'
> Then he opened their minds so they could understand the
> Scriptures. He told them, 'This is what is written: The
> Christ will suffer and rise from the dead on the third day,
> and repentance and forgiveness of sins will be preached in
> his name to all nations, beginning at Jerusalem.
>
> Luke 24: 44–7

The message we are called to bear is the message of the kingdom
(Matt. 10: 7), a message about Jesus as redemptive King.

The call of the gospel is a call to kingdom allegiance, that is,
to repentance and faith. The Baptist's message was to repent
and believe the gospel because its accomplishment was found
in the kingdom of God that had come. The response demanded
to the kingdom is the same response demanded by the gospel,
the message of the kingdom. The gospel of peace looks not
to truce but to a clash of the kingdom of righteousness and
peace with the kingdom of darkness and decay. For us to be
ambassadors of a gospel of peace is not to be brokers of peace
in some sort of shuttle diplomacy, but to announce peace. It
is to call people to a change of kingdom allegiances through
repentance and faith in Jesus Christ.

Paul's message in Acts 26: 20 that the Gentiles should repent
and bring forth fruit in keeping with their repentance follows
on the heels of Acts 26: 17–18: 'I will rescue you from your
own people and from the Gentiles. I am sending you to them
to open their eyes and turn them from darkness to light, and
from the power of Satan to God, so that they may receive
forgiveness of sins and a place among those who are sanctified
by faith in me.'

Evangelism is conducted in power, power to open eyes,
power to change hearts, power to set free from the bondage of
the present, evil age, power to deliver from Satan to God.

The hope of the gospel is the hope of kingdom promise, put on
exhibition in the flow and outcome of the book of Revelation.
Kingdom alignment is expressed by change of kingdom
allegiance through repentance and faith (Matt. 4: 17).

CLASH OF KINGDOMS

Paul makes it clear that at the heart of it all is a spiritual battle, fought against a spiritual foe, with spiritual weapons and spiritual power, for a spiritual cause.

> For though we live in the world, we do not wage war as the world does. The weapons we fight with are not the weapons of the world. On the contrary, they have divine power to demolish strongholds. We demolish arguments and every pretension that sets itself up against the knowledge of God, and we take captive every thought to make it obedient to Christ.
>
> 2 Cor. 10: 3–5

The picture of the kingdom of God given to us in Scripture is of a rock growing to fill the earth, of a small seed growing and spreading as shade to the nations. The nature of that growth is spiritual conflict. The kingdom of God grows at the expense of the kingdom of Satan.

Our enemy is not flesh and blood, but spiritual. He has been disarmed of his leverage of accusation because every charge against those of Christ's kingdom has been nailed to the cross and paid for in full. But our enemy lurks and prowls.

The kingdom of God speaks to the power of the new life, the age to come, breaking in to the death, decay, disintegration, and destruction of the present age. Right now these two ages overlap while God extends his kingdom and grows his church, against which the gates of hell will not prevail. But there will come a day when the old order of things will be done away with and the new will come in fullness.

For today, however, as long as it is called today, we take the gospel of the kingdom of God with its hope and call, to a world that is perishing. We who have been delivered from the power of this age will one day be delivered from its presence. At our Lord's return in glory the present age will be no more as the rhythm of time unravels into eternity.

KINGDOM MENTALITY

Being members of the kingdom of God gives us identity, power, and a mandate. It means that we must see ourselves as soldiers of the cross, enlisted for the cause of our King. It means we have a message to bear. It means a power and purpose beyond ourselves is at work in this world, at work in and through us. The command of bearing witness comes from the lips of him who subdued us to himself, conscripted us to his service and is at work through us to complete his work.[23]

Considering the nature and the opposition of the kingdom of God and the kingdom of Satan, while the age to come and the present age overlap, we cannot allow ourselves to countenance a peace-time mentality for ourselves or the church. The very nature of the growth of the kingdom of God and its extension through the work of evangelism demands we live life as though we were at war. The church on earth is the church militant. The church triumphant is the church at peace, enjoying the rest of heavenly glory won by Christ.

We grimace with guilt at the words of John Bunyan, author of *Pilgrim's Progress*, who describes the devices of the devil in his work, *The Holy War*: 'Let us but cumber and occupy Mansoul [the church], and they will make their castle a warehouse for goods instead of a garrison for men of war.'

The kingdom of God is real and present. It breaks into the present order with the power of the new life, and with the message of new life—resurrection life. It is expressive of the sure promise of the age to come. What is now inaugurated will one day be consummated. The old, fallen order of things will be done away with. The new, redeemed order of things will be ushered in in fullness. For now, we live in and work in the power of the age to come. We are workers in a counter kingdom, 'fellow workers for the kingdom of God' (Col. 4: 11). We are children of the King, subjects of the kingdom, servants for its Commander and zealots for its cause. And we lay siege to the kingdom of darkness that rules in power of this age.

Our battle is with a spiritual enemy, not physical. The kingdom of God qualifies our battle and our tactics and our weapons. In the milieu of this age, empowered and mandated by the kingdom of God, we contend with an enemy.

4

Unmasking the Enemy

I grew up at the beach. My home was three blocks from the ocean. I would drift off to sleep at night with the rhythmic pounding of the surf in my ears. Talk about a Jeckyl and Hyde town! In the summer the area bustled with activity. People poured in from all over the place. You could find license plates from across the country. The streets teamed with people, day and night. Then came winter. The shops had closed up. The hordes of people were gone, leaving the handful of locals behind. The bustle had turned to the rustle of the occasional movement of someone walking her dog. The hustle had become the hassle of finding something to do for amusement.

There was a certain charm to living at the shore all year round. An untouched blanket of fresh fallen snow on the beach was a thing of beauty. Watching the fury of the ocean during a nor'easter was fascinating. Plus, there's something to be said for peace and quiet. But as a teenager I didn't see it. I appreciate the beach and the town much more now that I have grown up and moved away than I did then.

All this created the problem of finding something to do during the barren winter. Just to show you how dull things were, when I was in my early teens we would seek out fun at the city dump. When darkness fell, my buddies and I would park in front of a pile of garbage, headlights off, and wait. After a period of calm and quiet, we would turn on the high beams, take up our weapons, rush out of the car toward the pile of garbage, and inflict blunt force trauma on the rats as they scurried to escape. Now that's a sport where trash talk would be encouraged.

I relate this rather pathetic and disturbing story to make one point: to effectively combat our self-appointed adversary we had to know what they were like. We knew they were fond of garbage. They were nocturnal. They did not like the light, so we had to be quick to act when the headlights were turned on. Our tactics and weapons were tailored to the nature of the enemy and the battle.

That's just the way it is when it comes to spiritual warfare in evangelism. We need to know the foe. Awareness of our adversary allows us to plan and prepare properly. In this chapter we zero in on the reconnaissance report our God gives us, not only seeing the opposition we face, but particularly scrutinizing the opponent. In studying the biblical profile of Satan, we are apprised and alerted to what we face as we look to engage others for Christ.

PROCEED WITH CAUTION

One word of caution is in order. For some strange reason we can have an inclination to morbid fascination with the enemy. My family and I had the opportunity to spend a couple of weeks in England, staying in one of the outer boroughs of London. London offers all kinds of things to see and do. We got to visit the typical tourist stops. The place that I found most fascinating was the Tower of London, which is not so much a tower as it is a fortress complex. It was also a place of historic torture and execution. That's the part that intrigued me most. In London, a variety of walking tours are available. Of the scores of offerings, my kids and I picked the Jack the Ripper walking tour that traced the steps of the notorious and brutal serial killer of prostitutes in London's East End in the late nineteenth century. What is it that attracts people to the macabre?

The same is true of our enemy, the devil. He is the epitome of evil. Just as people can be entranced with the human evil of Stalin, Hitler, and Jack the Ripper, we can be captivated with curiosity at the one who is identified for us as the 'evil one.' It's like playing with fire, watching the flame dance, forgetting how combustible is the material around us. In matters of sanctification, sometimes we see how close we can get to the flame of temptation without getting burnt. The same is true of an unhealthy preoccupation with the evil one in evangelism, who would sing his siren song to lure us away from the narrow strait of God's truth, onto the rocks of human error and contrivance, as we seek to reach others for Jesus Christ.

This morbid fascination seems to fit right into his intentions. It is like Satan the serpent fanning out his neck to mesmerize us and so draw us into his reach. We need to be careful not to cross the boundary from awareness to obsession. On this note of caution, we turn to examine the profile God gives to us of the enemy we face in the work of evangelism.

A FORMIDABLE FOE

Albeit judgmentally-impaired and psychologically questionable, the idea of taking on rats is not that intimidating. After all, they're relatively little and ordinarily not particularly combative, at least if they have a route of escape. However, the foe God describes for us is considerably different.

Vacationing in northern Vermont presented a different scenario to the doldrums-induced rat beating escapades of my youth. The setting was the same—a garbage dump, the opposition not. Although, I never verified it with my own eyes, rumor had it that the area dump was a favorite haunt for wild animals. These animals, however, were not rats. They were bears, big bears with big teeth and a bad attitude in the face of a meal.

When we think of the foe God calls us to face for the work of evangelism, we would do better to think of bears than rats. Our enemy, the devil, is strong, savvy, subtle, and relentless. We may be able to stand against a rat. It's a different story with a bear.

Yet, at the same time, while we should have a sober regard for Satan, we don't want to make him larger than life. We need to be on guard against glamorizing him or giving him more credit than he deserves.

A friend invited me to a professional baseball game. We met at the stadium and found our seats slightly below the tree line. The atmosphere was electric: the animation of the fans, the lights, the big screens showing film clips and replays, speakers alternately carrying music and the play-by-play, hungry patrons working out installment payments to purchase the food. It was fun. But what struck me was the players. I looked down from my perch to see these little uniformed specks of humanity spread across the playing field. I knew many of the names from the sports page. And it struck me: they are regular people, ordinary human beings like me, except they're rich.

Just as we can make celebrities larger than life, we can do that with our spiritual foe. The problem with that is we end up ascribing to him attributes he does not have and abilities we don't need to deal with.

What is our adversary like? We begin with what should be obvious, but is often overlooked. Satan is not God. Satan is not God's equal, the guy in the black hat to God's white hat. Satan is a creature, as in created being. The devil is a counterfeiter as we will see shortly, but he is not God's counterpart.

God created two types of beings, angelic and human. We belong to the latter, Satan to the former. Satan is a created, angelic being who rebelled against God (Jude 6). God permitted this rebellion for his own purposes. Other angels, God preserved for his own services. The Bible calls these 'elect angels' (1 Tim. 5: 21). Angel means messenger. Angels do not act on their own initiative, with their own agendas. They serve God's bidding and seek his glory. The angel Gabriel who visited the virgin Mary was sent by God with a message and on a mission.

Satan and his angels belong to the spiritual realm of angelic beings. By virtue of their fall, they are called demons. While the elect angels voluntarily serve God's bidding, the fallen angels purposefully rebel against God's directives.

In saying this, we need to tread carefully so as not to fall off the beam of biblical balance to the left or to the right. We don't want to get the idea that Satan and his fallen angels are autonomous, existing outside the pale of God's providence, which governs all events and entities. Scenes like Satan asking permission to afflict Job or to sift Peter are given to remind us who's in charge.

When speaking of Satan's evil functioning in the context of God's absolute sovereignty, we might find help in an important distinction God makes for us. The book of Deuteronomy takes special care to describe the prophetic office in protection of God's revealed truth (Deut. 13 & 18). Then, toward the close of the book God says this through the prophet Moses: 'The secret things belong to the Lord our God, but the things revealed belong to us and to our children forever, that we may follow all the words of this law' (Deut. 29: 29). In this statement, God is sorting out for us two 'wills.' The unknown things belong to the decree or plan of God, which serves his perfect purpose. These things are secret to us, not to God. It is to this secret will that Paul responds in awe and adoration after addressing God's plan in election:

> Oh, the depth of the riches of the wisdom and knowledge of God! How unsearchable his judgments, and his paths beyond tracing out! 'Who has known the mind of the Lord? Or who has been his counselor?' 'Who has ever given to God, that God should repay him?' For from him and through him and to him are all things. To him be the glory forever! Amen.[80]
>
> Rom 11: 33–6

In contrast to the secret will is the revealed will. The secret will has not been disclosed. It is secret to us, not God. The revealed will has been exposed to us. It is the revealed will that we are responsible to obey, and to inculcate in our children as we raise them in the nurture and admonition of the Lord.[24]

Satan, as with any responsible creature, can and does violate the revealed will of God. He cannot deviate from the secret will of God's eternal plan. Satan can only serve the decretive will of him who works out all things according to the counsel of his own will (Eph. 1: 11). Satan entered Judas to send Christ to his death on the cross, according to the eternal plan of God. Yet he did so willingly and culpably as part of that overarching plan of God. Isaiah tells us of God the Son as Suffering Servant that 'it was God's will to crush him and cause him to suffer' (Isa. 53: 10), reminding us whose purpose governs and prevails.

Our foe is fearsome and formidable. But he is a created being nonetheless. Only God is eternal and uncreated. While Satan may be strong, dispatched throughout the earth through his demonic minions, and an adept observer of human weakness and frailty, only God is omnipotent, omnipresent, and omniscient.

When we hear him described as a 'god' in God's revealed profile, we are not to think of him as a rival deity in some sort of Greek pantheon. Rather, the devil is an idolatrous created being, who operates with evil intent and insidious tactics, exclusively within the providential confines of the sovereign and true God. The fact that we must encounter and contend with spiritual opposition is itself part of God's overarching and superintending purpose, serving his eternal plan. When the Apostle Paul states, 'we wanted to come to you—certainly I, Paul, did, again and again—but Satan stopped us' (1 Thess. 2: 18), he is not suggesting that God has been dethroned or stymied. Rather, he is identifying the reality of spiritual warfare in evangelism and the foe to be faced in the work, all within the borders of the purpose of God's decree.[25]

COUNTERFEIT

The police in my area recently pulled off a sting to bust a major criminal operation. You're probably thinking drugs, weapons. No. Clothes. A whole warehouse full of jackets, sneakers, and caps made to look like their designer counterparts, complete with label and emblem. Most of the bogus apparel had to do with athletic wear, with some designer labels thrown in for good measure.

Without royalties or fees, the clothing could be hawked on the streets at a huge price discount. The thieves not only cut the commissions, they cut the quality. Those who bought the garments got what they paid for. The counterfeit clothing proved to be a dud, disappointing those who expected more. To top it off, the rightful manufacturers that were being ripped off lost money and, perhaps more importantly, reputation. Inferior quality clothes had the potential to bring dishonor and distrust to their name and products.

Satan is the king of counterfeiters. The major subject of his counterfeiting operation is God himself, particularly God as the author of salvation. Satan's targets are unsuspecting consumers of religious realities. His counterfeiting scheme can be seen in several ways in Scripture. Paul attests to one approach:

> For such men are false apostles, deceitful workmen, masquerading as apostles of Christ. And no wonder, for Satan himself masquerades as an angel of light. It is not surprising, then, if his servants masquerade as servants

of righteousness. Their end will be what their actions deserve.

2 Cor. 11: 13–15

Maybe Halloween is right up Satan's alley. He costumes himself in apparel contrary to his real nature, to carry out his sinister schemes. I laid out the statements bracketing this exposé so that we can note how people who are part of Satan's realm, who are part of this present, evil age, can be used as tools of the devil.[26] They serve the same ends as he, and will suffer the same fate for their alliance.

While God provides tactical profiles of our enemy, virtually everywhere his name is mentioned throughout Scripture, the most comprehensive report is presented to us in the Book of Revelation. It's a shame that Revelation has been relegated to the 'truth is stranger than fiction' section of the Christian's biblical library. Popular evangelical writings tend to treat it as a crystal ball rather than the rudder that God intends it to be to safely navigate the seas of life in this fallen world. Revelation does just what it says: it reveals, not conceals. We're just unaccustomed to the way it does it, with the vivid symbolism of apocalyptic writings, which are to be taken symbolically rather than literally unless the text requires otherwise.

What does Revelation reveal? It makes it clear that Jesus Christ has won the victory and reigns on high for his church. Also evident is the spiritual worldview of life and spiritual opposition at work. Revelation is a pastoral book given by Christ to alert us to spiritual conflict, to assure us of his resurrection victory, and to admonish us to stand firm in what is true and trustworthy—his saving work. While the end of the book, with its promise of a new creation liberated from the effects of sin, is tremendously encouraging, that's not the focal point. Our attention is directed to Satan as the real cause of persecution suffered at the hands of worldly tormenters. And more importantly, Revelation makes it abundantly clear that the true God will bring judgment. That means that all who aligned themselves with Satan and his kingdom will suffer his fate. Contrary to most depictions, Satan will not be the dispenser of eternal torment in hell; he will be a co-recipient.

At the center of Revelation hangs a portrait of Satan, displayed as a warning from the pastoral heart of God. Just as the wizard was exposed as a charlatan in *The Wizard of Oz*, so this portrait pulls back the curtain to reveal Satan as a pretender, a counterfeiter. Salvation is found in the triune God. Pseudo-salvation is found in the bogus satanic trinity, in which the red dragon, the sea beast, and the false prophet counterfeit God the Father, Son, and Holy Spirit. Here are a few parallels, found in Revelation 12–13 in reference to the rest of the book and the rest of Scripture.[27]

- The beast is the image of Satan, coming from the dragon, just as Christ is the image of God, begotten by the Father, the exact representation of his being, in whom the fullness of the godhead dwells.
- The beast has many crowns and Christ has many crowns, both claiming supreme and sovereign rule.
- The beast has blasphemous names while Christ has worthy names
- The dragon gives the beast his power, his throne, and great authority, just as Christ is given power, a throne, and authority from the Father.
- The beast has a healed fatal wound, counterfeiting Christ's resurrection. The beast's healing draws followers to him, just as the resurrection of Christ is vivid in the gospel message.
- Worship is directed to the dragon and the beast, just as Christians worship the Father and the Son.
- Satan presents himself as creator, but only God is Creator. Satan is a deformer and a destroyer, a perverter and a prevaricator.
- He is known as a false prophet, whereas the Holy Spirit is associated with prophecy but of truth.
- The false prophet also is called a beast, tying him in with the counterfeit Christ, just as the Holy Spirit is associated with the risen Christ (see John 14: 16–18).
- The false prophet desires that people worship not himself but the beast, just as the Holy Spirit looks to bring glory and focus to Christ and not himself.
- He works miraculous signs, counterfeiting the miracles of the Holy Spirit.

- He forces a mark on his subjects, just as Christians are sealed with the Holy Spirit. He seals them for damnation, while the Holy Spirit for eternal life.
- As a propagandist for the beast, the false prophet serves a counterfeiting witnessing function, while the Holy Spirit provides witness to the Truth.
- This false prophet also leads in false worship versus the real Spirit who leads in true worship of the true God.

In keeping with the apocalyptic genre, God doesn't give us a photographic image, but paints a symbolically rich figurative picture, exposing Satan to be a false god, offering a counterfeit hope. This is the enemy with whom we contend for the work of witness to a world blinded by his deceptions.

TITLES

We also learn more of our enemy and what to expect of him through the names given him in Scripture and his modus operandi, his method of operations, displayed there. Alexander was called 'Great' for a reason. Hank Aaron was given the nickname 'Hammering' for a reason. Titles can be telling. They communicate something that we should know about the person. How much more so with biblical monikers, where names convey a great deal of meaning.

God's Word gives a variety of names to the devil: accuser, adversary, devil, enemy, evil one, father of lies, a god, murderer, prince, Satan, tempter, Beelzebub, Belial, and the list goes on. Examination of a few of these provides us with a clear picture of his character and a good idea of what we're up against in the spiritual opposition we encounter as we seek to reach others for Christ.

Adversary. The proper name Satan generally means adversary, one who stands in opposition. Who is Satan's opponent? Ultimately God, especially Christ, and certainly us as disciples of Christ. The Book of Revelation makes this opposition vivid (Rev. 12: 1–17). There a monstrous red dragon, symbolic of Satan, crouches to devour the male child, symbolic of Christ, upon his birth. When the dragon failed to overcome the child and the child gained victory over the dragon, the dragon takes off after the woman who gave birth to the child, the woman being symbolic of the covenant community, the church, and the rest of her offspring. Opposition and oppression of the church by the devil characterizes the period of time between Christ's first coming in humility and second coming in glory.

Accuser. The name Satan more narrowly means accuser. The root is the Hebrew word for 'accuse.' Accusation describes a primary means by which Satan opposes God's people. He is the 'accuser of the brethren.' He is the prosecuting attorney to Christ's defense attorney. Satan is the accuser; Christ the advocate (1 John 2: 1–2). In Zechariah 3, Satan stands before the judgment seat of God to accuse. He is disarmed by the intervention of God to provide an alien righteousness, anticipating the work of Christ. Though disarmed, Satan continues his attempts at accusation to lead God's people away from the gospel that proclaims a righteousness by faith, and to weigh them down with guilt and so seek to discredit Christ and his saving work.

In some cases the names of Satan are multiplied serving as commentary for one another. For example, in one of his parables of the kingdom our Lord Jesus exposes the true culprit and explains his adversarial efforts.

> Then he left the crowd and went into the house. His disciples came to him and said, 'Explain to us the parable of the weeds in the field.' He answered, 'The one who sowed the good seed is the Son of Man. The field is the world, and the good seed stands for the sons of the kingdom. The weeds are the sons of the evil one, and the enemy who sows them is the devil. The harvest is the end of the age, and the harvesters are angels. As the weeds are pulled up and burned in the fire, so it will be at the end of the age. The Son of Man will send out his angels, and they will weed out of his kingdom everything that causes sin and all who do evil. They will throw them into the fiery furnace, where there will be weeping and gnashing of teeth. Then the righteous will shine like the sun in the kingdom of their Father. He who has ears, let him hear.'
>
> Matt. 13: 36–43

Jesus calls Satan 'the evil one,' 'the enemy,' 'the devil.' 'Evil' speaks of his character. He is the one who has been sinning from the beginning (1 John 3: 8). 'Enemy' shows his stance. 'Devil' is equivalent to 'Satan' and means slanderer or accuser, looking to his approach.

In John 8: 42–4 our Lord gives us a pithy profile of our enemy, from whose kingdom we have been rescued.

> Jesus said to them, 'If God were your Father, you would love me, for I came from God and now am here. I have not come on my own; but he sent me. Why is my language not clear to you? Because you are unable to hear what I say. You belong to your father, the devil, and you want to carry out your father's desire. He was a murderer from the beginning, not holding to the truth, for there is no truth in him. When he lies, he speaks his native language, for he is a liar and the father of lies.

Satan is a murderer, a father, a liar, and the father of lies.

The Bible brings us many more names and titles of Satan, but this sampling will suffice to betray his evil character and ill intentions. But how does he go about his efforts to oppose for evil and injury? Scripture also gives us intelligence on our enemy's tactics.

TACTICS

Our enemy the devil employs three primary tactics in his efforts to oppose us in our walk with Christ (sanctification) and in our work for Christ (kingdom service).

Accusation. This tactic is inherent in the name of our enemy as 'Satan' and 'the devil.' Satan is the accuser who prosecutes the offenses of our sin against those who would stand before the tribunal of God or hold their lives up to the plumb line of God's law.

In Christ, however, those offenses are removed from our record. By his sacrificial death, he atones for our sin. He purges our guilt. Though the sin is ours, the guilt becomes his. We are declared 'not guilty,' not because the holy God simply pardons us, but because he pays the debt of our sin in his Son. Satan as the accuser is left without ammunition. All charges against us are satisfied in Christ.

Still, our enemy would weigh us down with the guilt of our sin. In so doing, he tries to discredit and devalue the work of Christ. He seeks to contaminate God's grace with our efforts at obedience to satisfy the righteous requirements of God's law, inducing guilt feelings and efforts to try harder.

These accusations assault both us as God's instruments and our perception of the gospel. They work to discourage us because of doubts as to our suitability as God's instruments in evangelism. They cast doubt on the glory of the gospel as God's perfect provision for a sinner's need.

Against the devil's accusations we are to trust wholly in Christ's work. We are to believe that there is now no condemnation for those in Christ Jesus.

Deception. Our enemy is a deceiver. He tries to get us to believe and act on lies. These lies are often proffered through the world's system. Hence Paul's warning in Colossians 2: 8 that we discriminate between the teaching of the world that has an appearance of value and wisdom, and the teaching of our Lord that we are to hear and put into practice.

Satan's assault on the truth is often subtle. He embellishes and distorts a grain of truth to such an extent that it is unrecognizable, although the grain generates a ring of sensibility. Our introduction to Satan in Genesis 3 sets the stage for his approach. He poses competing counsel to God's, counsel that will bring death, not life, and so lure followers away from the safety and security of God's truth. The devil is a purveyor of lies. Those lies are the bait for the jaws of his trap. 'Did God really say?' is the first line of assault, the initial tear in the fabric from which the cloth is torn asunder.

Waging warfare witness is waging a war of words, the word of truth versus the wayword of error (1 John 4: 1; 2 Cor. 10: 5). Against the devil's deceptions, we are to stand firmly with both feet on the given truth of God's written Word.

Temptation. Satan is the siren who would lure us to the rocks of spiritual ruin and ministerial impotency. He tempts us, playing on the sin that remains in us—the lust of the eyes, the lust of the flesh, and the pride of life. He plays on the lust of the eyes that sees and yearns after the world's trinkets. The latest technological innovations or the trendiest fashions captivate us and we are drawn to want more, more, more. He plays on the lust of the flesh that indulges in anger and sexual impurity. Preservation of our rights and pursuance of our gratifications rage in our hearts, fueled by the temptations of our enemy only a mouse click away. He plays on the pride of life that is more concerned for pleasing men than God, more concerned for exalting self than God. We seek first our kingdom and our righteousness.

Against the devil's temptations, we are to be ever vigilant. We are to hold fast to our Lord, finding our strength in him, girding our minds for action as obedient children in pursuit of holiness, out of love for God.

As we survey this triad of tactics, we can well see how they complement one another and even overlap. Satan tempts us to find fulfillment in an activity or product, deceiving us through the prophetic advertising of the world with its empty promises. His temptations lead us into idolatry by which we establish ourselves as rivals to God. He seeks to lead us into that which can never satisfy.[28] Through these our enemy sidetracks us from delight in God and sidelines us from his work.

FORCES OF EVIL

Satan is also described as 'the ruler of this world,' 'the prince of the power of the air,' and 'the god of this age.' Clearly, he is depicted as the head honcho of evil. He is Beelzebub, lord of the flies. He is leader over the angelic demons. He is also ruler over human beings who by their fallen nature are part of his fallen realm. It is in this sense that Jesus says to those who are against him, 'You belong to your father, the devil, and you want to carry out your father's desire.'

There are many fallen angels. I'm not sure how many there are. That might be one of those 'how many (fallen) angels will fit on the head of a pin' questions. But no matter what the number, God directs our attention in the spiritual realm to Satan as the prince, the idolatrous god competing for the hearts of men and women that rightfully belong only to the living and true God.

There may well be an angelic hierarchy of military rank in this spiritual realm as some suggest. Jude 9 calls the elect angel Michael an 'archangel.' Ephesians 6: 12 may indeed describe 'hell's corporate headquarters, laying an authority structure in descending order.'[29] The authority structure, however, is not made clear by God in his Word and is never sorted out for separate and varying approaches in our dealing with spiritual opposition.

What that means for us is that we do not need to make any attempts to learn the names of any of Satan's subordinates as we would look to reach others for Christ or reach out into a particular area on evangelistic mission. We learn all that we need to know about our enemy from God's Word, both for facing our foe and waging battle for the kingdom of God inherent in evangelism. That Word gives us knowledge of the whole through knowledge of the one, the leader of the spiritual forces of darkness.

TAKE HEART

After the terrorist attacks of September 11, 2001, the United States adopted a 'Homeland Security Advisory System.' That system involves five levels of 'threat conditions,' each identified by a color and each putting into place protective measures corresponding to the level of threat. These terrorism alerts carry recommended responses by both the government and the private sector. The threat levels progress from low (green) to guarded (blue) to elevated (yellow) to high (orange) to severe (red).

Thus far we have been seeing red. In taking a close look at the enemy we face in our work of witness for Jesus Christ, we've spent much time under the highest level of alert. It's not a matter that our enemy 'might' oppose us, he does. God's Word cautions us to be constantly on guard and continually prepared. Our enemy the devil prowls about looking for someone to devour. In the environment of the age in which we live, sin is continually crouching at our door, ready to pounce, and it desires to have us. In this picture, the terror alert can never be lowered, even to orange. But let me close this profile of our enemy with a word of relief and encouragement.

Our enemy the devil has been defeated and disarmed. True, he has not been destroyed. As illustrated in the casting out of the legion of demons into the herd of pigs, Jesus has authority over Satan, but he has allowed him to continue to prowl and prod, all within the purposes of a sovereign God. In view of the horrific picture of the enemy we face, turn your eyes to him who is your refuge and strength, your conquering king: 'Since the children have flesh and blood, he too shared in their humanity so that by his death he might destroy him who holds the power of death—that is, the devil—and free those who all their lives were held in slavery by their fear of death' (Heb. 2: 14–15).

This reality for us who belong to the kingdom of God and his Christ is carried to conclusion in Revelation, where the wages of sin are dispensed to Satan and his followers, and the reward of Christ is lavished on his disciples whom he rescued. In other words, the terror alert is red now, but there will come a day for us in Christ when it will be green—no threat at all, for ever. The old order of things will be done away with and the kingdom of our Lord ushered in in its fullness.

Satan is powerful in ways Scripture does not fully reveal to us. We can gain a feel for his power through observing his activity in Job or Revelation. We are told not to fear those who can kill the body, but to fear him who can destroy both body and soul in hell (Matt. 10: 28). In Revelation we see believers suffering and dying at the hands of instruments of the evil one. But though they die physically, they will not and cannot die spiritually. We do want to fear God and not others. Yet at the same time God informs us and shows us believers experiencing physical death, just as believing Abel did at the hands of Cain who willingly allowed himself to be mastered by Satan. It is redemptively that we are strong in the Lord and in his mighty power against the assaults of Satan in our own hearts and in our evangelistic endeavors.

Satan works through deception, temptation and accusation. His primary leverage over us has been broken. He has been cast down from his position of accusation before the judgment seat of God by the redeeming work of our Advocate, Jesus Christ. In the old time movies the bad guy with the black moustache held the mortgage on the widow's home. The date was set for him to foreclose. Enter the clean-shaven hero to pay the bill she could not and rescue her from the bag guy's leverage, freeing her from his power over her. That's the gist of Christ's work on our behalf. But we have not only been freed from sin's condemnation, we have been liberated from sin's power. Our hero is Jesus Christ. In him, by his Spirit, we prevail against our enemy's deceptions, temptations and accusations. In Christ, we are empowered and greatly encouraged for the evangelistic mission he gives us.

The Apostle Paul cautions us not to be unaware of Satan's schemes (2 Cor. 2: 11). Why?—'lest he outwit us.' We live and serve our risen King in a fallen world, facing spiritual opposition. That spiritual adversary is real. The spiritual conflict is real.

The key to our battle is threefold: 1) that we beware of the real and present danger, 2) be aware of our enemy's character and tactics, and 3) bear the weapons and methods suitable for the task given to us by God.

II

EQUIPMENT

5

Plundering Christ's Spoils

Our enemy is spiritual. That doesn't mean he isn't real. It just means you can't see him. How do you fight a foe you can't see? Just asking that question lends itself to all sorts of fanciful notions of spiritual combat. But we must confine ourselves to what God has told us in his Word.

We prepare for the spiritual confrontation inherent in the work of witness by going to the armory and seeing what God has laid out for our use as we contend with our foe. The Apostle Paul stirs our interest when he says: 'For though we live in the world, we do not wage war as the world does. The weapons we fight with are not the weapons of the world. On the contrary, they have divine power to demolish strongholds' (2 Cor. 10: 3–4).

What are these weapons of God's own design that are so different from any the world has to offer? When we think of God's creating power and the power we see on the pages of redemptive history, from the parting of the Red Sea to the feeding of the 5000, we wonder what exactly are these weapons that are endowed with the power of God himself? What will we see when we open the door to God's spiritual armory? How will we know how to use them?

Before we take a close look at the weapons our Lord gives us for spiritual combat, we need to prepare ourselves for what weapons we can expect to find.

RIGHT WEAPONS

The United States began its military campaign in Iraq around mid-March 2003. In May 2003 the United States President declared that major military operations in Iraq were completed. In June the news continued to report skirmishes in which Iraqis and Americans were wounded or killed. Snipers posed a constant danger. Iraqi insurgents were captured and key Iraqi leaders rounded up. Even the search for Sadaam Hussein continued. Oil pipelines were sabotaged. The landscape was peppered with land mines. Fighting went on unabated.

How could the President say that the war was over when fighting continued? How could victory be claimed when the target of the military operations, Saddam Hussein, had not been killed or even accounted for? The answer is that though the ruthless dictator may still be alive, he was not in power. His tyrannical grip had been broken.

The same is true of our enemy, the devil. Though he continues to roam and be active, he is not in power. Satan continues to act in this present, evil age but the power of a liberating force has taken hold and so broken his hold.

What's that got to do with weapons? The point is this: different weapons are required for each stage of the war. When the campaign in Iraq was initiated, the capability and number of weapons used was astounding. The power of the warheads and the delivery systems for the missiles that carried them boggled the mind. The barrage of these munitions was relentless. GPS navigation systems carried explosives to a military target. Missiles launched hundreds of miles away could be diverted in-flight if intelligence warranted, all in service to the focus of the assault. But after the battle was won and the oppressive regime broken, these weapons and tactics ceased to be employed.

The same is true for us, in the spiritual battle our Lord calls us to fight, in our efforts to liberate men and women held captive in the bonds of sin and to bring them into the glorious freedom of children of God. The weapons we use are different from the weapons wielded by the One who came to bring freedom for those oppressed by sin's guilt and power. Ours is to plunder the spoils of his victory.

In order for us to appreciate the weapons given to us by our Lord for spiritual battle and how to use them properly, we must first understand the overcoming work of Jesus Christ.

THE DIVINE WARRIOR

The Scriptures characterize the incarnation and mission of Jesus Christ in military terms. He came to destroy the works of the devil. He rescued us from this age, liberated us from the kingdom of darkness, and established us in the kingdom of life and light.

To see exactly what weapons we have been given, how to use them, and for what goals, we turn to examine what our Lord Jesus Christ did in his emancipating work. We can make this statement at the outset: Just as the power of the kingdom of God resides in the resurrection of Jesus as the Christ, so the effectiveness of the mission resides in our weapons imbued with the redemptive purpose and power of Christ's work.

That's part of what it means to find our strength in the Lord and his mighty power—power of the new life and the age to come at work in this age, through us in the weapons we wield.

Our God is the Divine Warrior, the One who fights for his people.[30] A quick overview shows warfare fills the Old Testament history of God's liberating his people and establishing them in Canaan. Basic to that physical warfare was the principle that victory was found in the Lord. Moses instructed the people: 'Do not be afraid. Stand firm and you will see the deliverance the Lord will bring you today. The Egyptians you see today you will never see again. The Lord will fight for you; you need only to be still' (Exod. 14: 13–14). The battle was with the Lord. They were to trust and obey.

As the Egyptians pursued the Israelites through the Red Sea in the Exodus out of Egypt, the chariots got stuck in the mud, wheels came off, confusion reigned. They concluded they had to get away, because it was painfully apparent that the Lord was fighting for his people.

The victory song of those freed from the house of bondage celebrated the Lord as Divine Warrior, fighting for the objects of his mercy and grace against an oppressive foe:

> Then Moses and the Israelites sang this song to the Lord:
>> I will sing to the Lord,
>>   for he is highly exalted.
>> The horse and its rider
>>   he has hurled into the sea.
>> The Lord is my strength and my song;
>>   he has become my salvation.
>> he is my God, and I will praise him,

> my father's God, and I will exalt him.
> The Lord is a warrior;
> the Lord is his name.
>
> Exod. 15: 1–3

This same theme of deliverance of God's people by his mighty hand winds its way through redemptive history until it reaches its culmination in the cross. There God's Son secured ultimate and eternal victory for his people—and he did so alone. All the sheep had scattered as Jesus faced his foe. God would fight the spiritual battle anticipated by the physical battles of the Old Testament, a battle that he alone was capable of fighting.

WARLORDS

Surveying the field of battle at the turn of the testaments, we see two combatants, the incarnate Son of God and the evil one. But more is at stake than simply struggle between Jesus and the Satan. Scripture describes each as a ruler of a kingdom. Jesus is the Lord of a kingdom of righteousness, joy, and peace. Satan is called Beelzebub, lord of the flies, ruler of this fallen world. Each has his subjects. Satan has authority over those born into this fallen world, those born dead in sin, bound by its power. The subjects of Jesus are those of Satan's realm whom the Father has given him from before the foundation of the world.

Messianic Mission. In the fullness of time, the eternal Son of God took to himself human flesh and frailty by being born of a virgin, born under law. After Jesus' baptism at the Jordan, which initiated his public ministry, the Spirit led him into the desert for the first step of his Messianic mission. What did that first step involve? Notice the account given to us by Luke.

> Jesus, full of the Holy Spirit, returned from the Jordan and was led by the Spirit in the desert, where for forty days he was tempted by the devil. He ate nothing during those days, and at the end of them he was hungry. The devil said to him, 'If you are the Son of God, tell this stone to become bread.'
>
> Jesus answered, 'It is written: "Man does not live on bread alone."'
>
> The devil led him up to a high place and showed him in an instant all the kingdoms of the world. And he said to him, 'I will give you all their authority and splendor, for it

has been given to me, and I can give it to anyone I want to. So if you worship me, it will all be yours.'

Jesus answered, 'It is written: "Worship the Lord your God and serve him only."'

The devil led him to Jerusalem and had him stand on the highest point of the temple. 'If you are the Son of God,' he said, 'throw yourself down from here. For it is written: "he will command his angels concerning you to guard you carefully; they will lift you up in their hands, so that you will not strike your foot against a stone."'

Jesus answered, 'It says: "Do not put the Lord your God to the test."' When the devil had finished all this tempting, he left him until an opportune time.

Luke 4:1–13.

Jesus' first step in his journey to the cross involved battle.

What do we make of this encounter? What significance does it hold? Paul provides the key: 'For just as through the disobedience of the one man the many were made sinners, so also through the obedience of the one man the many will be made righteous' (Rom. 5: 19). The two men of whom Paul speaks are Adam, the first man, representative of the fallen creation and a fallen progeny, and Jesus, the second man, representative of a new creation and a redeemed people.

The dividing line, the distinguishing feature between the two men is obedience. Listen again to the apostle: 'Consequently, just as the result of one trespass was condemnation for all men, so also the result of one act of righteousness was justification that brings life for all men' (Rom. 5: 18). That obedience affects not only each man himself, but the entire population he represents. Every person represented by the first Adam in his disobedience fell under the dominion of sin. Everyone represented by the last Adam finds life and liberty. Elsewhere, in speaking of the resurrection life that gives the kingdom of God its power, Paul says: 'So it is written: "The first man Adam became a living being"; the last Adam, a life-giving spirit' (1 Cor. 15: 45).

We bring this key given to us by Paul to Jesus' battle with Satan as representative of the kingdom of this world and what do we learn? Just as the first Adam contended with the evil one over the command of God, so the last Adam begins his public ministry contending with the evil one concerning the law of God. The first man fought his battle in the lush surroundings of the Garden of Eden. The second Man fought his battle in the deprivation of the wilderness and 40 days without food.

Unlike the first Adam, Jesus won the battle with Satan. The text ends on the sober note that the adversary left him until an opportune time. Jesus had won the first round. Would Adam have faced further temptations as part of his probation? We'll never know. But Jesus as the last Adam faced the assaults of Satan until he breathed his last on Calvary's cross. The darkness of Gethsemane is blackened still more by the presence of the evil one trying to lead our Lord into the path of disobedience, and so disqualifying him as Savior. The King of glory who humbled himself for a season would remain obedient unto death, even death on a cross.

As representative of his people, his sheep given him by the Father, Jesus would stand alone to do battle. He would be the true David, bringing victory for his people, over the Goliath of the prince of the power of the air.

Messianic Might. The tone of Jesus' work as Messiah was warfare, confrontation with a spiritual foe. Christ came to subdue Satan in the hold he has over us because of the guilt and power of reigning sin in our lives. While we were impotent, Christ stood in our place.

Jesus provides a graphic picture of this in an encounter with the Pharisees, the religious leaders of the day. Jesus had been casting out demons, freeing the possessed from vivid demonic oppression. The Pharisees framed Jesus' work in terms of spiritual conflict; only they were saying that he was allied with Satan. Jesus sets them straight. In so doing, he describes the method of victory over spiritual opposition.

> Jesus knew their thoughts and said to them, 'Every kingdom divided against itself will be ruined, and every city or household divided against itself will not stand. If Satan drives out Satan, he is divided against himself. How then can his kingdom stand? And if I drive out demons by Beelzebub, by whom do your people drive them out? So then, they will be your judges. But if I drive out demons by the Spirit of God, then the kingdom of God has come upon you. Or again, how can anyone enter a strong man's house and carry off his possessions unless he first ties up the strong man? Then he can rob his house.'
>
> Matt. 12: 25–9

The kingdom of God is present with its King. Jesus' authority over the ruling party bore that out, but he also shows us how he conducts spiritual military operations—by binding, defeating, and disarming the enemy.

What our Lord displays for us in this analogy of binding the strong man in order to carry off his possessions is his work as Messiah. He is giving us an idea of his mission of rescuing his people from the imprisonment of this age. That mission had to do with subduing the one who had a legitimate hold over us because of the guilt of our sin. Jesus came to Satan's turf. He bound him by his unique saving work, sufficient to meet the law's demands by which Satan held us prisoner. And Jesus took from Satan those subjects of the kingdom of this world for himself and his kingdom, to be possessed of God.

The whole world is a prisoner of sin (Gal. 3: 22), lorded over by a tyrant. To this world came the Christ of God. By his saving work he breaks the bonds of sin that held them prisoner, condemned and awaiting the fate of eternal death. He rescues them, providing their deliverance. When the tyrant objects and pulls out the charges against those whom he claimed for his own domain, the paper is empty but for one phrase—'ransomed by blood.' As the liberated prisoners file out of the prison each is presented with a paper on which is this declaration:

> When you were dead in your sins and in the uncircumcision of your sinful nature, God made you alive with Christ. He forgave us all our sins, having canceled the written code, with its regulations, that was against us and that stood opposed to us; he took it away, nailing it to the cross. And having disarmed the powers and authorities, he made a public spectacle of them, triumphing over them by the cross.
>
> Col. 2: 13–15

The paperwork each of us holds as subjects of the kingdom of God speaks of deliverance by death and rescue by resurrection. It speaks of Christ's work, not our wiles. We are exclusively the beneficiaries of his unique mission.

KINGDOM CONFIDENCE

Before we start thinking how we might bind Satan to reach others for Christ, we need to grasp the nature and uniqueness of

Christ's mission. The method our Lord describes in his binding of the strong man does not give us a method for conducting spiritual warfare in the work of evangelism. No, his description gives a picture of his unique work as the Messiah of God.

Our work of witness operates on the basis of binding Satan, but not as something we do: it is what Christ has done to bring life and liberty to his sheep ready for slaughter. Listen again to these compelling words: 'Since the children have flesh and blood, he too shared in their humanity so that by his death he might destroy him who holds the power of death—that is, the devil—and free those who all their lives were held in slavery by their fear of death' (Heb. 2: 14–15). That freeing is defined by his substitutionary atonement for their sins.

Christ's binding of Satan is not our model, but our motivation for reaching others with the gospel of freedom from sin's tyranny. It is true that those 'others' we seek to reach are held captive by sin and are part of Satan's fallen realm. But nowhere in Scripture are we given instruction in binding for our efforts at reaching others for Christ.

One of the most beautiful expressions of the Christian faith is captured in the the first question of *The Heidelberg Catechism*:

Q What is your only comfort in life and in death?

A That I am not my own, but belong body and soul, in life and in death, to my faithful Savior Jesus Christ. He has fully paid for all my sins with his precious blood, and has set me free from the tyranny of the devil. He also watches over me in such a way that not a hair can fall from my head without the will of my heavenly Father; in fact, all things must work together for my salvation. Because I belong to him, Christ, by his Holy Spirit, assures me of eternal life, and makes me whole-heartedly willing and ready, from now on to live unto him.[31]

We are not liberators. Christ is. We are heralds of that liberation. Christ's work is our confidence. His work says that we have something to say. We don't proclaim the possibility of salvation in Christ. We proclaim the success of his mission for his sheep. The gospel as it focuses on Christ, does not offer a King who made people redeemable, but a Lord who actually redeemed his people, accomplishing their liberation.

When we approach someone to share the glorious news of the kingdom of God by sharing the gospel of life and liberty in Jesus Christ, do we face demonic opposition? Most assuredly, we do. But we do not face it as did Christ. We don't face the opposition of evil as a foe to be defeated. We encounter a defeated foe. We don't fight for victory. We fight in victory, in the Lord and the strength of his might—not the might of mere divine power, but the might of redemptive power.

Scripture informs us that we will do greater works than our Lord: 'I tell you the truth, anyone who has faith in me will do what I have been doing. He will do even greater things than these, because I am going to the Father' (John 14: 12).

We could read this and get the idea that we will be empowered to perform more spectacular signs and wonders than our Lord Jesus did in walking on water or raising the dead. However, the context constrains us to understand the 'greater' in terms of quantity not quality and application not accomplishment. Jesus will not leave us as orphans. He comes to us in the Holy Spirit, whom he sent upon his ascension to the throne in glory. The Spirit will not do something new in a redemptive sense but will bring to bear what Christ has accomplished.

Greater things will be done as the liberating work of Christ is realized in the lives of those whose prisons of sin are unlocked by the Spirit's key of regeneration. As Charles Wesley put it:

> Long my imprisoned spirit lay
> Fast bound in sin and nature's night.
> Thine eye diffused a quick'ning ray:
> I woke—the dungeon flamed with light!
> My chains fell off, my heart was free,
> I rose, went forth, and followed Thee.

In our efforts against spiritual opposition, neither do we accomplish anything new. We operate on the basis of what Christ has done and what his Spirit is bringing to bear through us in the lives of those we seek to reach for Christ.

KINGDOM POWER

When we pray in the model prayer Jesus taught us, 'for yours is the kingdom and the power and glory forever,' we affirm that real power is part of God's kingdom. That power belongs to the King who is present with us as his church by his Spirit. The

Spirit is not only a Spirit of truth, but of power. Christ was raised in and by the power of the Spirit (Rom. 1: 4). We have received the Spirit of power for our role as witnesses (Acts 1: 8). The gospel comes with power, as the Spirit makes its call effectual in the hearts of its hearers (1 Cor. 2: 4; 1 Thess. 1: 5).

In other words, we do fight with power in the war for men's souls. The prayers recorded for us in Ephesians will not let us forget that any evangelism is power evangelism, in which the Spirit of God applies the work of Christ to make alive those who were dead in sin. The power of 2 Corinthians 10: 3–4 ('The weapons we fight with are not the weapons of the world. On the contrary, they have divine power to demolish strongholds.') is a resurrection power and a redemptive power, armed with the purposes of God resident in the particular work of Christ. That power is not at our discretion, or for our purposes. It is the power of Christ, wielded by the Holy Spirit for his saving purposes, not ours.

IN HIS STEPS

But don't we see Jesus giving this power to his apostles, both to perform miracles and to drive out demons? Don't we read in the gospels: 'he called his twelve disciples to him and gave them authority to drive out evil spirits and to heal every disease and sickness' (Matt. 10: 1). Aren't we disciples of Jesus? If these are evidences of his kingdom, isn't his kingdom still growing, making these in evidence today and giving us the mandate to deal with demons in the kingdom work he has given us to do?

Certainly, we are disciples of our Lord Jesus. Assuredly, his kingdom continues to grow to this day as his saving rule is established in the hearts of those formerly known as sons of Satan. The Apostle Peter in his first epistle, which deals so much with witness to Christ where he has placed us, urges us to emulate our Lord: 'Christ suffered for you, leaving you an example, that you should follow in his steps.' But even here we are reminded that our suffering is in the pattern of Christ, but not in the place of Christ. Notice the larger context:

> To this you were called, because Christ suffered for you,
> leaving you an example, that you should follow in his steps.
> 'he committed no sin, and no deceit was found in his mouth.'
> When they hurled their insults at him, he did not retaliate;

when he suffered, he made no threats. Instead, he entrusted himself to him who judges justly. He himself bore our sins in his body on the tree, so that we might die to sins and live for righteousness; by his wounds you have been healed.

1 Pet. 2: 21–4

We fight in the same way, for the will of the Father, in the wisdom of God that seeks his glory, in a way of weakness that the world considers absurd. Yet our battle is not for victory, but in victory, the victory he and he alone achieved.

When Jesus gave his disciples authority over the demons, he was demonstrating their participation in the work of the kingdom and in his building of the church. Jesus spent the time of his public ministry preparing his disciples to carry on the work he had given them to do in the world. They would do greater things, as they fan out across the terrain of this age to carry the gospel of life and liberty to people. As ambassadors of Christ, their ministry would be his. They would act in his name, invested with his authority. Like these first-century disciples, we are enfolded into this kingdom mission.

We, however, are unlike the apostles and disciples of the early church in that theirs was a unique function. The signs and wonders, and casting out of demons were peculiar to the inauguration of the kingdom of God. These mighty works of power showed the reality and presence of the redemptive kingdom of God. We do not find instruction in the epistles of Peter or Paul, the two key figures in the book of Acts, to cast out demons, or to perform signs, wonders, and miraculous feats to attract the eye or gain entry into the lives of those of this age for the proclamation of the gospel of the kingdom.

IN THE NAME OF JESUS

You might say, 'I can see how Jesus is the one who binds the devil in his unique work as Messiah. But isn't there some sense in which we also bind the devil in his name? In other words, we don't pretend to do something new or in our own right. Rather, we apply the work of Christ and rely on his authority and binding power. Isn't there some place where our Lord instructs us to bind?'

There is not any example where our Lord instructs us to bind. But there is one where it is implied.

> And I tell you that you are Peter, and on this rock I will
> build my church, and the gates of Hades will not overcome
> it. I will give you the keys of the kingdom of heaven;
> whatever you bind on earth will be bound in heaven, and
> whatever you loose on earth will be loosed in heaven.
>
> Matt. 16: 18–19

Here our Lord gives encouragement in the binding we do. We
act on his authority. But what does it mean to bind?

First, we look at the context. Jesus is establishing the apostolic
witness to himself as the Christ of God as the foundation of the
church, against which the gates of hell will not prevail. Christ
is with his church to protect and preserve. A little later, we
find the same principle of binding in Matthew 18: 18, in the
context of church discipline.

We also notice that what our Lord speaks of involves loosing,
as well as binding. Is he saying that we are to bind Satan so that
we can loose the prisoners, liberate them from the shackles of
sin? It can't be that because the binding and loosing refer to
the same thing. Binding does not refer to Satan, and loosing to
sinners. Both activities refer to a single subject.

What, then, is our Lord saying when he speaks of what we
do when we bind? Binding, together with loosing, is referred
to as the 'keys of the kingdom.' In Matthew 16 we see the keys
of the kingdom given to Peter and the other apostles for whom
he is spokesman. In Matthew 18 we see these keys applied to
the work of kingdom correction, to the unrepentant citizen
of the kingdom.

The key to the keys of the kingdom is not to invest them
with the meaning we would like, but to ascribe to them that
meaning the context warrants and the original audience would
have appreciated. Clowney leads us in proper understanding:

> The government of the church corresponds to its heavenly
> form. Jesus did not give Peter the sword of military power,
> but the keys of spiritual discipline. They are the keys of the
> kingdom. Authority in the church is kingdom authority, an
> authority not of men but of God. Jesus speaks of 'binding'
> and 'loosing.' These terms were used by the rabbis in the
> context of community discipline and may be applied to
> persons or to actions. As applied to actions they refer to
> whether a certain practice is permitted or forbidden by
> God's law...To 'bind' is to declare that the action in view is

contrary to God's word. To 'loose' is to determine that the action is consistent with a Christian profession.

> As applied to individuals, binding and loosing are not concerned with possible courses of action but with actual behavior. The one bound is declared to have sinned... 'Loosing' [is] the declaration of God's forgiveness of sins to those who heartily repent and turn again to the Lord.[32]

When we are told by our Lord to bind, it is in the context of application of the Word of God to the conduct of citizens of the kingdom of God, not to the demons of the present, evil age. The actions of binding and loosing relate to what is permitted or forbidden in God's law. Binding declares an action forbidden; loosing declares an action permitted. The focus is kingdom ethics governed by the revealed Word of God, not kingdom combat.

Yet we do want to note that these keys of the kingdom are used in the face of the efforts of the gates of hell to prevail. We're reminded here of the battle of kingdom conflict and of the nature of the battle. But we are also alerted to the form that battle takes and get an idea of what a fit weapon would be for the opposition faced. Error is combated by truth, wrong with right, evil with good. We can see how appropriate this weapon is against the father of lies and master of deceit, the one we saw at work with the first Adam, of whom God admonished Cain: 'If you do right, will not your countenance be lifted up? But if you do not do right, sin is crouching at your door, but you must master it.'

REACH AND RESIST

We are not called to bind the devil. Peter, speaking to Christians undergoing persecution for their faith, includes in his pastoral counsel the element of spiritual opposition and not just the human oppression they were encountering. Notice how he directs us in confronting spiritual opposition:

> Be self-controlled and alert. Your enemy the devil prowls around like a roaring lion looking for someone to devour. Resist him, standing firm in the faith, because you know that your brothers throughout the world are undergoing the same kind of sufferings.
>
> 1 Pet. 5: 8–9

The prince of this world is at work throughout the world, through his tools, to cause suffering for righteousness' sake. The counsel of Peter here, and of James 4: 7, is to 'resist' him. God's counsel to us is not to rebuke but to resist the devil. What does it mean to resist? That's part of our spiritual weaponry by which we stand firm in the Lord and in his mighty power— humble before him, submitting to him, dependent upon him at all times and in every way. Resistance recognizes an opposing force and stands firm from being led astray.

For spiritual warfare in evangelism (and sanctification) reliance is on God. Paul in his evangelistic endeavors did not call upon his fellow believers to bind the devil so that the gospel could go forth unfettered. He did not have them address the demonic enemy at all. After identifying our foe not as flesh and blood, but as spiritual forces of evil, against which we are to stand firm in the power of Christ, Paul issues this request:

> And pray in the Spirit on all occasions with all kinds of prayers and requests. With this in mind, be alert and always keep on praying for all the saints. Pray also for me, that whenever I open my mouth, words may be given me so that I will fearlessly make known the mystery of the gospel, for which I am an ambassador in chains. Pray that I may declare it fearlessly, as I should.
>
> Eph. 6: 18–20.

Paul solicited the prayers of his fellow laborers in the gospel to the Advocate, not the adversary. Our prayers are to Christ not Satan.[33]

All this means we never need to shirk our call or shrink away from threat. Did we in our own strength confide, we would have reason to do so. What we do, the weapons we wield, carry Christ's power but only for the accomplishment of his purposes. We plunder his spoils for his sake. And we do so with the weapons of his design, invested with the power of his redemptive purpose.

6

Spiritual Weapons

I mentioned the Tower of London being one of my favorite places to visit in London. The history, the lore, the architecture are all fascinating. The facility stores the opulent crown jewels. The oldest of the buildings on the grounds is the White Tower built by William the Conqueror who ruled 1066–87. In the basement of that tower is a display of the weaponry of the time: suits of armor, arrows, swords, shields, maces, and an assortment of instruments of torture.

We might scoff a little at such weapons, especially in light of advancements through the ages, guns, tanks, smart bombs. And we can only imagine what developments lie down the road. But those weapons showcased in the Tower of London were arms suitable not only for the time, but for waging the kind of warfare that would be fought in that day. In other words, the weapons at hand were sufficient to meet the enemy's warfare.

How do we fight against the rulers, against the authorities, against the powers of this dark world, and against the spiritual forces of evil in the heavenly realms that oppose us in the kingdom work of witness? What weapons do we find at our disposal? Do we use tarot cards, silver bullets, wolf bane, garlic and crucifixes? How do we learn to use the weapons given to us? Do we take an exorcise class?

Let me begin with a word of warning. Our enemy the devil would try to disarm us of the weapons our Lord says are suitable for the task. In his usual tactics, Satan sows seeds of doubt and tries to undermine our confidence by saying, 'Will that really work? Isn't there something better or quicker or flashier or more fun that you could use? Isn't there a better way to use that weapon?' The irony rests in the idea that our enemy is the one who attempts to convince what will work against him. In the political realm that's called a conflict of interest. In the spiritual realm it's called foolishness to turn our ear from the Lord of life to the lord of lies. Christ is full of grace and truth.

BIBLICAL BATTLE GEAR

Although we live in the world, we do not wage war as the world does. The weapons we fight with are not the weapons of the world. On the contrary, they have divine power to demolish strongholds. We demolish arguments and every pretension that sets itself up against the knowledge of God, and we take captive every thought to make it obedient to Christ (2 Cor. 10: 3–5).

The more we keep this passage in front of us, the stronger will be our confidence in what God has provided for the kind of warfare he calls us to wage. As we prepare to open the door to the weapons room we want to remember:

- The weapons are provided by our King.
- They have divine power.
- They are capable of destroying enemy strongholds.
- They are employed on the battlefield of this fallen world.
- They are wielded according to God's plan and design.

What are the weapons God spreads out before us in his Word for dealing with spiritual opposition in evangelism? It's tempting to divide them into categories, such as protective, offensive, defensive. But God's weapons defy such pigeonholing. Let's take a sweeping inventory, beginning with the most powerful, pervasive, and prominent of all—the Holy Spirit.

THE SPIRIT

Think about when you came to a saving knowledge of Jesus Christ. What brought that about? I confessed Christ as God's only way of salvation and professed my faith in him when I was an adult (at least chronologically). I grew up in a home where religion was respected and practiced through various external rituals like going to church on Sundays. A vibrant relationship with God or a Christ-centered life expressive of saving faith weren't there. Religion was more part of civil socialization.

When I went away to college I jettisoned the religion thing and became rather argumentative. It wasn't so much that I was antagonistic to religion. I just enjoyed arguing, especially from what I considered the rational and logical higher ground. When I met my wife, one of the summer influx of college students to the beach town in which I lived year round, I saw for the first time a religion that flowed from the inside out. I continued to date her at the university we both attended. I enjoyed her Christian friends, especially because they were great patsies for my arguments—like sitting ducks.

Over the months, I was exposed to the teachings of the Bible. I saw people with genuine love for Jesus Christ. I was surprised to see people making decisions and setting goals on the basis of something other than self-interest. Before long I came to understand my own sinfulness and dire need, what God had provided in the work of Jesus, and the call for a response on my part. I still remember walking deep in thought on the tree-lined mall of the campus, going back to my dorm room, kneeling down by my bed, and giving my trust and myself to Jesus Christ.

What happened? What changed? Things I had heard many times before all of a sudden made sense. They had meaning, profound meaning. What swamped my cynicism with confidence and faith?

The Bible's answer is the Holy Spirit. His work is described in the catechism's definition of effectual calling: 'Effectual calling is the work of God's Spirit, whereby, convincing us of our sin and misery, enlightening our minds in the knowledge of Christ, and renewing our wills, he doth persuade and enable us to embrace Jesus Christ, freely offered to us in the gospel.'[34] I could fill out each of those operations of the Spirit with details of my personal experience, as no doubt you could, if you belong to Christ.

I share something in common with you and with everyone ever descended from Adam. We are born dead in sin. By dead, we mean without ability to understand or savingly embrace the things of God. Paul sums up our condition by saying, 'there is no one righteous, not even one; there is no one who understands, no one who seeks God' (Rom. 3: 10–11). The core issue is a spiritual one: 'The man without the Spirit does not accept the things that come from the Spirit of God, for they are foolishness to him, and he cannot understand them, because they are spiritually discerned' (1 Cor. 2: 14). The heart of the matter is a matter of the heart. And with the heart we're born with, we are not going to accept what God says, at least in the way that leads to life.

Life comes through the Holy Spirit directly operating in our hearts to give ears to hear and hearts to receive. Though we are dead in sin, the Spirit makes us alive. That's called regeneration or being born again. With that new life we now have the ability to understand, accept, and embrace for ourselves the gospel of life in Jesus Christ. Those religious ramblings we heard many times before that seemed so far fetched, naive, even odious to us started to become beautiful, appealing, and meaningful. Scripture describes this in terms of scent, attributing the fragrance to the work of Christ, and the ability to appreciate it to the work of the Spirit.

> But thanks be to God, who always leads us in triumphal procession in Christ and through us spreads everywhere the fragrance of the knowledge of him. For we are to God the aroma of Christ among those who are being saved and those who are perishing. To the one we are the smell of death; to the other, the fragrance of life.
>
> 2 Cor. 2: 14–16

Spiritual receptivity is made possible because of spiritual regeneration in the heart of those dead in sin. When we or anyone turns in faith to Christ and can legitimately claim to be children of God, we affirm with our God: 'Yet to all who received him, to those who believed in his name, he gave the right to become children of God—children born not of natural descent, nor of human decision or a husband's will, but born of God' (John 1: 12–13).

John goes on to illustrate that spiritual phenomenon in John 3 with Nicodemus, and Christ's explanation of the new birth as the sovereign, immediate, transforming work of the Holy Spirit, and in John 11 with the raising of Lazarus from the dead. Jesus could have stood outside the open tomb of Lazarus and called for him to come out until he was blue in the face. Unless Lazarus had been given the ability to hear and act, he would have stayed in the grave. And, being given the ability, while theoretically he could have not responded to the call of Christ, there was no way he was going to stay put. He came to his Lord.

No one can be delivered from the kingdom of this world and be established into the kingdom of God apart from the work of the Holy Spirit (John 3: 3). Just as we did not come to Christ on a whim, but because of the direct operation of the Spirit in our hearts to convince and convert us, so the Spirit must work in those we seek to reach for them to come to Christ. Only the Spirit of God has the power to make effective the weapons we employ, giving them power to deal with the spiritual opposition we face.

The weapon of kingdom warfare is the Spirit of the risen Christ. But we don't want to get the idea that we wield the weapon of the Spirit. Rather, he wields us. He makes our efforts effective. He accomplishes his purposes through us. The Spirit is the one who infuses the weapons issued to us with the divine power for doing what he wants to accomplish. The Apostle Paul admits that with great relief and expectation: 'I came to you in weakness and fear, and with much trembling. My message and my preaching were not with wise and persuasive words, but with a demonstration of the Spirit's power, so that your faith might not rest on men's wisdom, but on God's power' (1 Cor. 2: 3–5).

THE SPIRIT'S ARMORY

Gods and Generals is a film based on a book by the same name about the Civil War, chronicling the conflict between the northern and southern states to the death of General Stonewall Jackson before the Battle of Gettysburg. The movie did a good job of bringing out the harsh realities of war, humanizing the combatants, and dispelling idealistic notions with historical actuality. One of the minor depictions that struck me had to do with the uniforms of the opposing soldiers. An army clad in blue was not opposing an army clad in gray. There was no uniformity in the uniforms. Especially with the soldiers from the south, the uniforms were mix and match, ragtag ensembles put together for function not style.

That is not the case for soldiers of the cross. Our God supplies a uniform for the personnel of his army. We who belong to Christ's church are outfitted in kingdom clothing—the white robe of righteousness of Christ credited to us—designed for the expected opposition of the enemy. Here we want to see its functionality as a provision of God for spiritual warfare.

Kingdom Clothing. Satan aims his darts at our heart. As the father of lies, he touts our self-reliance. As the accuser, he posts our transgressions. As the enemy of Christ, he promotes our rival lordship. When we look at our lives we see sin. Doubts may plague us, guilt overwhelm us, or despair sideline us, but God outfits us with the breastplate of righteousness and the helmet of salvation. We are clothed in the righteousness of our Lord Jesus Christ. Our salvation is secure in him, bound up in his accomplished work on our behalf.

We don the kingdom clothing of discipleship by reminding ourselves of where we stand and how we do. We prepare our minds with the truth of God's Word from Romans 8, shore up our faith with John's first epistle, and assure our hearts with God's realized promises, like that of Hebrews 6: 17–20:

> Because God wanted to make the unchanging nature of his purpose very clear to the heirs of what was promised, he confirmed it with an oath. God did this so that, by two unchangeable things in which it is impossible for God to lie, we who have fled to take hold of the hope offered to us may be greatly encouraged. We have this hope as an anchor for the soul, firm and secure. It enters the inner sanctuary behind the curtain, where Jesus, who went before us, has entered on our behalf. He has become a high priest forever, in the order of Melchizedek.

Lest our enemy succeed in disqualifying us for the task and discouraging us in the battle, we must remind ourselves where our righteousness is found and why we come to bear it.

Another part of our battle gear is the shield of faith. Just as a police officer wears a bulletproof vest, so we wear a shield. To sustain ourselves from growing weary and losing heart, we must fix our eyes on our Lord Jesus Christ, in his victory, in his presence with us, and in his example recorded for us.

Faith gives us the perspective of those spiritual realities that are ours in Christ. Many times in the storms of life the dark clouds obscure our view. Yet, as anyone who has broken through the clouds in a jetliner to cruise at 30,000 feet can attest, the sun continues to shine with the light of God's truth, and the warmth of his abiding and abounding love.

The third article of clothing concerns our footwear. We wear boots in which to march. We live in this world in a state of readiness. God's Word alerts us to live in sober alertness, on guard and opportunistic for the sake of Christ: 'Be very careful, then, how you live—not as unwise but as wise, making the most of every opportunity, because the days are evil' (Eph. 5: 15–16). Ours are the feet of those who bring good news, in kingdom service in the kingdom of this evil age. We walk in a strategy of stewardship—of our resources of time, possessions, finances, inclinations, and abilities.

Kingdom Weapons. The armaments for the conduct of spiritual warfare fall into two general categories. These categories are not hard and fast, but they do give us a helpful distinction for understanding what our Lord has issued to us for the work of his kingdom.

With the advent of live television coverage the strategy and weapons of war are there for all to see. In the second Gulf conflict, some journalists even got in trouble for making too much known and thus jeopardizing the troops with whom they were embedded. In the coverage I noticed two types of bombing missions. One was by the B-52 bombers that opened their bays and scattered bombs over a wide swath of ground. The other was by so called 'smart bombs' that were directed by GPS coordinates to hit a needle in a haystack. These two bombing methods help us to see the two kinds of weapons provided for our use.

The first category is useful for scattered, generic assault. Have you ever heard the expression: 'he disarmed me with his charm'? Character and behavior consistent with the kingdom of God speak contrary to the kingdom of this world, and wage war against its ruler and his efforts. As we seek first the kingdom of God and his righteousness as the governing principle of our lives, we will live counter-kingdom lives. Such lives will be God-centered, Christ-serving, and Spirit-empowered. We will be zealous for the glory of God in all things present and future, public and private, secular and sacred. His righteousness will be our garment and our goal. We will desire to live such good lives before others that those of the kingdom of this world will see our distinctive behavior and glorify our Father in heaven.

Jesus had just affirmed his identity as Messiah to Peter's confession of Jesus as the Christ, the Son of the living God. He pronounced a blessing on Peter in his confession. Then Jesus laid out the game plan for his Messianic work: 'From that time on Jesus began to explain to his disciples that he must go to Jerusalem and suffer many things at the hands of the elders, chief priests and teachers of the law, and that he must be killed and on the third day be raised to life' (Matt. 16: 21).

Now instead of lining up with God's assessment, Peter takes a stand against God's plan. He has a better idea. Listen to how Jesus characterizes Peter's insubordination: 'Jesus turned and said to Peter, "Get behind me, Satan! You are a stumbling block to me; you do not have in mind the things of God, but the things of men."' (Matt. 16: 23). It's not that Peter transmogrified into Satan. Rather, he aligned himself with Satan's ways. To be in line with Satan is to be self-centered rather than God-centered. 'There is a way that seems right to a man, but its end is the way of death' (Prov. 14: 12). Seeking the kingdom of God is to seek God's glory, God's gain and God's goals—often contrary to what we feel like doing or the way the world does it. Let's explore some examples of kingdom character and conduct as a spiritual weapon against evil in reaching others for Christ.

Your colleague at work has just pulled the rug out from under you. She took credit for an idea you had. You are annoyed. But you know sin is crouching at your door and its desire is for you. You know your enemy the devil is prowling about seeking to devour you. You know that sinful origination of anger, or sinful expression of anger, opens the door of your life to your enemy, like the proverbial camel's nose in the tent. What do you do, especially with an eye to being light in darkness? God's counsel to you in Romans 12 is this:

> Bless those who persecute you; bless and do not curse. Rejoice with those who rejoice; mourn with those who mourn. Live in harmony with one another. Do not be proud, but be willing to associate with people of low position. Do not be conceited. Do not repay anyone evil for evil. Be careful to do what is right in the eyes of everybody. If it is possible, as far as it depends on you, live at peace with everyone. Do not take revenge, my friends, but leave room for God's wrath, for it is written: 'It is mine to avenge; I will repay,' says the Lord.
>
> Rom. 12: 14–19

That's the battle plan. But what's the weapon? Paul puts it in your hand in the last verse of the chapter: 'Do not be overcome by evil, but overcome evil with good.' God places the weapon of good in your hand to combat the evil that opposes you. You leave it to God to settle any score. Your concern is to seek peace to the best of your ability. That's the responsibility God sorts out for you in seeking first his kingdom and his righteousness. After all, his kingdom is a kingdom of righteousness, joy and peace (Rom. 14: 17). In seeking peace, you display kingdom character and conduct that by the Spirit's working will attract your co-worker's attention to Christ.

Love is another general assault weapon of God's kingdom. The love of the kingdom is the love of God, love of the unlovable. Do you know any people like that—unlovable? A mirror will show you one recipient of such love. When we were sinners, God set his love upon us, sent his Son to save us and his Spirit to claim us. The Scriptures are full of illustration and direction in such love, from God's electing love in Deuteronomy 7 and Romans 9 to the parable of the Good Samaritan.

Love is not something that happens to us. It is a servant of our will. We purpose to love. We love as we have been loved. Our love is not only in word but in deed, not only in sentiment but in practice. Our Lord himself is our exemplar for love. He explains what kingdom love looks like in action:

> But I tell you who hear me: Love your enemies, do good to those who hate you, bless those who curse you, pray for those who mistreat you. If someone strikes you on one cheek, turn to him the other also. If someone takes your cloak, do not stop him from taking your tunic. Give to everyone who asks you, and if anyone takes what belongs to you, do not demand it back. Do to others as you would have them do to you. If you love those who love you, what credit is that to you? Even 'sinners' love those who love them.
>
> Luke 6: 27–32.

We all know the love showcased in John 3: 16. Well, 1 John 3: 16–18 brings it home to us:

> This is how we know what love is: Jesus Christ laid down his life for us. And we ought to lay down our lives for our brothers. If anyone has material possessions and sees his brother in need but has no pity on him, how can the love

of God be in him? Dear children, let us not love with words
or tongue but with actions and in truth.

Righteousness, obedience, mercy—all those kingdom
characteristics are part of the arsenal we use against the forces
of spiritual evil in reaching those who are mired in the kingdom
of this age, with the goal of bringing them into the glorious
freedom of the children of God. In the spiritual struggle we face,
Paul's warning to elders applies to each of us as representatives
of the kingdom of God: our character and conduct is to foster
'a good reputation with outsiders, so that [we] will not fall into
disgrace and into the devil's trap' (1 Tim. 3: 7).

One other kingdom quality that has a special function
in kingdom conflict is kindness. Just as signs, wonders and
works of power gave testimony to the presence and character
of the kingdom of God, so we can conduct warfare through
deeds of kingdom kindness. Miracles served the function of
reversing the effects of the fall, bringing relief to those who
were beneficiaries and bringing credibility to the reality and
character of the kingdom of God.

In the same way, our deeds of kindness can testify to the
kingdom of God we seek and serve. We try to make others'
lives easier, giving them relief from the harshness of existence
in a fallen world, a cup of cold water to their parched throats,
a helping hand to their oppressive burdens.

Those acts of kindness can also serve as doors into a person's
life, by which we might have opportunity to give verbal witness
to the good news of the kingdom. While there is benefit in
the act of kingdom kindness itself, our goal is always to direct
people to Jesus Christ, as the Lord provides opportunity.
There are those who say that they bear witness by their lives.
But righteous deeds unqualified by verbal comment only
communicate to others how great we are or that salvation is by
works. Deeds of kindness can point to us. We want people to
see Christ in us, the hope of glory.

The second category of weapon provided by God is useful
for focused, specific assault. The first category dealt with arms
of kingdom character and conduct. This category addresses
those offensive weapons for direct assault on the spiritual
forces of evil that oppose us in the work of witness. These are
prayer and the Word.

Prayer is the dominant weapon of God's arsenal. It touches everything related to spiritual warfare, but now we turn our attention to the Word of God as a weapon in facing spiritual opposition. It is the Word of God that gives us prayer and instructs us in its use. The Bible is a handbook on spiritual opposition, an operations manual for conducting spiritual warfare. Throughout our study thus far, we have appealed to Scripture for proper understanding and direction.

But as a weapon, the Bible serves a particular function. Remember what Paul told us when he alerted us to the divine power of the spiritual weapons God gives to us: 'We demolish arguments and every pretension that sets itself up against the knowledge of God, and we take captive every thought to make it obedient to Christ.' What the Bible arms us with is truth, in opposition to relativism that is nothing but a counterfeit contender for our confidence.

Satan is a counterfeiter, a deceiver. He is a liar and the father of lies. His temptations often lure us to partake of that which offers the promise of life, liberty and fulfillment. But his offerings are bogus, empty.

As we saw in Revelation, Satan is portrayed as a huge red dragon. How is his assault on the church depicted? As a torrent of water that spews forth from his mouth (Rev. 12:15). That is a picture of deception, emanating from the mouth. The devil employs the same tactics as at the beginning, posing blasphemous and contradictory counsel to God, assaulting via his words.

God's Word is truth. It is seen as a weapon against the lies of the devil throughout Scripture. Our Lord Jesus uses Scripture to combat the devil in the desert. Two passages particularly instructive to us are given by the Apostle Paul. He tells Timothy that 'all Scripture is God-breathed and is useful for teaching, rebuke, correction and training in righteousness.' The Bible is the word of the living God, by which we might know and please him in every area of life. It shows us the way of truth (teaching), how we got off the way (rebuke), how to get back on the way (correction) and how to stay on the way (training in righteousness).[35] Everything we need to know for life and godliness, God has provided in his Word.

In addition, God's Word equips us to know and combat evil and error. While the text of the Bible is inspired of God in all its parts, chapter divisions are not. The break between the third and fourth chapters of 2 Timothy is ill-placed. After establishing the Bible as God's Word for all life at the end of chapter three, Paul then brings that Word to bear in spiritual combat in the beginning of chapter four:

> In the presence of God and of Christ Jesus, who will judge the living and the dead, and in view of his appearing and his kingdom, I give you this charge: Preach the Word; be prepared in season and out of season; correct, rebuke and encourage—with great patience and careful instruction. For the time will come when men will not put up with sound doctrine. Instead, to suit their own desires, they will gather around them a great number of teachers to say what their itching ears want to hear. They will turn their ears away from the truth and turn aside to myths. But you, keep your head in all situations, endure hardship, do the work of an evangelist, discharge all the duties of your ministry.
>
> 2 Tim. 4: 1–5

Paul is speaking of a conflict of kingdoms, and which one will endure. Christ will one day come again to usher in his redemptive kingdom in fullness. But that kingdom is present now, in conflict with the kingdom of this world. Those kingdoms are characterized in terms of what pleases God and what pleases people, what God says and what people think. Kingdom conflict pits truth against error. Every thought is to be taken captive to the obedience of Christ.

Look at the heart of the passage above. 'Sound doctrine' is pitted against 'what people want to hear,' 'truth' against 'myth.' The work of an evangelist is a readiness to correct, rebuke, and exhort. We'll say more about this later, but for now we want to notice that spiritual warfare has to do with combating error through the ministry of the Word.

We might also note in this context that new revelations are not needed to augment the written revelation of God's Word. God has given us everything we need to live to please him, and everything we require to confront the weapons of spiritual opposition. The enemy has not changed, nor have his tactics. Our prayer is not for new information, but for wisdom in understanding and applying God's Word, and in distinguishing truth from myth. Some believe we need fresh revelations of the

Spirit, but the written Word is the word of God particularly attributed to the Holy Spirit (2 Pet. 1: 20–1). It is the Spirit who has given us the Bible who declares it sufficient, meaning further revelation is unnecessary and not to be expected.

One other passage that highlights the clashing of the sharp sword of the Spirit, the Word of God, against the counterfeit sword of Satan is given by Paul in his epistle to the Colossians. In that letter, Paul sets the stage by contrasting the kingdom of light and darkness, freedom and bondage: 'For he has rescued us from the dominion of darkness and brought us into the kingdom of the Son he loves, in whom we have redemption, the forgiveness of sins.'[36]

Paul goes on to speak of our deliverance from the darkness into the light by our Lord Jesus. Then, he gives this warning: 'I tell you this so that no one may deceive you by fine-sounding arguments.' Kingdom conflict is framed along the lines of deception. Kingdom combat sets truth against error:

> So then, just as you received Christ Jesus as Lord, continue to live in him, rooted and built up in him, strengthened in the faith as you were taught, and overflowing with thankfulness. See to it that no one takes you captive through hollow and deceptive philosophy, which depends on human tradition and the basic principles of this world rather than on Christ.
>
> Col. 2: 6–8

Paul expresses the lordship of Christ in terms of obedience. No surprise there. Members of a kingdom are subject to a king. Servants of a kingdom obey their commanding officer. As we come to Christ as Lord, so our lives are to be lived under that lordship, denying ourselves and following him. That is the essence of discipleship. When Jesus called Peter 'Satan' and told him to get behind him, he went on to say: 'If anyone would come after me, he must deny himself and take up his cross and follow me' (Matt. 16: 25). We fall in line behind our Lord, laying aside our will and ways in deference to his.

But the world and its satanic system will try to lure us away and lead us astray, seeking to make us prisoners of war. The expression Paul uses is 'take us captive.' Those are fighting words. We live in constant conflict in this world that is trying to lead us astray, capture us with the net of deception and bind us with the cords of a lie. This is true both for our sanctification and service in the face of spiritual opposition. Paul exposes those lures as empty and misleading, setting them against the truth of Christ.

The Word of God, properly divided and not deceitfully twisted as Satan is prone to do, is our weapon against the enslavement of error. The Scriptures have divine power to demolish arguments and every pretension that opposes the knowledge of God. The power is not magical, but through communication, correction, and cultivation of truth in response to error.

Kingdom Company. A company is a body of soldiers. God has not sent us into battle as mavericks or mercenaries. He has enfolded us into an army, a company of fellow soldiers, fighting under the banner of the kingdom of God and his Christ.

God's provision for us in the work of witness means that we are not alone. Our Lord and King accompanies us. He is with us always until the end of this age for the carrying out of his mission, entrusted to us, to make disciples of the nations. We also have fellowship with one another, participation in a common salvation and for a common cause. We desperately need one another. Our enemy the devil continually exerts his efforts to make us deserters. We need the community of the company to watch our backs, to encourage us in the fray, to maintain *esprit de corps* with a proper focus on Christ lest we grow weary and lose heart.

In the Book of Hebrews Jewish believers are being persecuted for their faith. They are being harassed and lured away from Christ, urged to return to the former ways. But the writer reminds them of the nature of the work of Christ as fulfillment and urges them not to return to the shadow cast by the reality bound up in Christ. The shadow offers no hope. Only the reality of Christ's priestly work provides salvation. They are urged to stand firm against the lie and to endure suffering, as others had done through the same faith that believed God and persevered.

The incubator for this needed strength in face of opposition was the company, the encouragement of the one by the many. Notice the context and function of kingdom community:

Take care, brothers, lest there be in any of you an evil, unbelieving heart, leading you to fall away from the living God. But exhort one another every day, as long as it is called 'today,' that none of you may be hardened by the deceitfulness of sin.

Therefore, brothers, since we have confidence to enter the holy places by the blood of Jesus, by the new and living way that he opened for us through the curtain, that is, through his flesh, and since we have a great priest over the house of God, let us draw near with a true heart in full assurance of faith, with our hearts sprinkled clean from an evil conscience and our bodies washed with pure water. Let us hold fast the confession of our hope without wavering, for he who promised is faithful. And let us consider how to stir up one another to love and good works, not neglecting to meet together, as is the habit of some, but encouraging one another, and all the more as you see the Day drawing near.

Heb. 3: 12–13; 10: 19–25 (ESV)

The danger is clear and present. Together, we stand firm both for spiritual protection of the individual and for the spiritual advancement of the kingdom of God.

Our God has well-outfitted us for the spiritual combat he calls us to wage in evangelism, which necessarily involves a clash of kingdoms. From the military garments to the armaments to fellow participants, our King has provided what is necessary for the conduct of warfare witness in our everyday lives.

7

The Weapon of Prayer

It used to be that soldiers' rifles were their best friends. They had to care for their rifles with the tenderness and attention a husband should show his wife. Soldiers were expected to know their rifles inside and out, being able to take them apart and put them back together blindfolded. They knew everything about their rifles and how they worked.

That's how we want to know the weapon of prayer. We need to know what it is and how it works. We need to know how to use it effectively and the many ways in which it can be used. Prayer seems to touch everything in the Christian life. It affects us as God's instruments, touching everything from our motivation to our vitality to our stance in the work of witness. Prayer has been so designed by God that he uses it even to accomplish his purposes and to effect change. Prayer can be directed to self, others, present, future, hearts, circumstances, preventative and remedial, and the list goes on. Prayer is prominent and pervasive in the Christian's life and ministry.

Prayer is like bag balm. Several years ago we used to vacation in Vermont's northeast kingdom, a stone's throw from the Canadian border. The winters can be brutal up there for human and animal residents. To treat the udders of the cows in that weather, farmers use an antiseptic ointment called bag balm. I don't know what this stuff is, but its healing and restorative properties are remarkable. My wife, Linda, discovered that bag balm is also fit for human use and is marketed as such. She has become a bag balm banshee. Whenever our kids would have any sort of external problem, my wife would whip out the bag balm. I wouldn't be surprised if bag balm started ending up in some of her recipes.

Prayer is the bag balm of the spiritual world. It is to be applied to everything. Its God-given properties are astounding and, invested in prayer by the design of God, they are not only therapeutic. They are militaristic. Prayer is a weapon of the kingdom of God, suitable not only for the infirmary but for the field of battle. As a spiritual weapon, prayer is particularly powerful and indispensable to the spiritual combat inherent in the nature of kingdom conflict.

GETTING A GRIP ON PRAYER

What exactly is prayer? Growing up, prayers were things that I said, often recited without bothering my mind and certainly without benefit to my heart. When I came to Christ, however, my prayer life was transformed from 'saying prayers' to actually praying. If we're going to understand prayer as a weapon of the kingdom of God, endowed with divine power to demolish strongholds that we will encounter in the work of witness, we must have a biblically-informed understanding of prayer unencumbered by imported or distorted ideas foreign to Scripture.

'This is a football.' That's the famous line attributed to the professional gridiron legend, Vince Lombardi. Now you'd think that professional football players would already know that and be able to pick a football out of a line-up of a baseball, basketball, soccer ball, tennis ball, and golf ball. Lombardi's team, however, had just given a pathetic athletic performance on the field. The coach wanted to get his team back to basics.

Prayer is one of those basics of the Christian life, a staple for sanctification and service in relationship with God and dependence upon him. Prayer is also the most basic weapon against the spiritual warfare inherent in those aspects of the Christian life in a fallen world.

Prayer can be defined any number of ways, from any number of perspectives. For our purposes we can define prayer as 'personal, conscious awareness of and communication with the living and true God.' Prayer is the created capacity to commune with the Creator. Dogs can't pray. Water buffalo can't pray. Despite appearances, preying mantises can't pray.

We, however, are made in the image of God and we can pray. God has designed us for prayer, both in desire and ability. Communication with God is an expected feature of the Creator-creature relationship.

That relationship has been ruined by the fall. We are born into this present, evil age estranged from the God we were created to glorify and enjoy. However, the goal of God's saving purpose in Christ is to reconcile us to himself. The goal was not merely forgiveness of sin or eternal life. Those are glorious benefits. What God wanted was a restoration of relationship. Being delivered from this present age and brought into the kingdom of light and life had far-reaching consequences for us. Newness of kingdom realm meant newness of relationship. The Apostle Paul makes this clear. In his explanation to the Corinthians he says: 'Therefore, if anyone is in Christ, he is a new creation; the old has gone, the new has come!' God did this through Christ: 'God made him who had no sin to be sin for us, so that in him we might become the righteousness of God.' The result is: 'All this is from God, who reconciled us to himself through Christ and gave us the ministry of reconciliation' (2 Cor. 5: 17, 21).

Prayer is the product of a reconciled relationship with God. That's why we describe it as personal in our definition. Prayer is communication with God that cultivates communion with him. It is not simply parroting words in the direction of up. I was required to learn the biblical languages of Hebrew and Greek in my seminary studies. I started with summer Greek, an intense program of study designed to dispel any notion that you still had a life of your own for the duration of your tenure at seminary. First I learned the alphabet (an English word which is the first and second letter of the Greek alphabet, alpha and beta). Within a week I could read the entire Greek New Testament. I didn't say I understood any or all of it, but I could read it. Perhaps, it's better to say I could audibilize it, say the words out loud.

Sometimes prayer can be like that. We audibilize the words, but haven't a clue what we've said or to whom we are saying it. We can fall into that as believers, praying without thinking. If you doubt that, pay attention to how you sing hymns, many of which are prayers. Our voices can function independent of our attention. We often do the same thing in our prayer lives.

But God wants our prayers to be personal, conscious expressions of our hearts, communicated in attentive and intimate awareness of him as the one to whom we are speaking. This is especially true when we realize just what that relationship is to which he has brought us. Our God has lavished his love upon us to such an amazing degree that we are called his children—and that is what we are! By virtue of the reconciling work of Jesus Christ, we are sons and daughters of the living and true God, creator of all that is. That's why the model prayer our Lord Jesus gives us as a template for our prayer is so astounding. How does it begin? 'Our Father who is in heaven.' We are enjoined by our Lord to call his Father our Father. The one we address in prayer is our Heavenly Father, who receives us as his children and receives our prayers as the communication of his adopted kids.

For years I prayed the Lord's Prayer for one reason or another, sometimes saying it 10 or 20 times in a row. But when God brought me into a new relationship with himself that model prayer was revolutionized for me. It became new to me with the newness of life in me. The words became exceedingly rich and meaningful. The word 'Father' I took to my lips was steeped in grace and privilege, and endowed with an intimacy I had not known before. That's prayer as conscious communication as part of personal communion with the living and true God.

In our adoption, we receive all the rights and privileges as children of God. One of those rights and privileges is that of prayer. We have access to the ear of the Maker of heaven and earth, of all things visible and invisible. We have access to the throne of grace that we might have audience with the transcendent God of all creation, and do so as his own children. By its nature such prayer is intensely intimate. At the end of the semester, as the students were filling out class evaluations, one of my seminary professors jokingly made sure we knew that 'privilege' was not spelled with a 'd.' When it comes to prayer, 'privilege' should occur to us without suggestion as we see it contextualized in a reconciled relationship of grace.

Let me mention one thing about defining prayer as 'conscious communication.' Sometimes I love sitting in the room with my wife. We don't have to be talking. I just enjoy that she's there with me. In one respect, prayer is like that. We are deeply aware of the presence of our God as Father with us. We don't have to say a word. We may not even be particularly thinking about him. That's part of what it means to pray without ceasing. We may turn to God in prayer all the time, but frequently we just live our lives for him and before him, erupting in spontaneous expressions of thanks or praise or confession or affirmation as life warrants. That's been called practicing the presence of God. In him we live and move and have our being—as his children, adopted by his saving purpose.

But, while that may characterize prayer as we live to glorify and enjoy God, prayer as a weapon requires intentionality. We need to be deliberate and purposeful as we feel the grip of prayer in our hand. The prayer we want to get a grip on for the work of witness is decidedly active communication of purpose, not passive communication of presence. In what way is this active prayer necessary?

NECESSITY OF PRAYER

One of the characteristics of military service is obedience to the commanding officer. We do what we're told. The same is true of our relationship to Jesus Christ as our King and Commander. He says, 'jump.' We say, 'how high; help me to do it.'

The most obvious reason prayer is necessary relates to our relationship with our Lord. Christ is not a figurehead king like that of a constitutional monarchy. He is an absolute monarch who is to be obeyed. The working definition of discipleship given by our Lord involves denying ourselves, taking up our cross, and following him. If we love him, we will do what he says. If we call him 'Lord,' we will follow his commands. Jesus' curriculum for making disciples laid out in the Great Commission includes 'teaching them to obey every thing I command.'

God tells us to pray, so we pray. We could multiply examples of the orders of our God to pray. Two will suffice, one from the lips of our Lord, one from the pen of the apostle, both equally from the Spirit as the divine author of Scripture: 'Watch and pray so that you will not fall into temptation. The spirit is willing, but the body is weak' (Mark 14: 38). 'Do not be anxious about anything, but in everything, by prayer and petition, with thanksgiving, present your requests to God' (Phil. 4: 6).

In the first instance, 'pray' is in the imperative mood, meaning a command. In the latter, 'present' is also a command. When it comes to prayer as a weapon of the kingdom, we might think of our Lord commanding us to 'present arms,' to wield the weapon of prayer. A basic reason to pray rests on the orders of our Commander.

Aside from our Lord's command, wherein lies the necessity of prayer? Books have been devoted to the subject. For our purposes we can identify two reasons for prayer. First, prayer is a spiritual weapon invested with divine power, entrusted to us by God for the nature of the battle we face in the work of witness. How can we possibly break the grip of Satan on the lives of those who are part of his kingdom of this age? That's the case whether I am concerned for my next-door neighbor or a missionary's neighbor in Senegal. Prayer reaches where we are not and accomplishes what we cannot.

Prayer is an instrument of impotence, ours not God's. The power necessary for the work of witness is exclusively the power of God himself, divine power.

We seek the intervention and involvement of the One who is able to do immeasurably more than we could ever ask or even imagine. When we pray in this way, we step out of the way asking God to have his way. J. I. Packer expresses it this way: 'In evangelism...we are impotent; we depend wholly upon God to make our witness effective; only because he is able to give men new hearts can we hope that through our preaching the gospel sinners will be born again. These facts ought to drive us to prayer. It is God's intention that they should drive us to prayer.'[37]

The weapon of prayer is necessary at God's design, so that we can entreat him for what only he can do. It's like the access we have to a superior at work. Only our boss has the power to make certain decisions. With God, however, it's not only a matter of authorization but authority, of power to accomplish, creating power.

Paul recognized the spiritual opposition he faced in the work of witness: 'The god of this age has blinded the minds of unbelievers, so that they cannot see the light of the gospel of the glory of Christ, who is the image of God. For we do not preach ourselves, but Jesus Christ as Lord, and ourselves as your servants for Jesus' sake.'

Paul also recognized what was necessary for light to break though the darkened heart, something he was impotent to do. God had to intervene with creating power of the new life. God had to make the spiritually dead spiritually alive if our witness would find receptivity. 'For God, who said, "Let light shine out of darkness," made his light shine in our hearts to give us the light of the knowledge of the glory of God in the face of Christ.'

The apostle goes on to express the bottom line that prompts our prayer, spurs his own, and enlists others to pray for the work: 'But we have this treasure in jars of clay to show that this all-surpassing power is from God and not from us' (2 Cor. 4: 4–7).

Paul certainly knew this absolute dependence on God for the success of the mission God had given him.

> When I came to you, brothers, I did not come with eloquence or superior wisdom as I proclaimed to you the testimony about God. For I resolved to know nothing while I was with you except Jesus Christ and him crucified. I came to you in weakness and fear, and with much trembling. My message and my preaching were not with wise and persuasive words, but with a demonstration of the Spirit's power, so that your faith might not rest on men's wisdom, but on God's power.
>
> 1 Cor. 2: 1–5

No matter what we say, or how we say it, it profits nothing apart from God's power.

When we remember that the effectiveness of evangelism is entirely dependent on the enlivening and illuminating work of God, we are driven to our knees. We can speak to people dead in sin all we want, but no matter how loud, how eloquent or how persistent we are, the only way the dead will hear the voice of the Son of God is by the immediate work of God in their lives to enable them. So we pray. Prayer is our avenue to the power of God necessary for the success of the gospel in our exercise of the mission given to us by our Lord Jesus Christ.

Secondly, we must pray because God wants us to ask first. It's not unusual for dinner conversations at my household to include timely lessons on manners. Nathan, my 9-year-old, will ask for the fruit salad. My wife will ask him how he is supposed to ask. Nathan will say, 'Please.' Not content with disembodied pleasantries, my wife will ask, 'Please what?' Finally, when Nathan expresses his request in the politely prescribed manner, he will receive his fruit salad, as long as his siblings within reach of the bowl did not empty its contents in the interim.

God is our Father in heaven. He knows what we need before we ask. He knows what's in our minds before it hits our tongues. He knows what we want, but he still wants us to ask, and he wants us to ask in a particular way. Listen to our Father's instruction:

> You want something but don't get it. You kill and covet, but you cannot have what you want. You quarrel and fight. You do not have, because you do not ask God. When you ask, you do not receive, because you ask with wrong motives, that you may spend what you get on your pleasures.
>
> Until now you have not asked for anything in my name. Ask and you will receive, and your joy will be complete.
>
> So I say to you: Ask and it will be given to you; seek and you will find; knock and the door will be opened to you. For everyone who asks receives; he who seeks finds; and to him who knocks, the door will be opened. Which of you fathers, if your son asks for a fish, will give him a snake instead? Or if he asks for an egg, will give him a scorpion? If you then, though you are evil, know how to give good gifts to your children, how much more will your Father in heaven give the Holy Spirit to those who ask him!
>
> Jas. 4: 2–3; John 16: 24; Luke 11: 9–13

God wants us to ask, and to ask with the priority of seeking first his kingdom, his glory, and his will. Why would God want us to ask instead of responding without our asking? Don't earthly fathers do things without having to be asked, especially if they already know?

One reason why God wants us to ask has to do with relationship building. Communication is the lifeblood of relationship. Our relationship with God is strengthened and deepened through the communication of prayer. Certainly, God does act without our asking, but from our end he wants us to ask.

God makes the case a little stronger. We can have if we ask. We don't have because we don't ask. This means that prayer is necessary because we can't accomplish the mission without constantly seeking God. The resources are his. He dispenses them in response to prayer. The upshot of it all is that all the glory goes to God and our gratitude belongs to him. Part of the relationship-building God wants is a fear of God, that proper perspective and respect that recognizes God as God and ourselves as dependent servants, the end of which is his glory.

KINGDOM PRAYER

James' mention of motive in the passage cited above brings us another dimension of prayer—kingdom prayer. In one respect all prayer is kingdom prayer. Prayer is a privilege of the kingdom. It is a right of a child of the King. Kingdom prayer, however, looks not to context but to content, not to right of access but to what we pray for.

Kingdom prayer is prayer that seeks first the kingdom of God and his righteousness. There is a difference between what we might call therapeutic prayer and kingdom prayer. Therapeutic prayer is prayer that unburdens. You feel better when you pray and God invites us to cast our burdens on him because he cares for us. Therapeutic prayer unburdens us before our Father in heaven. We gain relief and refreshment in such prayer. As we were reminded above, when we are troubled and anxious we are to turn to God in prayer and petition with thanksgiving, knowing he is near and bringing his peace to serve as a sentry to our hearts and minds, keeping idolatrous thoughts from their destructive devices.

But even therapeutic prayer can never be an end itself. Kingdom prayer seeks not only relief, but relief for a reason. For example, let's say Aunt Mary has a goiter. We pray for her healing. In kingdom prayer we recognize that that goiter may be sidelining Aunt Mary from the work God has called her to do for the kingdom, whether it be hospitality or singing in the choir. We also know that her condition is not accidental, but has come to her at the hand of her God and Father. So how do we pray? We might ask God to use this infirmity to expose her weakness that she might better know Christ's strength and provision. We might know Aunt Mary has a tendency to worry and so we pray that she will learn trust or patience in the Lord.

We might ask God for a measure of relief so that she can get back in the fray in her usual industriousness for Christ.

Kingdom prayer looks not just to Aunt Mary but to the Christ-like character the God who works all things for her good as his child is working in her. Kingdom prayer also brings God and his purposes for Aunt Mary to the main course of the meal of his prepared purposes. Kingdom prayer deals with the essential and not just the peripheral, looking to seek and serve the purposes of God in those who serve in his army.

The model prayer in Matthew 6 through which our Lord teaches us to pray is a kingdom prayer. 'Your kingdom come' gives the prayer its theme. In this way, when Jesus gets to the part of 'give us this day our daily bread,' he is not changing the subject. Rather, he is saying that we make request for our daily rations, supplies and needs so that we can carry on in the work of his kingdom. We look to him for the daily manna of his provision for the mission he gives us.

The context of the Sermon on the Mount in which the model prayer fits reminds us that we are to seek first the kingdom of God. The following verse gives us our cadence: 'Therefore do not worry about tomorrow, for tomorrow will worry about itself. Each day has enough trouble of its own' (Matt. 6: 34). Day by day—that's the rhythm for the life of the disciple who is to take up the cross as an instrument of death to self on a daily basis, and for the subjects of the kingdom of God as they seek the provision of God. Each day will have trouble of its own, our Father alerts us. Just as the manna of Exodus, God's provision and strength is sufficient for the day and the demands thereof. And he wants us to ask him for it, to look to him for our needs in the struggles of kingdom service.

Notice how Paul's prayers are kingdom prayers, both in what he prays and why he prays them. His prayers for the saints provide models for us in praying deeper and richer than the therapeutic prayer that can major on the minors to the neglect of God's hand in and through us:

> For this reason, ever since I heard about your faith in the Lord Jesus and your love for all the saints, I have not stopped giving thanks for you, remembering you in my prayers. I keep asking that the God of our Lord Jesus Christ, the glorious Father, may give you the Spirit of wisdom and revelation, so that you may know him better. I pray also

that the eyes of your heart may be enlightened in order that you may know the hope to which he has called you, the riches of his glorious inheritance in the saints, and his incomparably great power for us who believe. That power is like the working of his mighty strength, which he exerted in Christ when he raised him from the dead and seated him at his right hand in the heavenly realms, far above all rule and authority, power and dominion, and every title that can be given, not only in the present age but also in the one to come. And God placed all things under his feet and appointed him to be head over everything for the church, which is his body, the fullness of him who fills everything in every way.

For this reason, since the day we heard about you, we have not stopped praying for you and asking God to fill you with the knowledge of his will through all spiritual wisdom and understanding. And we pray this in order that you may live a life worthy of the Lord and may please him in every way: bearing fruit in every good work, growing in the knowledge of God, being strengthened with all power according to his glorious might so that you may have great endurance and patience, and joyfully giving thanks to the Father, who has qualified you to share in the inheritance of the saints in the kingdom of light. For he has rescued us from the dominion of darkness and brought us into the kingdom of the Son he loves, in whom we have redemption, the forgiveness of sins.

Eph. 1: 15–23; Col. 1: 9–14

Paul's prayers are replete with kingdom content and are oriented to the needs of those in kingdom service. These prayers are illustrations for us of prayer as a kingdom weapon in that they give us a God-centeredness for life and service.

One of my favorite prayers for my children and congregation is a prayer of Paul's that seeks first the kingdom of God and his righteousness: 'And this is my prayer: that your love may abound more and more in knowledge and depth of insight, so that you may be able to discern what is best and may be pure and blameless until the day of Christ, filled with the fruit of righteousness that comes through Jesus Christ—to the glory and praise of God' (Phil. 1: 9–11).

God's glory, God's goals, God's righteousness, the strengthening and lengthening of God's kingdom in the hearts of others—these are the parameters of kingdom prayer. Inherent in such prayer is an awareness of the spiritual struggle and opposition we face in this present, evil age.

Kingdom prayer seeks the advancement of the kingdom of God, looking at self and life and needs in that light, toward that end. When we pray, 'Your kingdom come,' we seek our God for the subduing and strengthening work of his kingdom. We pray, 'Lead us not into temptation, but deliver us from evil.' This prayer escorts us into battle against the spiritual forces of evil that are at work to oppose us in mission.

Prayer engages us in the work of the kingdom. It also provides support to others so engaged, recognizing the need for God's power and protection. Paul's acute awareness of himself and the nature of the mission given to him led him to recruit prayer support:

> I urge you, brothers, by our Lord Jesus Christ and by the love of the Spirit, to join me in my struggle by praying to God for me. Pray that I may be rescued from the unbelievers in Judea and that my service in Jerusalem may be acceptable to the saints there, so that by God's will I may come to you with joy and together with you be refreshed.
>
> Devote yourselves to prayer, being watchful and thankful. And pray for us, too, that God may open a door for our message, so that we may proclaim the mystery of Christ, for which I am in chains. Pray that I may proclaim it clearly, as I should.
>
> Rom. 15: 30–2; Col. 4: 2–4

In the same way, we labor in prayer for ourselves and for others in the work of the kingdom. This tells us something not only about the necessity of praying, but also the nature of prayer in God's design.

PRAYER IN GOD'S DESIGN

> I'll never be able to thank America and the different Christians around the world who prayed for us, literally around the clock. I've realized that we really would not be standing here if people hadn't prayed for us. It truly was a miracle and I thank the Lord Jesus Christ for getting us out and answering all those prayers and for taking such wonderful care of us while we were there.

Those are the words of Dayna Curry at a White House reception held in honor of her and Heather Mercer. The Taliban had arrested these young witnesses for Christ in early August 2001 and held them captive until their rescue in mid-November. Her comments beg a few questions:

- Is she right? Did people's prayers really make a difference?
- Would Jesus not have acted on her behalf had people not prayed?
- Did the sheer number of those praying influence God's answer?
- Were around-the-clock prayers better in some way than one-time prayers? Could one person praying one time have had the same result?

These questions lead us to take out the scriptural screwdrivers and disassemble prayer. I saw a bumper sticker recently that said, 'PRAYER: It Works.' Most Christians could say 'amen' to that, but exactly how does prayer work? What makes it tick? Where does prayer fit into the bigger scheme of God's design? How does prayer function as a weapon in the arsenal of God's kingdom? Understanding this will help us to see where the true power of prayer is found and enable us to wield it more intelligently and appropriately.

We've already seen how prayer is the language of relationship, promoting intimacy and cultivating fellowship between us as reconciled sinners and our Creator God who reconciled us to himself in Jesus Christ. We've seen that prayer is urged and commanded, a staple of a Godward life. But there's more to prayer.

God is sovereign. He reigns in absolute, unaffected and abiding power over all his creation, creatures and circumstances. Joseph serves as a classic example. His brothers had sold him into slavery. They were responsible agents, making their own uncoerced decisions. Yet God superintended over their actions to the accomplishment of his purposes in providing for the needs of his people and in setting the stage for the prototypical old covenant redemptive event, the Exodus. The brothers sinned. The guilt was theirs. Yet God's sovereignty ruled, even over the responsible men. Sinful acts were part of God's plan, without him being the author of sin. The God who works all things after the counsel of his own will is sovereign over both means and ends, the goal and all that contributes to it.

God's Word gives example of this throughout. God's Word itself is an example. The prophet Isaiah affirms: 'All that we have accomplished you have done for us' (Isa. 26: 12). Think about that for a moment. We act because God does. After speaking of salvation being bound up in the humiliation and exaltation of Christ, the Apostle Paul calls believers to live out the fruits of grace, the ground and fountain of which is the handiwork of God himself: 'Work out your salvation with fear and trembling, for it is God who works in you both to will and to do for his good purpose' (Phil. 2: 12–13).

The Bible itself is an example of the relationship of men's actions to God's sovereignty. Who wrote the Bible? Men? God? Scripture answers with an emphatic 'yes.' Peter explains to us that 'men spoke from God as they were carried along by the Holy Spirit' (2 Pet. 1: 21). With the ideas that occurred to them, viewed from the perspective of the experience and personality God had given them, men wrote the Bible. Yet at every point the Spirit of God superintended so that the product would be the Word of God himself—holy, inspired, inerrant and infallible, down to the singular and plural of words.[38]

What about prayer? Where does it fit in to the works of God's sovereign rule that encompasses both our temporal expressions and God's eternal decree? What function does prayer play? Scripture provides the frame in which the picture of prayer is showcased. The epistle of James gives us two snapshots that make the point.

> Elijah was a man just like us. He prayed earnestly that it would not rain, and it did not rain on the land for three and a half years. Again he prayed, and the heavens gave rain, and the earth produced its crops.

> Is any one of you sick? He should call the elders of the church to pray over him and anoint him with oil in the name of the Lord. And the prayer offered in faith will make the sick person well; the Lord will raise him up. If he has sinned, he will be forgiven. Therefore confess your sins to each other and pray for each other so that you may be healed. The prayer of a righteous man is powerful and effective.

> Jas. 5: 17–18; 14–16

What do you notice about prayer in each of these texts? Prayer is depicted as a means by which God acted. God could have just withheld the rain in Elijah's day. He could have opened the skies when he was good and ready. But God used prayer as the catalyst to his answer and conduit to his actions, actions we might add that he had ordained from eternity. God does not plan things on the fly. His eternal plan includes prayer and uses prayer.

We see the same design in the prayer to which God calls the elders in James' epistle. God could heal at his own initiative, apart from the petitions of others. But he has chosen to use means, one of which is prayer. We'll see in a moment where prayer gets its power and effectiveness, but we can affirm here that the power of prayer is neither in the prayer itself nor in the faith of those praying, or prayed for.

But doesn't the Bible teach that God changes his mind and that he does so in response to prayer? Didn't God look on the human race in the days of Noah and think twice about making man? Didn't God change his mind about destroying Nineveh in the days of Jonah because they repented? How about this?

> 'I have seen these people,' the Lord said to Moses, 'and they are a stiff-necked people. Now leave me alone so that my anger may burn against them and that I may destroy them. Then I will make you into a great nation.' But Moses sought the favor of the Lord his God. 'O Lord,' he said, 'why should your anger burn against your people, whom you brought out of Egypt with great power and a mighty hand? Why should the Egyptians say, 'It was with evil intent that he brought them out, to kill them in the mountains and to wipe them off the face of the earth'? Turn from your fierce anger; relent and do not bring disaster on your people. Remember your servants Abraham, Isaac and Israel, to whom you swore by your own self: 'I will make your descendants as numerous as the stars in the sky and I will give your descendants all this land I promised them, and it will be their inheritance forever.' Then the Lord relented and did not bring on his people the disaster he had threatened.
>
> Exod. 32:9–14

Sometimes God's plan of salvation is seen as a plan B. The covenant of works didn't work. People didn't obey the law of God. So God put in place another plan, the new covenant. But Scripture makes it clear there is one covenant (Heb. 13: 20) and that the law was never meant to save but to show people they are sinners and in need of the Savior who would be born under that law and keep it. God's covenant promises would not be fulfilled by a plan B, but through the outworking of the single plan that would involve God doing what man could not. Prayer can be seen as pitching another plan.

God does have a single plan, ordained from all eternity. That plan encompasses everything. As that plan unfolds in time and space it appears to us time-bound creatures that God is scrapping one plan that didn't work and is implementing a plan B. But that change was on the books all along, in place at the wisdom and multi-faceted purpose of God Almighty. Scripture clearly affirms that God does not alter his plan or change his mind.[39]

Seeing how God acts in daily existence helps us to see the place of prayer. God works in two ways, immediately and mediately. When he acts immediately, God directly acts to do something. For example, when Jesus turned the water into wine he did so immediately, without an intermediary such as grapes or fermentation. When God acts mediately, he uses means. An illustration of this would be when he parted the Red Sea at the time of the Exodus from Egypt. God did not instantly part the sea and dry a pathway for the escape of his people. Rather, he caused a wind to blow throughout the night to cause the separation. That wind was a means, showing God's control over elements of nature to effect his purposes. Even God's use of means carried his intention to work in the hearts of all involved and to set the stage for his purposes for which all things work together.

Here's where the nitty meets the gritty when it comes to our prayer for the advancement of God's kingdom and the accomplishment of his mission. Prayer is a means by which God enfolds us into the outworking of his eternal plan. Prayer is God's means for God's ends. God executes his plan and accomplishes his purposes through the mediation of our prayers as his people. Prayer is intended by God to engage us in the accomplishment of his purposes for his own glory and goals.

We can put it this way: in the majesty and scope of God's design, in praying we can expect God to do something he would not have done had we not prayed. That statement seems to verge on blasphemy. God dependent on me? May it never be! God waits on no man. God's hands are not tied by my prayerlessness. God cannot be limited. Plus, didn't we say that his sovereignty is absolute and unaffected, that is, not contingent on anything outside of himself?

We can say that in praying we can expect God to do something he would not have done had we not prayed,[40] not to limit God, but to exalt the glory of his unfathomable providence that governs all causes, mediate and immediate. In other words, to suggest God waits on our prayers does not make God smaller. It makes him bigger than we could possibly fathom. Who is like God, governing means and ends, including the acts and prayers of his creatures, without violating their free agency and still maintaining their responsibility and culpability? Yet that is exactly the way God works and the way he shows us he works both in history and in his use of prayer—our prayers. We can take it a step further: God's sovereign plan not only does not invalidate responsible action, it establishes it because that is the way God has designed things. Prayer does work, not as an outside influence but in purposed congruence in God's eternal plan.

Listen to these quotes that may surprise you but which are in keeping with the Bible's teaching on prayer we've just laid out.

> Prayer starts the promises of God on their way to fulfillment! In prayer, God allows us to lay hold of his purposes as these are expressed in his promises. Each promise is a hook for pulling our faith into the heavens. By claiming God's promises as we petition him in prayer, we set God's work in motion. Unbelievable as it may seem, the omnipotent God permits our requests to activate the fulfillment of his mighty promises in history.[41]

> Prayer is not made pointless by the sovereign power of God. Our prayers, no less than their answers, are part of God's design. It is God's will and promise: prayer changes things in his world.[42]

> We are to pray, because only the sovereign Holy Spirit in us and in men's hearts can make our preaching effective to men's salvation, and *God will not send his Spirit where there is no prayer.*[43] [italics mine]

Are these men overstating the case? Are they limiting God? Or, are they simply affirming the place God gives prayer as a weapon of his kingdom, for the accomplishment of his purposes, against the opposition inherent in that work?

So, where does the power of prayer reside? The effectiveness of prayer is not found in numbers, frequency or fervency of those praying. Prayer finds its potency in the hidden will of God, his perfect plan that governs all things, for his own glory. That's why our prayers are always qualified by, 'Your will be done.' We submit our will to God's and trust that he will use what we have brought to act in accordance with his good pleasure and purpose. That's what we want. We want our prayers presented by the Spirit in complete and uncompromised conformity to the will of God to which we submit ourselves. We know full well that we do not know all. Only God sees the beginning from the end. Father knows best. The power of prayer is not resident in the prayer itself or in those praying, but in the eternal purpose of God himself. We don't need to somehow discern that purpose. Ours is but to trust and to pray. His will, will be done.

PRAYER'S PROMISE

Prayer can accomplish wonderful and amazing things. That's the way God designed it. He enfolds us into the work of the kingdom through taking up the weapon of prayer. Prayer holds great promise. That promise is to faith. Earlier James reminded us 'the prayer offered in faith will make the sick person well.' Faith is the operative element. When he began his epistle, James established the principle of faith: 'But when he asks, he must believe and not doubt, because he who doubts is like a wave of the sea, blown and tossed by the wind. That man should not think he will receive anything from the Lord; he is a double-minded man, unstable in all he does' (Jas. 1: 6–8).

Our Lord Jesus makes the statement even more strongly: 'I tell you the truth, if you have faith and do not doubt, not only can you do what was done to the fig tree, but also you can say to this mountain, "Go, throw yourself into the sea," and it will be done. If you believe, you will receive whatever you ask for in prayer' (Matt. 21: 21–2).

Clearly, faith is the animating feature of prayer. In that sense prayer is sacramental. It is operative to faith. It is not just an empty exercise, but carries with it the power and purpose of God that ordained it as a means.

But prayer does not work automatically, just by the recitation, simply speaking the words. To use our earlier distinction, prayer operates mediately as a means, not immediately as though it had power in and of itself as some sort of magic wand. That view of prayer is mystical and superstitious. It is more akin to the occult and to magical incantations. Vain repetition is neither heard by the Father, nor endorsed by him. But prayer does involve faith.

Faith is necessary for the function of prayer. But in what way? We want to dismiss one idea at the outset. Realization of the promise of prayer does not correspond to the strength of our faith, so that if we only have enough faith our prayers will be answered. The faith in which we pray is not some muscle that exerts force, so that the more faith we have the greater the likelihood of what we want happening. Our Lord Jesus makes it clear that it is not the size of the faith, but the presence of faith that matters: 'Because you have so little faith. I tell you the truth, if you have faith as small as a mustard seed, you can say to this mountain, "Move from here to there" and it will move. Nothing will be impossible for you' (Matt. 17: 20).

When we hear such things, again our mind is gripped with delusions of grandeur. The sky is the limit, we think. But a grounded understanding of faith dispels such ideas. Faith sees and seeks God. It does not have a life of its own, but takes its stand on something. Faith is that spiritual capacity given by God to take hold of his truth.

In this way faith is never the rebellious teenager believing she knows best or her way is the right way. Faith rests, receives, believes, submits, trusts, waits, and defers. In other words, praying in faith is praying with the conviction of God's hearing, the expectation of God's answering and the confidence that no matter how great is the thing we ask for, God is able to do immeasurably more than we could ask or think.

What a tremendous encouragement to us for the effectiveness of the God-given weapon of prayer. The God for whom nothing is impossible is at work through our prayers for the accomplishment of his purposes. That's what faith knows and how it functions in prayer. We pray with faith's focus on God.

Faith infuses prayer with great expectancy, because it knows God and knows that God has ordained prayer as his means to his ends. Such prayer identifies with the psalmist: 'In the morning, O Lord, you hear my voice; in the morning I lay my requests before you and wait in expectation' (Ps. 5: 3). God will answer: yes, no, not now, in this way, in this time. When we pray for a job for someone, faith will see God's enabling completion of a résumé or provision of a job interview as God's working and answering. Faith expects God to work and so looks for his working, accepting of his answers, in submission to his purposes.

Another way we could express the effectiveness of prayer in the hand of the God who has given it to us as a weapon is that it never misfires, nor does it ever miss. It always works. It always finds its target. The coordinates of our prayer originate in the heavenly realms and will find its mark under the guidance of God's infallible providence. There will be no collateral damage, no extraneous benefit or unexpected result outside of the perfect plan of God.

8

Wielding Spiritual Weapons

The little blue ball caromed off the wall, angling right at me. I reached back and swung with all my might, fully expecting the ball to rupture as it crashed into the front wall. Nothing. Whiff. I totally missed the ball. No contact whatsoever. The only thing that took a hit was my pride. I remember that first time I picked up a racquetball racquet. I was a sophomore in college, fairly athletic and apparently way too cocky. I figured racquetball was a piece of cake. After all, I was adept at other racquet sports: tennis, ping-pong, badminton. I watched others play and it looked easy.

When we look at the weapons of spiritual warfare, particularly the Word and prayer, we might think the same thing. What's the big deal? You read your Bible and you say your prayers. How difficult is that?

In one sense these staples of the Christian life are easy to use. Our particular challenge, however, is to learn to use them as weapons of the kingdom of God, for assault on the kingdom of the evil one, with the goal of rescuing those bound in sin and bringing them into the glorious freedom of children of God. And we can learn. God teaches us how to use them.

I eventually improved in racquetball. I learned how to stand, how to grip the racquet, game strategy, and the anticipation gained only by experience. That's how it works with the weapons of spiritual warfare. We learn by precept and practice, as we follow God's instructions and get down to the business of using them.

We're going to lay out some general principles for wielding spiritual weapons. Then, we'll take a look at some specifics for employing prayer and the Word of God in spiritual warfare.

INTELLIGENCE

There it is—a blip on the screen. As the line sweeps over the screen once more, it shows up again, only this time it's closer. The radar has picked up an incoming missile. The glowing green figure moves stealthily across the field. You look closely through the night vision goggles to follow his progress and figure out his intentions. The ultra-violet ray casts its light across the room. As it does, it exposes all sorts of trace elements and fingerprints of enemy involvement.

Constant monitoring is a necessary part of a country's defense system. All sorts of technology and techniques are used to keep one step ahead of the enemy. How much more true is this for a country engaged in actual warfare! Preventative and remedial measures are taken in response to resident and gathered intelligence.

Our Lord puts us in a state of alertness as well. We are told to be alert so that we can pray (Eph. 6: 18). Peter warns us: 'Be self-controlled and alert. Your enemy the devil prowls around like a roaring lion looking for someone to devour' (1 Pet. 5: 8). Paul warns us about our enemy's efforts to outwit us, and the necessity of being aware of his schemes (2 Cor. 2: 11). God calls us to keep our eyes on the radar screen, knowing that the air is filled with the flaming arrows of the evil one (Eph. 6: 16).

Alertness and awareness are fundamental to wielding spiritual weapons. In the face of spiritual opposition, our Lord calls us to pray to be alert (Mark 14: 38) and to be alert to pray (Col. 4: 2–4). Awareness comes from a sobriety that takes seriously our spiritual adversary and knows how he operates. It is the skill that looks at the blip on the radar screen and recognizes the missile, whether it be a deception, a temptation, or an accusation.

Our spiritual radar needs to be programmed with the data of God's Word, so that we might distinguish between truth and error (1 John 4: 1). The instruments of discernment are kept sensitive through a steady diet of Scripture in communion with our Heavenly Father. Speaking of God's Word, the writer of Hebrews highlights this need for us: 'But solid food is for the mature, who by constant use have trained themselves to distinguish good from evil' (Heb. 5: 14). Also necessary to maintain our spiritual discernment is constant cleaning from the corrosion of sin that dulls our spiritual senses.

The intelligence God gives us is not some sort of new revelation. Nor is it exposure of some demon crouching behind a bush. Rather, God provides us with the truth of his Word and the wisdom to use it to discern the lies and the errors of the enemy.

WIELDING SPIRITUAL WEAPONS

The spiritual weapons issued to us are wielded in two ways, in weakness and in wisdom. We'll see how weakness and wisdom apply to the Word and to prayer as we engage in warfare witness.

Weapons of Weakness. When Paul says we are to 'be strong in the Lord and in his mighty power' as we take our stand against the forces of darkness, that tells us our strength is not in ourselves, but in him who is with us to the end of the age. To be strong in the Lord means that we are not to be strong in ourselves, or in any other purported source of strength.

The nature of the weapons attests to our weakness. God gives us his Word because without it we will be left to our own assessment and devices. As we saw in the disassembly of the weapon of prayer in the previous chapter, the heart of prayer seeks the Lord of hosts for his power to make our efforts effective. These and any weapons given to us by God make clear that we are completely and continually reliant upon him for anything that he would deem successful. Paul spells it out for us: 'But we have this treasure in jars of clay to show that this all-surpassing power is from God and not from us' (2 Cor. 4: 7).

Evidently, we are prone to forget where our strength lies. Even the Apostle Paul, who makes such a ringing affirmation of it being all of God, needed God's providential prodding.

> To keep me from becoming conceited because of these surpassingly great revelations, there was given me a thorn in my flesh, a messenger of Satan, to torment me. Three times I pleaded with the Lord to take it away from me. But he said to me, 'My grace is sufficient for you, for my power

is made perfect in weakness.' Therefore I will boast all the
more gladly about my weaknesses, so that Christ's power
may rest on me. That is why, for Christ's sake, I delight
in weaknesses, in insults, in hardships, in persecutions, in
difficulties. For when I am weak, then I am strong.

2 Cor. 12: 7–10

God used the enemy as an unwitting tool to teach Paul that his
strength for the battle against Satan was found not in himself
but in Christ. We need to be reminded of that lesson all the
time. We delight in our struggles not as masochists but as ones
who need to be brought back to solid footing, knowing that
God gives us struggles to make that evident to us.

My family and I head to the Jersey shore for our annual
vacation. The beach is a guarded beach. Lifeguards are stationed
on elevated chairs giving them a bird's eye view of the water.
The lifeguard station stands centered between two flags, many
yards apart. These flags cordon off the designated area in which
people are allowed to swim. When we head down to the beach,
we usually set up camp between the two flags. That way we
can keep an eye on the kids and not have to go too far to hit
the waves.

What often happens is that I will be in the water riding the
waves, only to look up and see that the motion of the ocean has
carried me outside the swath of the flags. So I need to trudge
back to the safe area. That's how it works with pride. Pride
constantly carries us away from the safety and stability of
God's protection, driven away by the waves of self-sufficiency.
Distress will wake us up to our weakness and prompt us to
return to Christ's all-sufficient grace. Hard times expose our
weakness, exorcise our pride, exercise humility and explain
our constant need for the Lord and his mighty power.

Weapons of Wisdom. Wisdom is distinguished from foolishness
in Scripture. Wisdom begins with the fear of the Lord.
Foolishness enthrones us and elevates our thoughts and ways
over God's. Wisdom wields a weapon in God's way, to God's
ends, for God's glory. Wisdom is quite pragmatic. It doesn't
operate on conjecture, but on the basis of truth. It is true
knowledge applied truly.

What this means is that wisdom wields the weapons of
spiritual warfare in a down-to-earth manner as opposed to

fanciful and mystical. For example, wisdom does not handle the Word of God as a book of incantations or as a magic talisman. While the Bible talks about supernatural things and is used of God in a supernatural way,[44] it is a book that requires understanding through proper methods of interpretation. God has recorded his revealed Word to us in conventional ways that are to be understood through rules of grammar and interpreted through the expanding contexts of sentences, paragraphs, and the like. Interpretation must take into account the single Author, the multiple human authors, the genre employed, and the immediate audience. The interpretation is enriched through various lenses, such as that of redemptive history that brings a Christ-centeredness to it.[45] Scripture is not to be ripped out of context or twisted to serve our own ideas.

We can take a superstitious approach to the Bible in any number of ways. We might seek guidance by opening the Bible randomly and deciding to turn left because the verse we fingered had the word 'left' in it. Such tactics have more in keeping with a Ouiji board than God's written revelation. Some chant the name 'Jesus' or 'plead the blood,' as though simply saying the words produced some sort of magical effect. Others mysticize the original languages of the Bible, Hebrew and Greek, as though those languages were something other than ordinary media of communication. Or, in our witnessing to others we might get the idea that if we use the exact words of the Bible that will have a mystical impact that our communication and explanation of the gist of the text would not.

In the same way the Bible is to be brought to bear in a conventional way that accurately reflects the communication of God, prayer is not to be used in a superstitious fashion that exceeds the bounds of normal sense. It is the way of the cult to twist the Bible to arrive at desired doctrine. It is the way of the occult to use prayer as incantation. It's common to see spiritual warfare conducted by praying the name of Jesus in some sort of incantional invocation, but that approach violates the very faith said to empower it.

Yet many believers fall into this trap in other ways. How often do we use the phrase 'in Jesus' name' without thought and simply as a prelude to an 'amen'? Our Lord in his instruction on prayer in the Sermon on the Mount does not include that phrase to conclude the prayer he gives us as a pattern. The point behind praying in Jesus' name[46] is to pray the way Jesus prayed and through Jesus as the way. We pray for the will of the Father as did Jesus, seeking the glory and kingdom of God as Jesus did. We want the will of God's perfect plan to be accomplished.. That means we will defer to however God wants to answer our prayers. To pray in Jesus' name is to pray as he did, 'not My will but Your will be done.'

Another aspect of praying in Jesus' name is acknowledgment that Jesus is the one Mediator between God and man, and that we can approach the Father directly through him.[47] Of course, this means that every prayer is qualified by the name of Jesus, in whom and through whom we pray. We do need to pray in Jesus' name, but we don't need to pray 'in Jesus name'. We do not actually have to invoke the name of Jesus or supply some heavenly formula for the prayer to be effective.

WIELDING THE WEAPON OF PRAYER

Three wishes! Anything I want. The sky's the limit. Now, where will I start? Of course, any Miss America contestant will begin by asking for world peace, but I've got different ideas as I take in the offer of the genie who emerged from the lamp. Since it's a genie I should probably look back to the beauty of Eden for my wish list, but what will I ask for?

We've seen how the weapon of prayer works, but how do we handle it? Our Lord says this to us: 'You do not have because you do not ask.' 'Ask and you will receive.' 'Ask whatever you will in my name and it will be given to you.' Our eyes might get as big as saucers when we hear these things and our imaginations run wild. We've just rubbed the lamp and the genie has told us he will grant us not three, but an unlimited number of wishes. Do these statements give us carte blanche, a blank check signed by our Lord for whatever we want?

We already have our answer. Above we noted that wisdom wields a weapon in God's way, to God's ends, for God's glory. Our use of the weapon of prayer must be in keeping with the kingdom of God, to which we are subject and which we serve.

The first thing we want to get straight is that it is Jesus and not a genie that solicits our requests. A genie serves us. Jesus is served by us. We receive a genie's offer with an eye to what we want. We take in our Lord's offer knowing who he is to us and for what purposes he extends the offer he does. It is the will of our Lord that qualifies our requests and governs his answers: 'This is the confidence we have in approaching God: that if we ask anything according to his will, he hears us. And if we know that he hears us—whatever we ask—we know that we have what we asked of him' (1 John 5: 14–15). God answers our prayers to serve his purposes. That is the scope through which we must aim our weapon, with God's perfect will in the crosshairs. As we saw above, proper motive keeps our prayers pointed in the proper direction.[48]

With that in mind, allow me lay out several principles in taking up the weapon of prayer. First, our prayer is to our King, not to the prince of this world. We are not called to address Satan to bind him or command him to go away, to let go, to do anything. Our petition is to our King who has promised to be with us and in whom is our strength.

Our Lord Jesus does not stay at headquarters when he dispatches us to engage in evangelism. No, he is with us. He lives in us by his Spirit. When we face spiritual opposition we look to him, asking him for strength. We turn to him for protection. We trust in him for provision. If we see how the enemy has blinded the eyes of one we're trying to convince of the truth, we don't blurt out to our foe, 'Let her go, you fiend, and stop pulling the wool of your deceptions over her eyes.' Instead, we turn to our Lord and beseech him to frustrate the efforts of the evil one and to penetrate the darkness of her mind with the light of his truth—all in keeping with his sovereign good pleasure and purpose.

Second, as best we can, we want to aim the weapon of prayer and not to discharge it indiscriminately. In no way does this suggest that we have a limited supply of ammunition or a cut off to our requests. Rather, the idea is simply to pray intelligently. When a friend asks you to pray for an upcoming job interview, you pray for that interview. You pray discriminately on the basis of the information you have. You might also pray specifically for things related to the interview (safety in travel, finding the interview location) and for the interviewee (not to worry but to trust in God, peace, honest representation of himself).

We pray as we think best, in keeping with the revealed will of God. We don't need to seek some secret knowledge. If we believe Jerry is making a foolish decision, we pray what we think appropriate, in view of that information. God will receive and use our prayers as he sees fits. Our job is to content ourselves with his answer.

Prayer as a weapon of the kingdom of God is prayer conducted in knowledge—knowledge of our Savior, of ourselves, of Satan and of situations. Such prayer knows the times and takes into account what it sees, bringing it to our Lord.

Not only do we want to pray aware, we want to pray against. Satan is a liar and a destroyer. The perversion of the gospel which Paul laments in Galatians 1: 6–9 is consistent with the ruler of this present, evil age cited by Paul a few verses earlier. Satan twists and corrupts what God has made good and declared as truth. That means much of our prayer contends against the devil's efforts. For example, let's say you've been talking to Carla for some time about spiritual matters. She finally agrees to take and read a booklet you've wanted to give her. How do you pray against? You know that Satan will try to keep her from reading it and certainly from understanding it. His desired intention is get her to revile and reject it. That intelligence will help you to frame your prayers as you seek your Lord in opposition to the spiritual adversary. Any prayer can take into account the agenda of Satan and values of his kingdom, against which you can pray.

Third, God instructs us to pray 'in the Spirit':

> And pray in the Spirit on all occasions with all kinds of prayers and requests. With this in mind, be alert and always keep on praying for all the saints.
>
> But you, dear friends, build yourselves up in your most holy faith and pray in the Holy Spirit. Keep yourselves in God's love as you wait for the mercy of our Lord Jesus Christ to bring you to eternal life.
>
> Eph. 6: 18; Jude 20-21

What does it mean to pray in the Spirit? Are we being informed of the need to enter some sort of prophetic trance and pray with ecstatic utterance?

Praying in the Spirit is a simple reminder to us of the ground and power for our prayer. Prayer is spiritual activity. We pray as ones indwelt and enlivened by the Spirit. We pray in communion with the Spirit. Our prayers are brought to the Father and conformed to his will through the Spirit.[49] To pray in the Spirit is to pray in profound awareness of our redemptive relationship with God, in deep dependence upon him, and in perfect submission to his desires.

Praying in the Spirit means one other thing for wielding the weapon of prayer. We must pray along the contours of God's Word. Of the three persons of the Triune God, the Spirit is the one identified as the author of the Bible. Our prayers are to be structured by Scripture and saturated in Scripture. In Ephesians 5 Paul speaks of the spiritual conflict inherent in this age and calls upon us to make the most of every opportunity because the days are evil. In that context, he insists we have a clear mind and that we be filled with the Spirit.

Prior to saying that, he warns: 'Therefore do not be foolish, but understand what the will of the Lord is.' To be filled with the Spirit, is to know the will of the Lord. As we saw in Deuteronomy 29: 29 that will is not the secret, hidden will of God's plan, but that which is revealed—in other words, the Bible. The parallel passage in Colossians, the sister epistle to Ephesians, bears this out. There, parallel to Ephesians' 'be filled with the Spirit' is the command to 'let the word of Christ dwell in you richly.'

A wonderful example of this sort of Scripture-rich prayer in the Spirit is given by Matthew Henry, praying mainly for ourselves as God's instruments against the efforts of the evil one to sideline us and disarm us:

> Lord, lead us not into temptation. We know that no man can say when he is tempted, that he is tempted of God, for God tempteth not any man; but we know that God is able to make all grace abound towards us, and to keep us from falling, and present us faultless. We therefore pray that thou wilt never give us up to our own heart's lust, to walk in our own counsels, but restrain Satan, that roaring lion that goes about seeking whom he may devour; and grant that we may not be ignorant of his devises. O let not Satan sift us as wheat: or however, let not our faith fail. Let not the messengers of Satan be permitted to buffet us; but if they be, let thy grace be sufficient for us, that where we are weak, there we may be strong, and may be more than conquerors through him that loved us....And since we wrestle not against flesh and blood, but against principalities and powers, and the rulers of the darkness of this world, let us be strong in the Lord, and in the power of his might.[50]

Fourth, we are to pray persistently. Sometimes it takes more than one chop of the ax to fell the tree. Our Lord encourages perseverance in prayer in the parable of the judge who seems to have forgotten why he is on the bench. He lays the premise of the parable at the outset: 'Then Jesus told his disciples a parable to show them that they should always pray and not give up' (Luke 18: 1ff).

While we are not to pray with vain repetition, saying the same thing over and over, that does not preclude repeated prayer. Such prayer keeps us in the fray. We labor in prayer before God, who urges persistence. He will answer in his time.

The salvation experience of many of us bears this out. Christ died for us corporately in the fullness of time, but it was the timetable of God by which the Spirit applied it to us. We may have heard the gospel many times, but it was the timing of God's plan that drove it home to our hearts readied by his grace and power. In the same way, God answers our prayers in the timing of his perfect will. Sometimes I get irritated with my kids if they keep asking for something, especially if I've given them an answer. But with our Heavenly Father, if it's on our hearts, we don't need to fear keeping it before his face. It's all part of his intention for us and his working through us.

PATTERN FOR PRAYER

My children are as different from one another as the four suits in a deck of cards. They all belong to the same deck and bear resemblance to one another, but when it comes to personalities they are each a suit of their own. I have often stood amazed at my daughter Sarah when she was in her teens. She could talk on the phone for hours. That in itself is quite a feat, totally foreign to me who doesn't like talking on the phone much at all. But the amazing part is that she could talk that long, in a steady stream of words, and not say a thing. Don't ask me how that's possible. You'd have to be there.

Our prayers can be like that. We can ramble. But prayer as a weapon of the kingdom is focused prayer. There is a difference between persistence in prayer and rambling on in prayer. Jesus instructs us to pay attention to the art of prayer. He tells us our prayers are not for public performance to draw people's attention and admiration to us. He also says that we are not to 'keep on babbling like pagans.' In other words, our prayers are not to be random acts of mindlessness. We are to be focused.

As a corrective to rambling prayer, our Lord provides us with a pattern for prayer. Although this model prayer serves as a general pattern for prayer, it also gives us guidelines for employing prayer as a weapon of the kingdom of God. It helps us to focus our prayer. Allow me to put this prayer before you and show you what I mean as we would use it as a framework to direct our prayer for others who have not bowed the knee to Jesus Christ (Matt. 6: 9–13 (ESV)):

> Our Father in heaven,
> Hallowed be Your name.
> Your kingdom come,
> Your will be done, on earth as it is in heaven.
> Give us this day our daily bread,
> And forgive us our debts,
>   as we also have forgiven our debtors.
> And lead us not into temptation,
>   but deliver us from evil.

Our Father in heaven. Pray that God would rescue them from the family of their father, the devil, and bring them into the glorious freedom as his adopted children. Pray for the mercy of God in their lives to prepare a heavenly home for them.

Hallowed be Your name. Pray that they would be made ones who honor the name of God instead of ignoring or dishonoring it. Pray that they would cease to suppress the truth about God in their unrighteousness and recognize him as the Creator God who is to be forever praised.

Your kingdom come. Pray that the kingdom of righteousness, joy and peace under the rule of Christ would dawn in their hearts and subdue them to Christ. Pray that God would extend his kingdom by adding those who are being saved and as the catechism states, 'that Satan's kingdom may be destroyed'.[51]

Your will be done, on earth as it is in heaven. Pray that God's saving purposes would be accomplished in their lives. Pray that they would submit their wills to God in repentance and faith, and that they would believe on the One he has sent.

Give us this day our daily bread. Pray that they would come to see that man does not live on bread alone but on every word that proceeds from the mouth of God. Pray that they would see Christ as the living bread who would eternally satisfy their hunger.

And forgive us our debts, as we also have forgiven our debtors. Pray that they would see the debt of their sin against a God whose name is holy and see their desperate need for forgiveness. Pray that they would see their spiritual bankruptcy in their being able to satisfy that debt and their need for the gospel of forgiveness and righteousness bound up in Jesus Christ.

And lead us not into temptation, but deliver us from evil. Pray that God would rescue them from the grip of the devil enabled by the power of reigning and enslaving sin in their lives. Pray that God would thwart the tactics and schemes of the evil one in their lives that blind them to their need in Christ and give them a false sense of security.

No doubt many things occurred to you as we walked through the framework of this prayer. That's exactly how the structure is supposed to work. Our Lord has given us a model prayer, not one only to be recited. Every time we lay this prayer before us, moving from petition to petition as we would make the circuit of workout stations the content will likely be different, infused with general and specific requests related to those for whom we are praying, as the Spirit would lead us in prayer.

Certainly, this model prayer can be directed in ways other than evangelistically. We can use it as a pattern to pray for ourselves, our families, our church, missionaries, Sunday's worship services, and the list goes on. But it does function to bring a kingdom perspective to our petitions and to lay out a variety of areas in which to pray as we seek that kingdom. The Lord's model prayer for us encourages an economy of words as we seek our God for his saving work in the souls of those we seek to reach for Christ, under the banner of his redemptive kingdom. Other prayers recorded in the Bible can be used to guide us as well. The psalms are particularly suitable for prayer as a weapon of the kingdom of God against the kingdom of Satan, remembering that our enemy is not flesh and blood but the spiritual forces of evil that oppose God and our mission in his name.

CORPORATE PRAYER

God's Word directs us to pray privately, in our prayer closets and in our hearts along the path of daily life lived in fellowship with him and in dependence upon him at every point. But we also find corporate prayer illustrated for us in Scripture, believers praying with one another. How does a group of believers, banding together, wield the weapon of prayer? Is there greater power or value in prayer as the many express the amen of agreement in concert of prayer?

Emphasis is sometimes laid on our Lord's teaching on prayer in Matthew 18: 19–20: 'Again, I tell you that if two of you on earth agree about anything you ask for, it will be done for you by my Father in heaven. For where two or three come together in my name, there am I with them.'

Jesus seems to make an extraordinary promise specific to corporate prayer, which he defines as 'two or three coming together in his name.' It is true that the larger context refers to church discipline, but in the statement above our Lord appears to be applying a general principle to a specific situation, that being the exercise of church discipline.

What is our Lord telling us about prayer? The key relates to the context. Matthew 18 illustrates the Lord's concern for the kingdom, its character and its subjects. The kingdom is most visible in the church. These are those who claim to have bowed the knee before the King. Church discipline addresses allegiance to Jesus Christ, and is exercised through the application of the constitution of the kingdom, the Word of God.

The gathering of two or more is a holy convocation of the kingdom of God under the constitution of that kingdom in service to the King. Jesus promises to be with them in that gathering, for the sake of the kingdom. With them for what? With them for the work inherent in making disciples, just as he promises his presence in the Great Commission at the close of the Gospel of Matthew.

The application to prayer simply brings to bear the petition of the model prayer, addressed corporately to 'our Father' and asks for his 'will to be done on earth as it is in heaven.' Two or more gathered in the name of Christ is an expression of community and solidarity with one another in the kingdom of God, standing on his Word, in the authority of the presence and power of the King, Jesus Christ. The 'two' of verses 19–20 are likely the 'two' of verse 16 who bring testimony in respect to the person and the Word of God. The 'asking' is no different from the asking we have already seen, and is governed by the same kingdom qualifications. Christ's promised presence and answer to prayer is a welcome reminder that they are not alone. He will lead his church against the intrusions of the counter-kingdom as they act in his name.

We would be hard pressed to make a case on this text for greater power through corporate prayer, as though our agreement constrained the hand of God. The benefit of corporate prayer is communion with Christ and one another, and the blessing of laboring together in the work of the kingdom. For prayer, believers assembling for a common cause enjoy the assurance that they are not on their own, but that their Lord is with them for the building of his church. He is with them to guide and provide in response to their prayers. Though error and sin infiltrate the church, the gates of hell will not prevail.

Prayer is a powerful weapon for the kingdom. It can be wielded privately or corporately, but in each case the power resides in the Lord and his purposes, not in the prayer itself or in the agreement of numbers.

WIELDING THE WEAPON OF THE WORD

The Word is what places prayer in our hands, instructs us in its use and assures us of its power. But the Word is itself a weapon for the kingdom.

I don't know what I was thinking. My wife and I flew British Midland Airways from Heathrow to Edinburgh for a few days together in Scotland. We arrived at Heathrow and were proceeding through the security checkpoint with our carry on luggage. The next thing I know the guard had opened my suitcase and was riffling through all my unmentionables. Before long she had in hand the object of her search, to which she had been alerted by the x-ray machine—manicure scissors. She said she had to confiscate them. I protested, pointing out how little the blades were and that they were even rounded on the tips, but to no avail. My little metal companion of many years and I were separated, never to be reunited. I should have known better, considering the post 9/11 climate, but I didn't see the harm.

God has given us a weapon against spiritual terrorism, his Word. His word is living and active, sharper than any double-edged sword, able to penetrate and expose even the thoughts and intentions of the heart. By his Word, the Spirit of God searches our hearts and shows us where we have permitted our enemy a toehold, where we have erected idols that compete for allegiance to our Lord Jesus.

The weapon of God's Word also enables us to detect error among truth. By knowledge of the truth of Scripture, we can discern the elements of error. What did we say are Satan's tools and tactics? Deception, accusation, and temptation. It is by the Word of God that we can discern and address error, finding God's corrective and directive. The more well versed we are in the Word, the better we will be able to detect even the small and seemingly innocuous error.

Basic to use of the Word is proper handling of it. We cannot use it in any sort of superstitious fashion. God's Word is Truth. We understand that truth through sound principles of interpretation. A clear view of the truth will give us a good grasp for dealing with error. The question for us here is, truth in hand, how do we wield it?

Truth is communicated through teaching. Let's say you're talking to Fred. Fred says he believes in God, but the God he believes in would never send anybody to hell. You've just entered the arena of warfare. What do you say? First, you might do as Nehemiah did and utter a 'popcorn prayer,' saying, 'Lord, give me words. Be at work through me.' God's Word has exposed a dangerous object of error. Your job, as the Lord provides opportunity, is to try to dislodge that error with the corrective of God's truth.

You don't want to badger Fred. You want to present the truth of God's Word to chip away at the edifice of error he has erected and sought refuge. God instructs you to try to rebuke and correct with gentleness, respect, great patience and careful instruction. You want to advance the truth in Fred's thinking, seeking to take his thoughts and ideas captive to Jesus Christ.

The Apostle Paul serves as our model here. The philosophers in Athens loved to argue. They took no greater delight than debating the latest ideas. As he walked around the city, Paul noticed all sorts of altars to their polytheistic, mythological gods. He has spotted a miscellaneous altar to an unknown God. They certainly wouldn't want to chance offending any god they may have forgotten or weren't aware of. Paul's radar picked up the mine left by the enemy and he capitalized on it. What did he say? 'What you worship in ignorance, I'm going to explain to you.' Then he launches into the presentation that was suited for the audience of Greek philosophers. Listen:

> The God who made the world and everything in it is the Lord of heaven and earth and does not live in temples built by hands. And he is not served by human hands, as if he needed anything, because he himself gives all men life and breath and everything else. From one man he made every nation of men, that they should inhabit the whole earth; and he determined the times set for them and the exact places where they should live. God did this so that men would seek him and perhaps reach out for him and find him, though he is not far from each one of us. 'For in him we live and move and have our being.' As some of your own poets have said, 'We are his offspring.' 'Therefore since we are God's offspring, we should not think that the divine being is like gold or silver or stone—an image made by man's design and skill. In the past God overlooked such ignorance, but now he commands all people everywhere to repent. For he has set a day when he will judge the world with justice by the man he has appointed. He has given proof of this to all men by raising him from the dead.
>
> Acts 17: 24–31

You see what Paul is doing, don't you? He is contrasting their view of God with the truth about God. They had fabricated a god made in their image, a 'Mr. Potato-Head' god, built to their own specifications. But Paul introduced them to the God in whose image they were made, a solitary God, a sovereign God, a God who would call them to account.

Paul let the chips fall where they may, where God wanted them to fall. The result was some embraced the message, some rejected the message, some were intrigued and wanted to hear more. The same message, differing responses, as God willed.

How did Paul wield the weapon of truth? He sought to dislodge the error with the truth. In our kingdom building, we can try to raze the error and raise the truth in their minds. Or, we can look to push out the error with the truth as the dead leaves of an oak are discarded through the new sprouts of spring.

In our interactions with others, we want to attend, to listen, to discern deviation from the truth of God's Word. Key areas for inspection are their views of God, the person of Christ, and the way of salvation. Try to communicate the corrective of God's truth. Communication is not just talking; it's getting through, at least to the degree of knowledge, not necessarily their agreement with it.

One other way the Word can be used as a weapon for spiritual warfare is ammunition for prayer. If Fred has bought into the lie of Satan regarding the character of God and so invested his life in a scam, we can use God's Word to pray against what we see happening. All those descriptions of the spiritual enemy's titles and tactics can serve as a springboard for prayer. In this way, prayer is the hand that wields the weapon of the Word.

For example, God informs you: 'The god of this age has blinded the minds of unbelievers, so that they cannot see the light of the gospel of the glory of Christ, who is the image of God' (2 Cor. 4: 4). How might you use this in tandem with prayer? You might pray: 'Lord God Almighty, you created the world and all that is in it, by the word of your power. You are the Creator of all things, visible and invisible. You are the only true God, full of grace and truth, rich in mercy and abounding in love. O Lord, remove the scales from Fred's eyes. Enable him to see the glory of your being and the glorious salvation of Your Son. By the regenerating power of Your Spirit, penetrate the darkness of his heart and flood it with the light of life in the gospel of the glory of Christ.'

Descriptions of our enemy from God's Word can be a springboard for our prayer in the face of the enemy's efforts, evident in the lives of others we engage for Christ. Other portions of Scripture can be brought to the service of prayer. In every case, however, we want to remember that we are opposed in this age by the spirit of the antichrist, whose tactics are lies and deceptions, distortions of that truth, offering a contrary and counterfeit hope.

Warfare witness is communication of God's truth, particularly his Messiah as the way, the truth and the life, in the face of spiritual opposition with the weapons God has issued to us suitable for the task, wielded in the way of his design. Having reviewed our enlistment papers and examined our equipment for the conflict, we now turn to the engagement of others in the exercise of our divine commission.

III

ENGAGEMENT

9

The Theatre of Operations

For weeks and months US troops said goodbye to wives, husbands and children as they were deployed to the Persian Gulf region, positioned to enter the country of Iraq. Hugs and tears were the order of the day. Employers had to scramble to cover bases for those employees of the military reserves called up to active duty.

Why all the packing and preparation? Why all the separation anxiety? Why go half way across the world to Iraq? Because that's where the conflict was—over there. It wouldn't come to us. We had to go to it. Troops and equipment were deployed to where the war was to be fought.

As we look to engage in the kingdom battle of reaching others for Christ, where is our destination, our field of battle? Where does our Lord and Commander send us to engage others in this operation of liberation? We can find the coordinates of the theatre of operations by reminding ourselves of the nature of the battle.

KINGDOM BORDERS

What are the geographical boundaries of the kingdom of God? How about those of the kingdom of this world? If the everlasting kingdom of God and his Christ has been inaugurated and is like a rock growing to fill the whole earth, as Scripture describes it, then it must have boundaries that can be measured to trace that growth. But what are those boundaries?

There are houses in my older neighborhood that are large, almost sprawling. But they weren't always that way. At one time, when the neighborhood was first built, they were the same size as mine. It's not like today where houses in my area are all built large, larger and huge. Over the years the owners added to them, a garage here, a new room there, and maybe a screened-in porch for good measure. With each addition, the houses grew. The square footage of the building could be seen and measured for its growth.

But the kingdom of God is not like that. It is a kingdom of redemptive rule measured not spatially but spiritually. I live in a burgeoning area. Housing projects are springing up everywhere. The roads are insufficient to handle the traffic demands created by the increasing population. Evidently, the phone lines were insufficient to handle the telephone traffic as well. With multiple lines, cell phones, faxes, and computer hookups, the phone company was running out of numbers to assign. Their answer was to create a new area code, not by geographic region as before, where all those in the same vicinity had the same area code, but by individual phone line. The new area code would overlay the existing codes. Homes with the new code would be interspersed throughout the region. The upshot was that your new neighbors across the street could have a different area code from you, and you'd have to dial ten digits instead of seven to call one another.

The kingdom of God is a spiritual dominion that overlays the kingdom of this world. We live as children of God and citizens of heaven amidst the children of Satan and citizens of a fallen kingdom. We are in the world but not of it. We might live next door to an unbeliever but have a heavenly calling rather than a worldly one. Scripture describes an overlay of those sealed by the Spirit of God amidst those bearing the mark of the beast. These are signs of ownership and citizenship.

What that means is the kingdom of this world that we engage for the cause of our King is not over there but right here. Our engagement with it is not then when we get there, but right now because it's where we are. We don't need to pack up our gear and kiss our loved ones good-bye as we set out for the theater of operations. We enter the field of battle when we set foot out the door and even when we set foot on the floor from our beds.

IN YOUR GOING

As his disciples, our Lord Jesus has given us marching orders. The Great Commission of Matthew 28 rests on the kingdom authority and actuality of the risen and reigning Christ. Those orders not only tell us what to do, they tell us when to do it.

If it's Tuesday night, it must be time to go out and bear witness. In my Christian life I have been part of several evangelism programs. I benefited greatly from the training I received. Learning an outline of the gospel and gaining an outlet for its presentation were wonderful. I learned by watching and by cutting my teeth on actual encounters for Christ. These programs emboldened me, giving me the content, confidence and courage that would serve me well for mission.

But these programs had their drawbacks. Although I'm sure this was not the intention and a violation of everything the designers of the programs stood for, I found myself on a time clock of witness. My evangelism was tied to the time frame of the evening or to the duration of the program. On Tuesday evenings, I was on-duty. Any other time I was not. I know this reveals something about my heart. But judging from others in the program and from those not in the program, I know that I was not alone in this notion of being on-duty for witness.

One contributor to this frame of mind was an improper understanding of the Great Commission. Let's take a closer look at those marching orders given to us by our Lord. His final command is expressed this way: 'Therefore go and make disciples of all nations, baptizing them in the name of the Father and of the Son and of the Holy Spirit, and teaching them to obey everything I have commanded you. And surely I am with you always, to the very end of the age' (Matt. 28: 19–20).

What is the command? It is two-fold. First, we are to 'go.' Second, we are to 'make disciples' through establishing converts in the local church[52] and instructing them in the true faith. Or, so it seems. Actually, the only finite verb is the single word in the original, 'make disciples.' 'Go' is a participle that gains its stature as a command from the command to make disciples. The 'go' tells us not only what, but especially when and where we are to carry out our Lord's command to make disciples.

We might express it this way to capture the sense: 'in your going, make disciples,' or 'as you go, make disciples.' It's like my telling my kids to go and pick up their clothes. They could think that I am directing them to their bedrooms, where they are to gather up the clothes that never made it to their dresser drawers. They can't do that until they get to their rooms. In the meantime, their obedience waits to be exercised. But if I tell them to pick up their clothes as they go, that engages them right here, right now as they move throughout the house. It causes them to look at the whole of the house and where they are at the moment.

In the sense of the Great Commission our disciple-making looks to the whole of life and where we are at any given moment. In other words, it is as we go about daily life as the witnesses we are that we are to bear witness to our Lord Jesus by what we say and do. That means we are witnesses on Tuesday night and on Tuesday morning. We are witnesses at 7:24 and 24/7. We are witnesses whether we are officially part of the evangelism training program or not. We are witnesses.

That also means that the harvest of which our Lord spoke when he tells us to open our eyes and look to the fields ripe for harvest is not something for which we need binoculars or satellite spying capability. The harvest is right under our noses. We walk in the midst of it every day.

A MIGHTY FORTRESS

A mighty fortress is a great thing when it refers to our unchanging, almighty Creator and Redeemer. A mighty fortress is a travesty when it describes the ministry of the church. The church has been called a fortress in which the people barricade themselves, allowing admittance only to those who come to them and who are like them.

But when we repent of such a notion and venture out into the highways and byways for ministry and witness, what do we find? We find fortresses out there as well, fortress of thought and fortresses of lifestyle. Contending with our own fortress mentality is only part of the challenge.

For people today in the twenty-first century Western World, religion is either irrelevant or simply a matter of personal preference. Religion has been relegated to the Siberia of man's existence, exiled from real life, accorded a place, to be sure, but just as surely kept in its place. How many times have you read or heard someone speak of religion as merely a matter of personal preference? The very notion of evangelism and proselytism is foreign to the current dogma of tolerance.

We are consumer societies with ourselves as the final authority. Personal decision and choice are the by-laws; 'rights', the constitution. We might assert, 'The Bible says,' but if its authority is not recognized its message will not gain a hearing.

A related barricade is isolationism. So, not only are people sovereign cities unto themselves, they are cities walled with the brick of protectionism and the mortar of autonomy. These bricks take different forms, from the isolationism of telephone answering machines and other technological 'advances,' to the harriedness of overflowing schedules, to foundational matters such as personal rights that offer no forum for scrutiny and debate. I believe what I want. You believe what you want. Contradiction? No problem, just as long as it works for you.

To top it all off, not only is there a cultural resistance and challenge to the mission of witness on which our Lord sends us, there is a spiritual one as well. Once we break through the walls of resistance and protection we find ones who are described by the Bible as 'dead in sin,' without the capability of responding or even hearing. Fortresses—gated, alarmed, guarded, impenetrable to ordinary means. Your job is to go and breech them and bring the gospel.

KNOW AND THE DOOR SHALL BE OPENED

Why don't we like telephone canvassers? They're only doing their job, trying to eek out a living like the rest of us. No doubt there are many reasons for our disdain, ranging from initiative to intrusion. We didn't seek them out. We want to enjoy our dinner in peace.

But is it just the fact that they're telephone canvassers that fosters our disdain? What if you sit down to dinner and the phone rings? You cringe but get up to answer the call. On the phone you hear your best friend. She tells you she's got a job representing a company and proceeds to tell you about their product. She's a telephone canvasser! Your guard goes up reflexively, but you listen. Why? Because of the relationship. The strength of your relationship overcomes your aversion to the unwanted sales pitch, at least temporarily. You listen to the message over the growls of your stomach because you know and care for the messenger. The relationship has breeched your castle walls.

I realize that's a little far fetched. For some of you, that may kill the friendship right then and there. But you get the idea. You feel the difference, the softening and even receptivity to what would ordinarily make your skin crawl.

Relationships are essential as a context for communication. That's true of mass evangelism. That's true of personal evangelism. People listen to Billy Graham because they know Billy Graham, not just his celebrity. They trust him. He engenders confidence. People are inclined to lend him their ears. A big reason for that is his character, communicated mainly by what has not appeared in the headlines. He has never betrayed their trust with sexual indiscretion or been convincingly accused of misappropriating funds. There's not a personal relationship there, but there is a relationship nonetheless. That relationship keeps people from changing the channel and may even motivate them to attend the crusade in their area.

I can say things to Jim that he probably wouldn't take or at least take seriously from many other people. Jim and I have played tennis together for years. I've been to his house, met his wife, petted his dog, asked him for favors. We have a history together. Jim's not a believer. He admits that without apology. He holds a certain disdain if not antagonism for the Christian faith and religion in general. Yet Jim will listen to me as I share my faith in Jesus Christ. He even takes a degree of interest in it since it's important to me.

Why is Jim willing to listen to something in which he has no interest? It's because it comes from one in whom he does have an interest—me. Our relationship gives me liberties I would have no right to ordinarily.

Each of us has those relationships that serve as a natural context for our communication of the gospel. That context does not guarantee acceptance of what we say, but it does provide for opportunity to say it and even to be heard.

For this sort of license where people lower the drawbridge of their lives for our entry, it's important that the relationships are real. I don't think too many people are drawn in by the 'how are you today?' of the telephone canvasser. Manufacturing relationships for ulterior motives can be manipulative and misleading. For us as Christians, we want our relationships to be relationships of love where we genuinely care for others. To some degree, we will have access to their lives and they to ours. We genuinely enjoy them and don't want to use, misuse, or abuse them. But we do want to love them as Christ loved us.

PROVIDENTIALLY POSITIONED

Special teams play an extremely important dimension in a football game, right along with the offense and defense. Integral to good special team play is each player staying in his lane as he runs up the field to cover a punt or kick-off. If the entire team converges on the ball, the returner could break free of the containment and find no one to stop him on his way to the end zone. The same holds true of military campaigns. Platoons are positioned strategically by commanding officers for the benefit of the battle plan.

I saw the movie; now I'm reading the book. *The Killer Angels* by Michael Shaara describes the men and maneuvers of the four days in the summer of 1864 when the troops of the North and the South met at Gettysburg, Pennsylvania for the watershed battle of the war. Both the film and the book convey the harsh realities of war. They also graphically portray the value of holding the positions assigned them by the savvy commanding officers, who knew the value of the ground they occupied.

Our God is sovereign. He is infinitely wise. Just as churches are outposts of the kingdom of God, providentially stationed by him for the work of the kingdom, so are we strategically positioned by our Commander in this world for the campaign of his kingdom. I know we are the ones who decide what houses to buy and what gym we go to. But ultimately, it is by the providence of God that we go where we go and know whom we know. His guiding hand leads not only in the way of righteousness for his name's sake, it leads us for the way of righteousness, positioned for the good news of kingdom proclamation.

This means not only that we live in the theatre of operations for the kingdom of heaven, we have been strategically stationed there by the wise providence of God. He has established us on the high ground in which we are beacons of light. Our engagement for the cause of Christ is not extraordinary to life, but part of ordinary, everyday life. Those encounters and relationships in ordinary life, 'in our going,' provide us the forums for engaging others for Christ. God has planned it that way. He has put us in their way.

Saturday morning. You can't wait to meet Jane on the courts for your weekly tennis game. After a long week of work, your body longs for recreational activity. You enjoy Jane a great deal. She's easy to get along with. Her game presents a challenge for you. You've had opportunities to talk and get to know her. One of those tidbits of knowledge is that Jane is not a believer. She knows you are. She knows you know she's not. That tennis engagement affords you far more than getting some exercise. It provides you opportunity to share a love other than the zero score of tennis. You can share the love of God filling the cross of Christ. Your time at the net takes on a whole different character as it affords opportunity to bear witness to your Lord and take note of the devil's lies which she has believed, and the hope in which she has invested.

Tennis is but one of the areas of life. Every area of your ordinary life is a forum for impacting others for the cause of the kingdom of life and light. We might call these your life-spheres—areas of activity and relationship that make up your life. Examples of life-spheres are our family, our neighborhood, our workplace, our activities, our recreation, the marketplace. Each of these is a sphere of influence for us. Spheres of influence are those arenas of life in which God has providentially placed you, where you operate and have contacts, and where you have special opportunity to influence others for Christ.

God has raised us up in the lives of those around us as beacons of light and bastions of truth. I see Matt all the time. As long as I drink coffee and continue to enjoy the coffee where Matt works, I will likely run into Matt. I have a question for you: Why don't you pray and plan to be a more active witness to Matt? You never open your mouth to him. You never pray for Matt's spiritual welfare. Why not? Probably because you don't know Matt. God has not situated you in his life. God has put me there. God has given me that special opportunity to influence Matt for Christ. I need to be a faithful steward of the opportunity and an obedient servant of my Lord Jesus.

While we are stationed as soldiers of the kingdom of God in the battleground of the kingdom of this world, we are not all in the same place. Like that 484 area code overlay, we are spread out, living among those residents of the kingdom of this age. We want to be faithful where God has put us. We want to stay in the lane to which God has assigned us. If he grants us other avenues and opportunities, we want to be faithful there as well. We don't want to be derelict supposing someone else will cover those whom God has placed in our lives.

We each have our spheres of influence, arenas of life where we have peculiar opportunity to influence others for Christ. The question is, how do we take stock of those life-spheres?

LIFE-SPHERE MAPPING

Although research bears out the truth that the more believers grow in Christ, the more they tend to grow away from unbelieving contacts and friends, we still have plenty of relationships that afford opportunity to reach others for Christ. We can chart these relationships by way of life-sphere mapping.[53] Look at the diagram below:

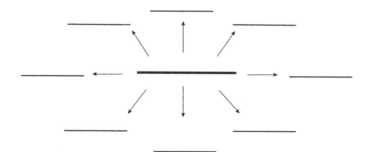

Put your name on the bold line in the center. On the lines surrounding you, write your various life-spheres, such as your immediate or extended family, the neighborhood in which you live, where you work, your church, places of recreation, marketplaces you frequent, organizations to which you belong, and so on. Each one of these is a sphere of influence for you.

Now write down names of people in each of these spheres whom you believe to still belong to the kingdom of this world or of whom you're not sure. Obviously, you can't know their hearts, but you can see the fruit of their lips and lives. On the basis of this fruit you make a determination, which may well be adjusted down the road. In naming names, you have identified potential targets God may use you to rescue from the present, evil age and bring into the glorious freedom of the children of the King. Of course, the Holy Spirit is the agent of change. You are the instrument. Your completed map may look something like this:

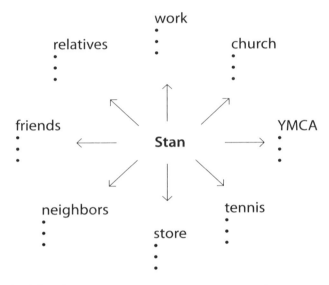

This life-sphere mapping gives you a more proactive posture in the theatre of operations in which you find yourself. It brings the theatre of operations to your doorstep and establishes you in the field for the sake of the kingdom of God. It helps you to take stock of real people with whom you can build relationships and draw near in mission of love for Christ and neighbor.

MISSION VERSUS MISSIONS

Often when we think of the mission of the church, our mind goes to missions and our eyes look to foreign shores. Missions happen 'over there.' We can go over there and join in the work of missions. We will join in when we get there. We can support those who are over there with our funds and prayers and expressions of encouragement.

However, the mission of the church into which we are enfolded is not only over there. It is right here, right now. It is where we live. It is foreign and domestic. It is wherever we are, whenever we are. We want to live with a mentality of mission, an attitude of active duty.

Cultivating a proper attitude is essential to making witness a part of the comings and goings of everyday life. I remember trying to be of help to a fellow believer in some struggles he was having in his life. He had a lot on his plate, but he was his own worst enemy. He looked at things negatively and pessimistically. In our discussions, I turned the subject to his attitude. You would have thought I just told him his mother wore army boots. He went ballistic, berating me for taking him to task. How dare I say he had an attitude?

I was using the word 'attitude' in a traditional sense of a way of thinking or looking at something. An attitude in this sense is neither good nor bad. It's just a lens that gives perspective, one of those half-empty, half-full kinds of things. This guy understood the word 'attitude' in the contemporary sense of negative disposition. So jaundiced was he that even with my explanation I never did gain his ear.

The attitude we need to cultivate is not one of belligerence. We don't want to rile ourselves up into some fighting mood. The attitude we need is a practiced way of thinking by which we remind ourselves of the kingdom perspective our Lord wants us to bring to everyday life. That perspective speaks to who we are, who Christ is, the mission we're on and the whole nine yards. It colors all of life. Paul expresses this attitude of alertness: 'Be very careful, then, how you live—not as unwise but as wise, making the most of every opportunity, because the days are evil' (Eph. 5: 15–16).

God's Word reminds us of the battleground that is life, but also of our stance and responsibility in the arena as the children of light we are. Our witness for Christ as part of our service in the kingdom of God occurs in the enemy territory in which we live. We are always on active duty. We are never off duty. There are no reserves in Christ's army who serve one weekend a month and two weeks in the summer. We cannot even expect retirement after 20 or 30 years.

Satan not only blinds the minds of unbelievers, he puts blinders on the minds of believers making us oblivious to our calling and surroundings. He convinces us through his agents of the world and his ally of our flesh that it is 'not my job' or 'I'm off the hook because somebody could do it better.' That's pretty effective. After all, who of us doesn't have someone who could do something better? But that reality does not relieve any of us from the responsibility given by God.

Another of our enemy's distortions that has greatly affected the effectiveness of the church as a military institution for spiritual service is Satan's success seen throughout the church and infiltrating the church's infantry. 'Christ is to serve me.' Christ is reduced from Lord to lackey. The church is redesigned from military post to mall where we want a full-service church that offers all we want. In this mentality we have lost the concept of sacrifice and hardship. This prompts withdrawal into the fortress. We don't want to make eye contact with those around us because if we do they might demand or take advantage. Our attitude as Christ's soldiers must be shaped by his truth and not the enemy's propaganda.

ENEMY ENCOUNTERS

As we speak of the 'enemy,' we always want to remember who that enemy is—not other denominations that are different branches of the armed services of Christ's kingdom, not unbelievers. Unbelievers are called to account for their actions by God, yet they are also characterized as pawns and prisoners of the evil one who has taken them captive to do his will. Our enemy is not flesh and blood, but the spiritual forces of evil.

10

Rules of Engagement

Becky worked in the same office as a member of my church. They got to know each other over time. Their discussions at break times would often gravitate to spiritual matters. Becky was particularly intrigued by our church as her co-worker described it to her, and, before long, took him up on his invitation to visit. She liked the church very much, especially the people and the atmosphere of worship. She kept coming until she could be considered a 'regular attender.'

Becky had visited the church several months before I decided to make an evangelistic visit. I had visited her once before just as a welcome and follow-up to her attending the church, but it had not been an evangelistic visit, with the express purpose of presenting the gospel message. Our visit started out well, friendly and relaxed, but I soon had backed her into a corner (in a gentle and loving way, of course) and was dumping the gospel load on her.

I became aware of the icy wall of protection that was shooting up around her, but I persevered, determined to carry out my responsibility to evangelize. We parted with cordialities, and, although I was unsettled, I chalked it up to the appropriateness of my evangelistic invasion, mixed in with a trace of satisfaction at having discharged the gospel missile and scoring a direct hit.

I never saw Becky again. I tried to contact her, but to no avail. I was kept informed about her through the member of my church, but that became a dead end when she left that job. Her co-worker did tell me how turned off she was at my visit.

Was Becky turned off by me or by the gospel? After all, doesn't the Scripture speak of the gospel being the fragrance of life to those who are being saved, but the stench of death to those who are perishing? That must be it—Becky must be one of those 'perishing' people. Could be, but I'm pretty sure the offense for her was not the cross; it was the communicator. Something was wrong.

How do we go about communicating the message of the kingdom of God in the face of spiritual opposition? The first thing is remembering who the opposition is. I didn't regard Becky as the enemy, but I was treating her as such. I was using the Bible as a blunt instrument to pummel her into submission. I was wielding the sword of the Spirit as the world would wield a sword of steel. Instead of speaking the truth in love, I treated Becky as a target. I manhandled her with truth.

Maybe the worst offense of all is that I tried to usurp the role of the Holy Spirit. The Spirit is the one who convinces, convicts, and converts sinners, not me. Yet I pressed on, even when I saw I was driving Becky away, as though I was the one who changed hearts. It was all up to me and this was the one opportunity. In other words, I was acting as agent, not instrument.

Mixed in with my presuming upon the role of the Spirit was a superstitious use of his Word. If I could only discharge the whole clip of ammunition, get the whole gospel out there, she might surrender. If I could only get the Word out, chant the incantations on the Scriptural signposts, the spell would be cast. If Becky were the elect, she would select and not reject Christ.

The whole world is under the control of the evil one, Scripture informs us. Satan is a prince over subjects, a father over children of kindred spirit, at home together in an evil age. The Beckys of this world are in bondage to sin, blinded by their fallen nature, of their father the devil, and in need of emancipation. In their rebellion they need to surrender to King Jesus, bowing the knee in a new kingdom allegiance of repentance and faith. In their bondage they need deliverance from sin and rescue from this present, evil age. They are not the enemy. They are in the oppressive hands of the enemy. We are to have compassion on them, regarding them the same as we would want to have been treated when we were in their shoes before conversion.

Yet, bringing biblical teaching to bear, the Beckys of this world are willing subjects of Satan, agreeable idolaters of a false god of this age. This means we must work on two fronts as we seek to be used of God for the sake of his kingdom. We must address the spiritual opposition of the forces of darkness, and the flesh and blood people who have been taken captive to do the enemy's will. How do we do that in practice? We just saw in the previous chapter that our life-spheres are our personal spheres of influence. How can we go about making these relationships and making the most of them for the cause of Christ?

BUILDING RELATIONSHIP

Relationships provide context for communication. Conversely, communication provides for strong relationships. Any marriage counselor worth his or her salt knows that communication is the blood flow of a relationship. As communication is cut off for whatever reason, the relationship typically withers and eventually dies, with gangrene leading to the amputation of the other from each person's life. Divorce court is filled with such cadavers.

Communication not only builds relationships, it builds understanding. One of the basic rules of engaging others for Christ is clear communication. This presents all sorts of challenges, especially trying to articulate biblical truth in a largely biblically illiterate society. The twenty-first century English-speaking world is secularized. Whereas two generations ago people were somewhat versed in biblical jargon and familiar with Bible stories, nowadays we can't assume anything. I'm not talking about use of heavy words like 'propitiation.' I am talking about simple words like 'Christian' that may conjure up political party or be encrusted with all sorts of negative connotations.

That's why listening is key to communication. The writer of Proverbs admonishes us: 'He who gives an answer before listening—that is his folly and shame' (Prov. 18: 13). It's like starting to scratch someone's itch without finding out where it itches. Ronald Johnson hits the nail on the head in the title of his book, *How Will They Hear If We Don't Listen?* How can we apply the corrective treatment of truth without proper diagnosis of the error typical of Satan's counterfeit kingdom?

Listening is hard work. It takes time and focus and energy. Listening is akin to love in that it is patient and unpresuming. It is giving, sacrificing of our time and self. Our listening needs to be active and not passive. Passive listening is where we hear the words, but we don't listen to what's said. Active listening works to understand, asking questions to promote understanding. It enters the world of those to whom we incline our ear with interest and compassion.

In addition, communication involves not only the impartation of information, but the reception of that information as well. A forward pass in football is not completed because it leaves the quarterback's hand. It must be secured in the hands of the receiver. Then it is completed. How do we know if the pass is completed? We confirm it by inspection. At least in televised games, we know it by the dozen instant replays from a myriad of different angles and the wearisome insights of the commentators. We know whether we have communicated by the same means, inspection. We know through the examination of more active listening and probing.

Information given is not necessarily information received. And even if it is received, that doesn't mean it's information understood. Anyone who has ever regurgitated information from short-term memory for a test in school knows this quite well. We can ace a test without really knowing a thing. The communication we want for the building of relationship and the benefit of others requires understanding. Not that that happens all at once or only from our lips, but that is the goal.

Another feature of communication is conveyance, the way we communicate. When I throw the ball with my kids I take into account several things. I throw differently depending on whether they are two or twelve or twenty years old. It makes a difference if I am standing five feet from them or fifty. I'm not going to rifle a baseball at them with all my might if they're five feet from me. If I do, it's not going to be any mystery as to why they didn't catch it. We want to convey in a way that facilitates and maximizes communication.

Mary Poppins instructed us in song that a spoonful of sugar helps the medicine go down. She may have learned that from the Apostle Paul. He was a master communicator. Paul listened to the altar of the unknown god in Athens to know the thoughts and intentions of the hearts of the citizens and to scratch their itch for truth. He knew he had to speak clearly, with content conformed to Scripture, and that no matter what he said or how well he said it, it would find genuine acceptance only by the Spirit of God. But Paul also knew the importance of tone in speech. In his letter to Philemon on behalf of Onesimus he spoke words of great diplomacy and conciliation, not demanding or heavy-handed as he may well have had a right to do by virtue of apostolic authority. The way something is said can gain a hearing. We may be invested with the authority of Christ as his ambassadors, but that does not mean it's appropriate for us to bark truth at people.

Certainly this is true with the truth of the gospel, the message of the righteous reign of the Prince of Peace that brings joy and life and peace to those who embrace it. Scripture in several ways qualifies presentation of the truth.

The overarching and overruling feature of the communication of truth is love. We are to speak the truth in love. What does that mean? Certainly, love speaks to the motive for our message. We share Christ not out of self-aggrandizement and not for self-glory. We bring the words of life to bear for the welfare of the other. But how do we convey the truth in love?

We could turn to 1 Corinthians 13, the classic chapter providing us with an operational definition of love. There we find the blueprint that enables us to grasp what the conduit of love looks like. God identifies four features flowing from love that are to govern our communication of his truth.

The first two are found in a discussion of truth in general, particularly as it is brought to bear against error: 'In the presence of God and of Christ Jesus, who will judge the living and the dead, and in view of his appearing and his kingdom, I give you this charge: Preach the Word; be prepared in season and out of season; correct, rebuke and encourage—with great patience and careful instruction' (2 Tim. 4: 1–2).

Love is patient. Love rejoices in the truth. When we speak with others about the truth, we want to exercise great patience with them. We want to take our time. We don't want to shake the dust off our feet in exasperation at the first glimmer of rejection or unreceptivity. We don't want to allow a raised eyebrow or furled brow to deter us. We want to be tolerant of resistance, allowing room for the Spirit. We want to explore the barriers of background or belief that might be impeding understanding or acceptance. We want to challenge and cause them to examine and question what they believe. That can take time.

Not only are we to be patient, we are to provide careful instruction. That means we're not satisfied to tell people they are wrong. We do not achieve our goal by exposing their error. We want to take pains to lead them in what is right. People don't need only to escape the quicksand. They need the solid foundation of the rock of truth on which they can take their stand.

We don't just talk at people. We talk with them. We engage in dialog, the give and take of communication. We don't want it to degenerate into point-counterpoint, but to foster understanding. This goal is pursued through presentation of the truth of the Word in great patience and careful instruction.

I can stand opposite my nine-year-old son, Nathan, ten feet away and throw the baseball to him with all my might. As he fails to catch it over and over again, I can be patient by putting up with his drops and by persisting in throwing it to him. I can instruct him in how to catch it, positioning his mitt properly and telling him to keep his eye on the ball. In other words, I can try to wing the ball to him with great patience and careful instruction, but he will likely still fail to catch it.

But God introduces two other qualifiers to our communication of truth that facilitate its reception, if not its embrace. Peter lays them out for us: 'But in your hearts set apart Christ as Lord. Always be prepared to give an answer to everyone who asks you to give the reason for the hope that you have. But do this with gentleness and respect' (1 Pet. 3: 15). Note how we are convey the words of life: with gentleness and respect.

As I hear these words again I grimace at my evangelistic manhandling of Becky. Gentleness is the opposite of coercion, trying to ram something down someone's throat. Speaking of throat, my dentist serves as a perfect illustration. I've had my share of dental work done over the years. I'm sure I've bankrolled several exotic vacations for my dentist and his family. But I'm glad to do it because I wouldn't part with the guy. He is extraordinarily gentle. I've been to dentists who have injected novacane in my gums in preparation for committing unspeakable dental atrocities in my mouth. While the novacane did its numbing work so that I felt nothing at the time, I was in serious pain when it wore off. What happened was that the butchers would just jab the needle in my gum and depress the plunger like they were late for tee time on the golf course. My current dentist, however, would gently prepare my gum for the needle and then gently depress the plunger on the needle while the fluid slowly worked its way to the nerves without causing havoc to my gum that I would feel later.

It is with such gentleness that we are to convey the truth of God's Word, allowing the power of the Word to do its work at the hand of its Author rather than trying to accomplish anything with the brute force of our knowledge.

We don't want to give the idea that gentleness means absence of force. Even putting the right puzzle piece in place requires a degree of pressure by our thumb. How much more so can we expect resistance as we bring to bear a message that runs counter to the kingdom of which they are a part and contrary to the right of self-determination they hold as a value! Our points do have force. Our arguments carry weight. We just don't want to be argumentative. We don't want to force a puzzle piece in place for our own goals and by our own efforts that is not in keeping with the Designer's picture.

A major contributor to this gentleness will be the other aspect of communication, respect. Sometimes in evangelism or in other things we hold with conviction, we can talk at people instead of with them. They become targets. Respect, however, humanizes and personalizes those with whom we are speaking. It doesn't treat them as objects of scorn as the Pharisee did of the tax collector in Jesus' parable. They will not end up as notches on our gospel gun. We will treat them the way we would want to be treated.

Respect is a by-product of love. It employs the Golden Rule of doing unto others as you have would them do unto you. Respect is ready to listen. Respect is the eye contact of loving communication. Respect is the willingness to become all things to all people for the sake of the gospel.

Gentleness, respect, patience, instruction—these are the elements of the delivery system that God gives for launching those spiritual weapons capable of destroying strongholds. The Apostle Paul gives us the model that reinforces our need for patience in the presentation of the gospel.

FARMERS FOR CHRIST

It's not too much of a stretch to mix the military and agricultural metaphors for the work of witness. After all, the prophet Joel speaks of beating plowshares into swords for the need of the hour (Joel 3: 10). Only later, would Micah speak of the reverse of beating swords into plowshares (Mic. 4: 3) in anticipation of the eternal peace of the age to come. But that's not where we live and serve in this day, in this age for Christ's kingdom.

The field of battle into which we head out as soldiers every day is also a field of harvest into which we are sent as workers by our Lord for his kingdom. The agricultural metaphor serves us well for learning more rules of engagement.

Not surprisingly, we face the opposition of the evil one under this metaphor as well. God's Word informs us that Satan is the one who plucks up the seed of the gospel sown. He sows weeds among the wheat. Satan undermines our efforts and seeks to frustrate God's purposes in the gospel. As we have seen, however, he actually ends up serving and furthering the purposes of God in the seed of the gospel and the harvest of the kingdom. Still, he works to oppose us. We are called to take that into account in engaging others for the cause of Christ.

In terms of what we are called to do in the face of such opposition, the Apostle Paul shows us the process of planting: 'I planted the seed, Apollos watered it, but God made it grow. So neither he who plants nor he who waters is anything, but only God, who makes things grow' (1 Cor. 3: 6–7).

What's the first thing you notice about this picture? It gives us relief in knowing that it doesn't all rest on our shoulders, but on God's. At the same time, however, the picture painted by Paul calls us to faithfulness. It may not all depend on me, but that does not excuse me from faithfulness in handling the responsibility I do have. This picture provided gives relief and responsibility. God makes the gospel grow; I don't and can't. But God uses me in the process.

This metaphor instructs us in several ways relevant to our engaging others with the gospel of the kingdom. First, you notice many hands at work over time. This tells us that the work of kingdom proclamation is progressive. Evangelism is not an event. It is a process. It involves a variety of activities over a period of time.

Second, we see many hands carrying out different responsibilities. Paul planted; Apollos watered. If I can stretch this metaphor a mite, we might think of the variety of activities related to communication of the gospel. You might be the first person to share the good news of what God has accomplished in Jesus Christ. In this you might be cultivating the soil or spreading the seed. At that person's next encounter with a believer, he might have some of the weeds of error pulled up. Another encounter might find the rich fertilizer of God's truth being spread about. There may be those who water that seed of the gospel every day through prayer. It may well be contact number 72 that God uses to harvest that person and usher them into his kingdom, as he draws them to face the warmth and brightness of the Sun of his love, emanating from heavenly glory.

Again, the process stands out. We don't need to dump the whole truckload of fertilizer. Been there; done that. We dispense just enough for the need of the moment. As we approach them with gentleness and respect, we'll see whether we need to use a teaspoon or a backhoe to fill the hole dug by God. What this says is that in our conversations with others about spiritual matters we need to be faithful in dealing with the need at hand, in keeping with the opportunity God has provided.

And, of course, we have that huge encouragement that this is God's work. By his design, we are his tools. The waiter was taking our drink order. My wife, Linda, and I were the guests of friends at a place they frequented. The husband friend engaged the waiter in conversation. It came out the waiter wasn't particularly religious, but he did relate one time he sat by a river to read a book, the Bible. It was meaningful to him. What jumped to my mind immediately was when Philip in Acts 8 found out what the Ethiopian eunuch was reading and asked if he understood it. I thought to ask the waiter what he was reading and if he understood it. Perfect, right? Although it jumped to my mind, it did not jump-start my mouth. I let the opportunity pass. I'm still disgusted with myself. My consolation (not an excuse by any means) is that God's salvation will not be frustrated by my dereliction. Christ will lose none of those the Father gave to him. But the bottom line as far as I was concerned was that I blew it.

If we blow it, God will not. But that calls us to faithfulness not faithlessness, to activity not avoidance. God's love and design should provoke in us determination, not dereliction. We need to expect involvement and anticipate opportunity as we sojourn in our life-spheres. We want to see and seize the opportunities he gives us. It's all part of participating in mission. That involvement basically falls into two areas, bound together and buttressed by a third. Peter provides these two areas of engagement for us.

PETER PRINCIPLES

Peter was writing to people like us—aliens and sojourners. One probable difference from us, however, is that they were aliens and sojourners because they were persecuted. They were more like the Pilgrims in that sense who came from England to America for freedom from religious persecution. Nonetheless, this world is not our home. We are strangers. We're here on a mission, looking forward to the eternal rest of our heavenly home.

Peter's letter to the pilgrims provides great encouragement and direction in dealing with suffering. Situations of distress and deprivation do not let God's people off the hook when it comes to obedience. Some may get the idea that suffering places us on disability, sidelining us from the work of mission. Peter will allow no such thing. He begins his letter by addressing the elect of God, displaced from their homes, enduring persecution for their faith. The first words out of his mouth are all-encompassing for the life of the believer, taking in past, present and future. Christians have the sure hope of a home in heaven because of the electing love of God the Father, the resurrection power of God the Son and the sanctifying work of God the Spirit. That inheritance is kept for us and we are kept for it.

But Peter's pastoral focus is on today. We are chosen for obedience. Peter says so in the letter's salutation. Suffering in the Christian life does not sideline us from the fray. In fact, we can expect suffering. Our Lord himself is held out as our example.[54]

> To this you were called, because Christ suffered for you, leaving you an example, that you should follow in his

steps. 'he committed no sin, and no deceit was found in his mouth.' When they hurled their insults at him, he did not retaliate; when he suffered, he made no threats. Instead, he entrusted himself to him who judges justly.

1 Pet. 2: 21–3

Our suffering is not to spring from unrighteousness, nor is unrighteousness to spring from suffering. Just as Christ persevered in trust and obedience, Peter's counsel to us is: 'So then, those who suffer according to God's will should commit themselves to their faithful Creator and continue to do good' (1 Pet. 4: 19).

Trust and obey—these are rules of engagement against the efforts of the evil one. Situations of suffering provide a forum where our handling of things in a way different from those without God and without hope in this world allows us to stand out. We can point to Christ as our hope, our confidence and our strength.

Don had been diagnosed with Lou Gerhig's disease, a debilitating and life-threatening nervous system disorder. Sales manager over a national work force, Don touched many lives in the home office and throughout the nation, both by his extensive travel and regular telephone contact. His physical symptoms and diagnosis made him stand out. It was under the glare of that spotlight that Don's faith sparkled so wonderfully to the glory of God. His tenacious trust in God, submission to his purposes and perseverance in his ways sparked many a conversation about Jesus Christ. He was able to show and share his faith—and his Father in heaven was glorified. He entrusted himself to his faithful Creator and continued to do good, conducting spiritual warfare through righteousness that rested on God.

Enfolded in this scenario of suffering are the two principles Peter lays out for our witness in the trenches of daily life. The first of these principles is our practice, faith exercised in a life of obedience, salvation showcased by lives in the grip of God's grace: 'Dear friends, I urge you, as aliens and strangers in the world, to abstain from sinful desires, which war against your soul. Live such good lives among the pagans that, though they accuse you of doing wrong, they may see your good deeds and glorify God on the day he visits us' (1 Pet. 2:11–12).

Our lives combat the flow of life in this age away from God. The way we conduct ourselves in any and every situation bears witness to our kingdom ethic. In conducting ourselves in righteousness, we conduct spiritual warfare against the world, the flesh and the devil.

We are to be intentional in living lives as sore thumbs, sticking out so that people will notice us. We want to be accepting of the spotlight of suffering placed on us by our God for worldly consumption, using it to draw attention to him. Of course, when we face accusation of wrongdoing, we must have made sure it is unfounded. What we want people to see is not us but Christ in us, the hope of glory. Our lives are to be governed by the revealed will of our God recorded for us in his written Word. God's design is that people will see our good deeds and glorify him as our Father in heaven. In so doing, we are putting feet to the model prayer our Lord taught us for the kingdom of hallowing the name of our God and living in his will.

A related means of assault on the kingdom of this age are planned efforts to do good to others. By deeds of kindness, we want to ease burdens of life in a fallen world. Our good deeds are to be not only active in our lives and so seen by others, not only reactive in response to persecution and suffering, but proactive in an agenda of deeds of unmerited, unexpected, undeserved kindness. Try offering to mow your neighbor's lawn because he hurt his back and see if that doesn't shake him up.

In other words, the righteous obedience of our lives is not only defensive; it is offensive as well. Just as signs, wonders and works of power that reversed the effects of the fall evidenced the inaugurated presence of the redemptive kingdom, so our deeds of kindness demonstrate that reality and bring relief to those of the kingdom of this age.

This brings into the picture Peter's second principle for our daily witness. The first dealt with our practice. This one speaks to our position. Some are quite content to stop at the first principle. In fact, they refuse to go further, insisting they witness by their lives. Their deeds demonstrate devotion to Christ. The problem with that, though, is righteous living by itself is insufficient for salvation, just as the general revelation of creation is insufficient for salvation without the special revelation of Scripture. At best the good deeds of righteous living send no message; at worst they send the wrong message.

To what do good deeds point? They can announce what a great guy I am. They draw people's attention to me—my character, my values, my lifestyle preference. Or, good deeds can point to a salvation by works. I'm obeying God so that I can earn my way into heaven. My efforts at law-keeping are what merit salvation for me. In other words, deeds unqualified by words have the potential of pointing people to us instead of Christ, and to works instead of grace. That's why Peter says: 'But in your hearts set apart Christ as Lord. Always be prepared to give an answer to everyone who asks you to give the reason for the hope that you have. But do this with gentleness and respect' (1 Pet. 3: 15). Deeds validate. Words verify. Authenticating deeds beg opportunity for interpretive word giving the deeds their position in mission.

We need to be prepared to give an answer for the hope we have, a hope explained by Peter in the opening verses of his letter. That hope is salvation rooted in the triune God. The idea is for the light of our lives penetrating the darkness to draw attention so that people will ask questions. And we need to be prepared to give an answer.

The rules of engagement in warfare witness call us to live lives of light in the darkness of the age in which we live. These obedient lives are not snuffed out or obscured by suffering but made brighter by it. We advance against the forces of darkness by displaying the glory of God's grace. All the while we expect and look for engagement by explanation, pointing to Christ as the reason for the hope we have.

This means that we need to be prepared to give an answer. If I expect rain, I will have an umbrella with me if I want to stay dry. If I boast about my wonderful wife and kids, I need to have pictures and commentary with me when people finally take the bait and ask me about them. In the same way, the hope we have is the hope of the gospel. We need to be prepared to present the gospel to others.

CATALYTIC PRAYER

Dynamite has its cap. A grenade has its pin. A gun has its trigger. Stable chemicals have their catalyst. Witness has its prayer.

Involvement in witness for the kingdom of God in the kingdom of this fallen world basically falls into two areas, bound together and buttressed by a third. Binding together and fortifying our witness by word and deed is prayer. Our deeds are made effective through prayer. Our words are made effective through prayer. Prayer is an armament of the kingdom that touches everything we do, at every point in the doing. This is the cardinal rule of engagement for the kingdom of God in reaching others for Christ: prayer must be pervasive. We are to pray for ourselves, for others, for the message. We need constant contact with our Lord whose battle it is. Peter tells us as pilgrims in this present age to cast our cares upon Christ and, standing firm in the faith, to resist the devil. These calls are admonitions to prayer.

We want to establish two general rules for the use of prayer as an armament of the kingdom under rules of engagement. The first of these rules we want to reinforce is that prayer is not to be wielded in lieu of action but in light of action.

Jan is looking for a job. Going through a time of transition in her life, she needs to find a source of steady income. She has put her need on the church's prayer sheet and asked those in her small group to pray that God would provide a job for her. Of course, she herself continues to labor in prayer before the throne of grace, casting her cares upon her Father in heaven, laying before him her need and imploring his provision. What if Jan stopped at that point? What if that were the extent of her job search? While it is true that prayer in itself is action and not inaction, prayer cannot be a substitute for effort we are able to make. Jan knows that and so she diligently looks for work. Her job is finding a job, for which she prays and acts in keeping with her prayer.

Again, prayer is not wielded in lieu of action but in light of action. That's the biblical portrayal. In the model prayer of Matthew 6 we pray for our daily bread. Yet Paul says to the Thessalonian church that if they will not work, they will not eat. They cannot expect to pray and to have a plate of food appear before them, complete with beverage and utensils. Nehemiah says the same thing in showing prayer and action working in tandem. In light of the opposition the people of God faced to the work he called them to do, we read: 'But we prayed to our God and posted a guard day and night to meet this threat.'[55] Prayed and posted, asked and acted—that's the biblical paradigm.

The rule of engagement is that prayer does not preclude action; it presupposes it. We don't just pray for someone's salvation. We pray and act in light of that prayer as we have ability and opportunity, expectant of God's working for his purposes. We want to talk to God for people and we want to talk to people for God. Both cases involve prayer.

The first rule shows the necessity of prayer and participation in tandem. The second rule for the use of prayer as a weapon has to do with the essential conflict between the kingdom of God and the kingdom of Satan. The antagonistic and adversarial nature of the kingdoms suggests that our prayer must be not only prayer *for* but also prayer *against*.

I remember a pastor opening in prayer before his sermon. He prayed, 'O Father, do not allow the evil one to steal the seed of the gospel being sown this morning.' That's prayer against. Knowing that Satan stands opposed to us and our efforts for the kingdom of God, we want to seek the face of our King to thwart his efforts to undermine us. We know the tactics of our enemy. We are not unaware of his schemes. In that knowledge, we want to pray specifically that God will keep the evil one from deceiving and distorting.

We pray for the success and strength of our efforts in submission to the purposes of God. We pray for the failure and futility of the efforts of the devil in submission to the purposes of God.

Jim is a young man living with his girlfriend. You work with Jim and have got to know him, including his living arrangements. Recently, your conversations have moved to issues of the faith. He's seen your life and the peace that guards your heart, and he finds that contentment and stability in life attractive. That has opened up occasions for you to lay key biblical truths related to the gospel on the table before Jim for discussion. You can tell something's happening. Jim isn't being as stubborn or argumentative as usual. There seems to be genuine thirst for knowledge, a searching on his part.

God has alerted you to spiritual opposition as you draw near to others for Christ. How might you pray against that opposition as you draw near to Jim? You may well pray for that spiritual understanding necessary for acceptance of the things of God, that God would give Jim ears to hear. In your discussions with Jim, you've learned that he is intrigued but threatened at the prospect of having to give up his immoral lifestyle. He's the one who has brought it up, knowing it relates not to salvation but to following Christ as Lord. Your discussions have made that clear. But Jim believes his relationship with his girlfriend is a greater source of delight and satisfaction than a relationship with Jesus Christ. He has believed a lie. Your prayer against might be that God would show Jim the inferiority and emptiness of Satan's perversion of God's good design. You could pray that God would make the known sin in his life unbearable and draw him to the enduring and life-giving beauty of Christ.

What obstacles or barriers erected by Satan do you find in those you seek to reach for Christ? Pray to God to remove them, against Satan's schemes. Pray for opportunities to bring the corrective truth of God's Word to bear. Wherever you find the distortions and deceptions of the evil one, wield the weapon of prayer against them. Use Scripture as a script or a springboard for prayer relevant to the deceptions, accusations and temptations of the devil in the lives of those you seek to rescue for Christ. Bring prayer to be a catalyst to change in their lives, change only God can accomplish.

IN STEP WITH THE SPIRIT

I can't dunk a basketball. I used to be able to get over the rim in my younger days, but no longer with my one-inch vertical jump. As a result, when I find myself on a rare breakaway I have no pretensions that I will elevate and slam the ball down the cylinder. I don't even try. It would be silly to try.

This brings us to our final rule of engagement in our efforts to reach others in the face of spiritual opposition. We must play within ourselves. We can't try to do what we can't do. We've seen this in the power required in conversion to infuse spiritual life where there is spiritual death. That's also true in engaging others with the gospel of life in Christ.

Contrasting models illustrate this principle. The first model is that of salesperson. I still remember the eagerness of the young man who sat opposite my wife and me as he enthusiastically described replacement windows and suggested our current windows were losing us a small fortune through heating bills. As he wrapped up his 15-minute presentation in 45 minutes, he beamed his 'it-would-be-foolish-to-say-no' smile, fully expecting us to rush to sign on the dotted line. When we hesitated, he found second wind to make clear what should have been obvious to us. When it was apparent we were still not convinced, he asked to use our phone, from which he explained to his manager in our hearing the deal we were passing up.

What is noteworthy about this sales model? The success of the encounter rested squarely on the shoulders of the salesman. Buttonhole and cajole—those were his methods. He would not take no for an answer and he would do whatever was in his power to seal the deal.

The second model is that of midwife. My wife and I have four children. I have been present with her at the delivery of each one, serving as coach and cheerleader. In all four births I have made an astute and profound observation: each child was born when he or she was ready to be born (a prelude, no doubt, to the dynamic of parenthood to come). Nothing my wife or I could have done would have hastened the moment. But when it was time, the personnel had better be ready.

In contrast to the sales model that greatly depended on the ability and effort of the salesman, the birth model depended on the child made ready by all the physical factors that bring about such events. A midwife does not control but simply keeps in step with the whole birth process. She submits to and works with what is happening at God's design.

The rule of warfare witness is that we are to keep in step with the Spirit, waiting upon his good pleasure, working according to his measure. That puts us in the role of spiritual midwives instead of spiritual salespersons.[56] We cooperate with the Spirit. We seize the teachable moment he has fashioned. We scratch the spiritual itch he has irritated. We fill the spiritual mouth he has opened wide. It may be he will give us the privilege of helping a newborn babe in Christ into the fold by leading them in prayer. Maybe not. It is up to the Spirit and we are content to have it that way.

I still have flashbacks of an evangelistic encounter I had, much like the one I described with Becky to open the chapter. Only this time I was a trainee. The trainer and I visited a couple as part of an evangelistic training event. It all started out well enough. The couple was relaxed and engaging. Then the trainer shifted gears to the presentation of the gospel. Tension saturated the air. It was as if he backed the gospel truck up to the couple's laps and dumped the entire load, without any beeping sounds warning of its coming. Before long the couple was numb, too polite to run. After the spiel, the trainer took a breath and asked if they wanted to receive the gift of eternal life in Christ. They both said yes. However, after they prayed the prayer and we left their home, I knew they didn't have a clue what they had done. That was confirmed when I returned the following night on my own to talk with them.

That happened before my Becky incident, so it shows you how quick a learner I am even after my being so turned off by that assault. But I do know that the Spirit is the agent. I know I need to remind myself of that and adopt an attitude that brings that perspective to bear. We are the instruments. The Spirit works at his pace, for his purposes. The rules of engagement help us to remember that and to work within the confines of his mission, not ours.

11

Flying the Colors of the Cross

Patriotism after the September 11th attacks on the World Trade Center in New York and the Pentagon outside Washington, DC was off the chart. The skyline of Manhattan would never be the same. Neither would the American mentality. Those attacks infused a new resolve and sense of identity and union into the national mindset. Rather than panic, the poles on which the flag flew were driven deeper into the soil of the heart of America.

The colors of the flag pervaded the landscape of America and throughout the world, as other countries showed their support and solidarity. The Stars and Stripes could be seen adorning cars and lapels and every sort of apex imaginable. Patriotic songs could be heard in gatherings of all sizes in all places. The color combination of red, white, and blue was spread across the land.

The display of colors was not a fashion statement, nor was it a decorating preference. The colors of the flag spoke of the freedom and courage that brought the country into existence and that courses through the veins of American life. America was born from the womb of religious oppression, the seed of religious conviction grown to religious liberty. American history chronicles an escape from the shackles of tyranny. When people rallied around the post 9/11 flag, they rallied around what the flag represents in the history and fabric of the nation for which it stands.

The history of America is a history of struggle for the sake of political freedom. As Christians, citizens of heaven, subjects of the kingdom of God and disciples of Jesus Christ, we too have a history. Our history looks to the emancipating work of Christ, freeing us from the tyranny of the devil, the bondage of sin, and the sentence of eternal death.

Though the message of the Statue of Liberty, which has welcomed oppressed people everywhere to the melting pot of America, has been muted of late, America continues to hold out a promise of freedom. In similar fashion, the kingdom of God continues to hold out a sure promise of spiritual freedom from the spiritual bondage of the kingdom of Satan. That promise will continue as long as it is the day of salvation, as long as the Lord tarries in coming to usher in his kingdom in fullness.

Freedom beckons. Whether it be political freedom or spiritual freedom, freedom comes with a message, a declaration of deliverance and an invitation of new allegiance. The gospels of the New Testament loudly affirm and proclaim the arrival of the redemptive kingdom of God. The epistles describe the charter and character of this new kingdom. The book of Revelation impresses upon us the present conflict but enduring victory of this kingdom and eternal blessing of all those part of it. The bells of freedom sound throughout the record of Christ's victory and reign.

FREEDOM UNFURLED

As Christ's ambassadors, that message of freedom in our hearts is to be on our lips. As subjects of the kingdom of God we need to be able to give a reason for the hope we have. The hope we possess comprises the message we profess. Christ's army does not march to conquer, but to communicate the victory of our King who has conquered sin, death, and hell. We advance to shout the news of life, liberty and the pursuit of holiness in a restored relationship with our Creator, and his purposes for those made in his image.

'I'm a pretty moral guy. I don't drink or smoke. I watch my language. I don't believe in sex outside of marriage.' Craig is convinced he will go to heaven, that his efforts and lifestyle make him stand out from others less desirable and render him worthy of heaven. He sits across the table from you, fully ready to listen to your evaluation of what he has said he believes and to an explanation of what's involved in having a sure hope of eternal life. Craig believes the Bible is the only authority for belief and believes it is true and accurate for the most part. His attention is on you. What do you say to him? Where would you start? Are you ready to give an answer for the hope you have?

I once heard a pastor say that the congregation's preparation for personal evangelism has to be better than memorizing the pastor's phone number.[57] In presenting the gospel, the good news of freedom in Jesus Christ, all of us as Christ's ambassadors need to be prepared to explain it. We need to be able to lay out a logical outline, ready with supporting Scripture, perhaps buttressed with examples and illustrations. The gospel is logical. The reason for the gospel is not logical in that God set his love on the unlovable. God's grace is illogical. There is a disconnect between what we deserve in our sin at the hands of God's justice and the outpouring of his grace. In his mercy, God does not give us what we deserve. In his grace, he gives us what we do not deserve. While grace is gloriously illogical, the gospel is thoroughly logical, flowing from one truth to another, each 'since' leading to a 'therefore.'

Our responsibility as soldiers of Christ is to unfurl that gospel in its logical framework. We can do that generally and we can showcase the gospel as it has dawned in our own hearts, giving our personal story of experience of God's grace.

GETTING OUR ACTS TOGETHER

The books of Luke and Acts form a unit of kingdom announcement. Luke's Gospel announces the accomplishment of the kingdom, Acts the advancement of the kingdom. Acts shows us how to carry out our mission of proclaiming the good news of life and liberty in Jesus Christ recorded in Luke.

The focal point of the Gospel of Luke is the final chapters with the death and resurrection of Christ. The entire book flows to that climax. The focal point of Acts is the first chapter as that good news is carried at Christ's commission. The entire book flows from that source of the water of life. The key passage of Acts comes from the lips of the risen Lord: 'But you will receive power when the Holy Spirit comes on you; and you will be my witnesses in Jerusalem, and in all Judea and Samaria, and to the ends of the earth' (Acts 1: 8).

The accomplished redemptive rule of Jesus Christ is a rock thrown in the water that sends concentric ripples from Jerusalem to include Jews and Gentiles alike. The widening concentric circles reach out to embrace the 'ends of the earth.' The reference here is not so much geographic but ethnic. In Acts 13, the outpouring of the Holy Spirit from Pentecost, marking the movement of the gospel, reaches the Gentiles, whom Luke identifies as the 'ends of the earth': 'For this is what the Lord has commanded us: "I have made you a light for the Gentiles, that you may bring salvation to the ends of the earth." When the Gentiles heard this, they were glad and honored the word of the Lord; and all who were appointed for eternal life believed' (Acts 13: 47–8). The gospel is not for the Jew only. It is for Jew and Gentile.[58] Both have been appointed to eternal life at the saving plan of God.

Notice how this message of the gospel is kingdom-qualified. The message was that Jesus was the Christ, the promised and anticipated Messiah of God, the Anointed One who would liberate from the oppression of the kingdom of this world. That's the crux of the apostles' preaching. 'The apostles left the Sanhedrin, rejoicing because they had been counted worthy of suffering disgrace for the Name. Day after day, in the temple courts and from house to house, they never stopped teaching and proclaiming the good news that Jesus is the Christ' (Acts 5: 41–2). Paul quotes Jesus in explaining his mission from Christ as an ambassador of his kingdom in this way: '…to open their eyes and turn them from darkness to light, and from the power of Satan to God, so that they may receive forgiveness of sins and a place among those who are sanctified by faith in me' (Acts 26: 18). The message was about the King and his kingdom and the benefits thereof. It was about deliverance and provision of what was necessary to inhabit the kingdom of God.

How was this message of Jesus Christ, crucified, risen, reigning, and returning communicated? In two ways, His-story and my story in him. Each of these means of making known the good news of the kingdom of God relates to us as we would communicate the gospel to others.

An example of the presentation of the gospel is found in Acts 17: 16–34. After listening through observation and conversation, Paul applies the truth of God's Word as a corrective to the false understanding of the pagan philosophies. There is but one God, not many. He is sovereign, ruling over his creation, not distant. The true God is self-sufficient, not dependent upon his creatures in any way, at any point. Conversely, we are totally dependent upon God for every breath we take. We have a tendency to make God in our image, but we are the ones made in his image. As image-bearers of God, we not only have the ability to commune with him, we have the responsibility of allegiance to him. As ones made in his image, a mark of ownership, God demands repentance from rebellion against him. He will judge with justice. The evidence for that is the resurrection of Jesus Christ. It is appointed for men to die once, then comes judgment. Christ was judged in respect to sin, righteousness and guilt. He will come again to bring judgment on all those who have not found refuge in his work.

The response to Paul's presentation of the gospel was threefold: some believed and followed, some did not believe and belittled, some were intrigued and wanted to hear more. Notice in this case that there was no explicit call to respond to the gospel through repentance and faith. But the proclamation of the gospel always carries with it that undertow to truth.

There can be a variety of ways to approach and explain the gospel. The centerpiece is always Jesus Christ and his saving work. We are to tell His-story. For us, the point is that we need to be able to lay the message of the way, the truth, and the life out on the table. We relate what God has done in Christ.

The second way we see in Acts of communicating the gospel is through my story in Christ, my testimony of God's work of grace in my life. A personal testimony speaks to what God did in my heart to bring the salvation of his Son home to roost, where by his Spirit God claims me as his own, having been purchased for him by the Son.

Paul provides us with the example of his personal testimony of liberation from sin's guilt and power when he appeared before King Agrippa in Acts 26. Paul's story of conversion falls into three sections: 1) his life before Christ, 2) his encounter with Christ, and 3) his new life in service to Christ. Each section of Paul's testimony expresses the theology he lays out in Ephesians 2: 1–10.

First, in Acts 26: 9–11 Paul describes something of his life before his conversion, when he was still dead in sin (cf. Eph. 2: 1–3). He speaks of his zeal as a persecutor of the faith and his efforts in keeping with that zeal. For us, we might ask questions like: How did I live for self rather than for Christ? What fulfilled and motivated me in life?

Paul didn't get into gruesome details as he might have. He didn't try to sensationalize his life before Christ or try to glamorize sin. But he did give the king a good feel for his life in rebellion against the lordship of Christ, in keeping with his bondage to sin.

Perhaps you were raised in a Christian home. You can never remember a day when you did not know and trust Jesus Christ for your salvation. The first section of your story seems rather anemic to you. What can you say? Remember, that salvation is not by socialization. As with every believer, God worked immediately in your heart. You were born dead in sin and you are alive because of the Holy Spirit to unite you to Jesus Christ. You can praise God for his early mercies to you. In this case, your testimony is filled in more by what God your Father tells you about the days before he adopted you, just as an adopted child might not remember the orphanage from which she was rescued. She would need to be told about it by her father and would relate that to others.

Next, Paul relates the time when he met Jesus Christ on the road to Damascus. In Acts 26: 12–18, he tells of how he was going about business as usual, carrying out the agenda of his religious zeal, when Christ came to him. Here he provides some of the details about his encounter with Christ.

What details might you include? If you were knocked to the ground in a dramatic conversion, you would tell the story. For most of us, however, we grow to know. Over time, through different situations and a variety of people we learn more. The sin that seemed delightful becomes repugnant. The guilt of our sin becomes oppressive. The Christ who was only an historical figure starts to become real and beautiful. For this section, we might ask ourselves questions like: What people, events and factors did God use to change my thinking and my opinion about Christ? In what ways did the Spirit convince me of my need for Christ? Was there one thing that I particularly became convicted of against the backdrop of my life before Christ? All this expresses the theology of Ephesians 2: 4–9, where by God's grace and power, death gave way to life, darkness to light, works to faith.

The final section of Paul's testimony points to new life in Christ. What does it look like now that I am a citizen of heaven and am seeking first the kingdom of God and his righteousness? Paul in Acts 26: 19–23 pointed out that now, instead of fighting against the kingdom of God, he fought for it. He became an advocate for Christ and held a radically new interpretation of Scripture from what he did previously.

Ephesians 2: 10 informs us that there will be fruit of salvation by grace through faith. A new lifestyle will characterize us because of the power of the new life at work in us. Here we might ask ourselves: How does my everyday life now reflect God's changing work of grace? How am I different now that I am a child of God?

We want to be careful here not to communicate any sort of contribution we make to our salvation, as though my life contributes to Christ giving his life for me. But at the same time, we want people to know the handiwork of God's grace. Saving faith is fruitful faith and we want people to taste and savor the Savior, to whom belongs all the glory. Faith rooted in God's grace will grow and manifest itself in the fruit of God's grace.[59] The call of discipleship for those with ears to hear is to come and follow Christ.

I can't tell how many times I have heard people lament their dull or tame testimony of salvation in Christ. They almost would rather have lived a more wretched life so that their testimony would shine brighter and be a more worthy witness. We want to understand that there is no dull testimony. Every account of personal conversion testifies to the resurrection power of God to bring life from death. It speaks of one dead in sin, supernaturally being made alive in Jesus Christ. Every testimony magnifies the grace of God to the undeserving and the love of God to the unlovable. The brightness of a personal testimony is the glory of God in the face of Christ against the blackness of a sinful heart and the bleakness of eternal damnation.

DISPLAYING THE COLORS

Monuments of all sorts fill the Civil War battlefield at Gettysburg, Pennsylvania. Some are quite simple and austere. Others are complex filled with stone soldiers in poses that send a message and create a story. Frequently in these monuments, carved in relief on a stone façade or in full dimensional form flying from the pole of the flag bearer, you will see the colors of the various state regiments. Those colors themselves, often tattered and torn, told a story and represented men and mission. The flags spoke of a history, stood for a cause and reached for a future.

As Christians, soldiers of the cross, we too march under a flag of the kingdom of God. The flag is not literal, pictured for us on some glossy insert in our Bible or described in the vivid symbolism of the Revelation. But the flag is real nonetheless.

As did the battle flags at Gettysburg, the colors of the cross speak of a history, stand for a cause and look to a future. John alludes to this flag in his Gospel: 'Just as Moses lifted up the snake in the desert, so the Son of Man must be lifted up, that everyone who believes in him may have eternal life' (John 3: 14–15). Whenever John speaks of Jesus being 'lifted up' he refers to the cross. The cross was the method of execution for a sinless Christ on behalf of a sinful people in whose place he stood. By the cross the justice of God was satisfied, the guilt of sin atoned for and the wrath of God poured out. On the cross Jesus took to himself the cup of wrath, taken from our hand, and drank it to its dregs. He fully satisfied the justice of God in regard to our sin. In our hand, he places the cup of blessing, something we celebrate every observance of the Lord's Supper.

Just as the bronze snake in the desert was God's provision, his means for life, the cross is the culmination of his promise from Genesis 3: 15 to bring salvation and eternal life to those who were steeped in sin, helpless to save themselves, devoid of hope. The cross rises from the promises and provisional types of Old Testament history. It speaks of victory. The accomplished work of Jesus Christ in the fullness of time establishes a future and hope for all those under its banner. The colors of the cross give us our mission, for the cause of God's saving purposes and the liberation of those still under the tyranny of the devil.

The gospel, which speaks of Jesus Christ and him crucified, is the force undergirding the arsenal of the church against the forces of spiritual darkness. The gospel testifies to the finished, victorious, liberating work of Jesus Christ. It is not a blueprint. It is not a battle plan. The gospel is a record of Christ's work to provide all that is necessary for liberation from the bondage of this age and is a receipt of those for whom Christ died, whose entire debt of sin is paid in full. The gospel is the proclamation of Jesus Christ as the way, the truth and the life—a message of assault on the kingdom of Satan and all that it stands for.

For us to fly the colors is to hold aloft for the world to see the finished work of Jesus Christ and the promise of deliverance it holds for all who will believe. We march under the banner of the gospel calling people to fall in behind us as King Jesus leads his people in triumphal procession through this world, as a display of his grace. The colors of the cross are rich in meaning and laden with hope, the hope of the finished work of Jesus Christ who has sat down in victory at the right hand of the Most High.

THE COLORS OF THE CROSS

Ireland's flag is pretty simple, three equal vertical bands of different colors. The green band on the left represents the Roman Catholic population of the country. The orange band on the right stands for the Protestant portion of the country, associated with Great Britain and a former monarch, William of Orange. In the center, between the Roman Catholic and Protestant factions stretches a band of white. White speaks of peace. Since 1848, the Green, White and Orange has flown over the Republic of Ireland, testifying to its history, its people, and its dream.

What exactly are the colors of the cross? If we were to assign pigment to the flag of the kingdom of God, we would find three dominant colors. These colors are pregnant with the truth of God's Word and capture the history, the future, and the kingdom cause the cross represents.

If we were to design a battle flag under which to march for the sake of the kingdom of God as we lay siege to the kingdom of Satan, we could include many colors. In Sunday School my children have received little rawhide bracelets, woven through beads of different colors to explain the gospel. For example, green represents growth, gold eternal life. Three of these colors, however, form the crux of the gospel and find inclusion in the banner under which and for which we march. The colors of the cross are red, white and black. Let's take a brief look at each color.

Red. The heart of the gospel is the cross of Christ. On the cross, Jesus poured out his life as a sacrifice for sinners, standing in their place, taking upon himself the penalty for their sin. At his last Passover meal, Jesus as the true Lamb of God said these words: 'This is my blood of the covenant, which is poured out for many for the forgiveness of sins' (Matt. 26: 28). The good news of the gospel is written in the blood of Jesus Christ. Notice how the Apostle Paul summarizes the provision of God for sinners in that great watershed passage of the book of Romans:

> But now a righteousness from God, apart from law, has been made known, to which the Law and the Prophets testify. This righteousness from God comes through faith in Jesus Christ to all who believe. There is no difference, for all have sinned and fall short of the glory of God, and are justified freely by his grace through the redemption that came by Christ Jesus. God presented him as a sacrifice of atonement, through faith in his blood. He did this to demonstrate his justice, because in his forbearance he had left the sins committed beforehand unpunished—he did it to demonstrate his justice at the present time, so as to be just and the one who justifies those who have faith in Jesus.
>
> Rom. 3: 21–6

The blood of Christ speaks not of an excoriated back or a nail-pierced hand or a spear-stabbed side. The blood of Christ speaks of the death, the sacrificial death, of the eternal Son of God, incarnate to die to satisfy the justice of the holy God as a substitute for sinners who deserved that sentence. Forgiveness of sin is bound up in that death. Forgiveness does not come from mere confession of sin but from the finished work of Christ that satisfied the wrath of God.[60] The vibrancy of the flag of the kingdom of God is the red of Christ's blood.

Black. Someone wearing a white sheet with a cross burning on a lawn in the background communicates something quite different from a small person wearing a white sheet holding out a bag half-filled with Halloween candy. What are the differences? Chief among them is the context. Context is crucial to proper understanding.

Such is the case with the gospel. The red of Christ's blood stands out in sharp relief only against the color of context.

That color is black. The world into which the King of Glory came was a fallen world. Christ became incarnate as a man in this present, evil age.

The bulk of the Bible is a history of redemption, with teachings and types that set the stage for the drama of the cross. That history emerges from and is set against the backdrop of the first three chapters of Genesis. To the consternation of many, those chapters don't give us as much information as our curiosity craves about the subject matter therein. But they do give us what is necessary as a backdrop for salvation history. They show an eternal, supreme and uncreated Godhead, human beings made in his image for relationship with him, the fall of the created order, and a promise of redemption expressed in terms of spiritual warfare. Without that backdrop, God's promise of salvation would not make much sense.

The same is true with the blood of Christ. The nature of his death as an atonement, a propitiation, a reconciliation would not make sense apart from the holiness, justice and wrath of God that abides on us because of our sin. For example, there are those who have little regard for the integrity of the Bible as the holy, inspired, inerrant, and infallible Word of God. In their efforts to manufacture God as they would like him to be, they cannot tolerate a God of wrath. They ask us which we would prefer, and have us choose between a God of wrath and a God of love. The problem is that Scripture never forces us to choose between these attributes of God.

The love of God makes fullest sense only against the backdrop of his justice and wrath. Notice the context in the following passages for the love of God: 'For God so loved the world that he gave his one and only Son, that whoever believes in him shall not perish but have eternal life' (John 3: 16). The context of perishing forms the bleak backdrop against which the love of God shines so gloriously. Remove the perishing and the love lists to only the blessing of eternal life, apart from the balance of the curse Christ took upon himself for his sheep. Paul provides a similar picture in which the blood of Christ is framed.

> But God demonstrates his own love for us in this: While we were still sinners, Christ died for us. Since we have now been justified by his blood, how much more shall we be saved from God's wrath through him! For if, when we were

> God's enemies, we were reconciled to him through the
> death of his Son, how much more, having been reconciled,
> shall we be saved through his life!
>
> Rom. 5: 8–10

God's wrath abiding on us as sinners explains the demonstration
of his love and the mechanics of the saving work of his Son.
The context into which the love of God in Christ dawns in
history and in our hearts is the utter blackness of sin, guilt,
condemnation and abject hopelessness and helplessness.

White. Just as the flag of Ireland has white to communicate
peace, so does the banner flown by the kingdom of God. In
the gospel, God provides a spotless and perfect righteousness,
apart from law. That righteousness is the perfect record of
law-keeping merited by Jesus Christ. White speaks of peace,
the peace of the work of Christ through which God reconciled
us to himself. The Prince of peace came to bring peace and
usher in a kingdom of righteousness and peace. That peace is
the fruit of a restored relationship with God and a peace that
runs contrary to the present, evil age. Those in Christ have
peace with God and the peace of God rules in our hearts, giving
us comfort and confidence in the conflict of the day and bright
hope for tomorrow.

The three colors of the cross, however, are set up differently
from the colors that make up Ireland's flag. Ireland's flag
displays the colors as vertical bands parallel to one another, but
the banner of the gospel of the kingdom displays its colors
front and back, communicating the message of hope and life.
The back of the flag shows the red on black, the background
of Christ's historical accomplishment. The front displays the
white of the new life in Christ who have that background, who
now enjoy new life, forgiveness of sin, a perfect righteousness
and an eternal home with Christ in glory—all because of the
historical reality of the cross that stands behind the Christian
hope. The white on the banner of the gospel is the white of
Christ's redemptive victory and spoils, in which we participate
by grace through faith in union with him.

Red, white, and black—the colors of the cross. They are
the banner which swept us up from our worldly prison. They
are the colors we fly as we march out into our life-spheres in
kingdom commission, ready to explain the hope we have in

our Lord's accomplished victory, pointing people to what Christ has done and the blessings he brings.

KINGDOM ALLEGIANCE

Ordinarily when you see a white flag, such as the face of the battle flag I just described, you think of surrender. In this case, however, surrender is to be the response of those who by God's power, want to come under the banner of its deliverance and protection. That surrender is surrender to the righteousness of Jesus Christ, bowing the knee before him and his redemptive rule.

At issue is two divergent kingdoms, one temporary, one eternal; one righteous, one unrighteous. The gospel of peace, as the colors of the kingdom of God, looks not to a truce but to a clash of the kingdom of righteousness, joy and peace, ruled by the Prince of Peace, with the kingdom of darkness ruled by the prince of darkness. As was mentioned earlier, to be ambassadors of the gospel of peace is not to be brokers of peace in some sort of shuttle diplomacy. It is to announce peace. It is to call people to a change of kingdom allegiances. That change of allegiance is effected by God's Spirit and expressed in repentance and faith.

Repent of what? In bowing the knee before Jesus Christ, we repent of our own saviorship and our own lordship. We renounce any effort, any contribution we could make to our own salvation. We repudiate our rebellion and idolatry and fall in step behind our Lord Jesus as his disciples.

Not only do we turn, we trust. We rest in Christ's work and his alone to save us and to spare us from the wrath of God we deserve. We purpose to serve and honor him with our lives. We deny ourselves, take up our crosses as instruments of death to self, and follow him. He is our King; we are his subjects. He is our Commander; we are his soldiers. The spoils of war he alone waged belong to us by grace.

COMMUNICATION NOT CONVERSION

We want to remind ourselves of a basic rule of engagement we explored earlier in proclamation of the good news of the kingdom of God. Our goal is communication, not conversion. We can carry out our responsibility to communicate.

Conversion, the change of heart reflective of a changed heart, is beyond the pale of our responsibility and ability.

I've been guilty of it myself, more than once. In my zeal for bringing the other person to make a decision, I have shortchanged the gospel message on which the decision is made. When we talk to someone about the gospel we are appealing to faith. Throughout our explanation and interaction, there runs a constant pressure of what will they believe. As we lay out the truths of God's Word related to the gospel, we are wooing them from error to truth, from false hope to a valid hope, from idols to the living and true God. Like the undertow of the ocean, the waves of truth in which we wash them look to draw them from the shores of self-sufficiency and self-service into the vast waters of God's love in Jesus Christ.

Faith has an object. Faith rests on something. Faith in this sense is not an entity but an action. The response of faith is to believe on Jesus Christ. Back when it seemed that winters were colder, my friends and I would look forward to consecutive days of freezing temperatures. After a cold snap we'd venture down to Silver Lake and take a look to see if it was frozen enough for us to go ice skating on. We'd huddle at the edge of the lake and discuss the prospect. Eventually, however, one brave soul would need to take that first step and venture out onto the ice. Would that ice hold him up? He had faith that it would. But his faith was only as valid as that ice was strong. He put his faith in something: the look of the lake, knowledge of the temperature, the number of consecutive days below the freezing point.

Faith is the call to take a stand, to rest on something. Just as repentance abandons a position, faith adopts a position. All this is to say that in bringing the gospel message to bear in someone's life, we need to remember two things. First, we don't want to be afraid of doctrine. Doctrine is biblical truth. We don't need to use big words, but we do need to speak the content expressed in those big words that captures the truth of the gospel. Our goal is to communicate the truth of God's Word, in reliance upon the Holy Spirit, with gentleness, respect, patience and careful instruction.

The second thing we need to remember flows from the first. We want to be patient in presenting truth, satisfied that those with whom we share the good news have a firm foundation on which to take the stand of faith. This reminds us that evangelism is a process, not an event. Some people may already have some understanding of the biblical truths that make up the gospel on which we can build. For others, we will need to address more basic issues.

I recently installed a CD changer in my car. While the radio unit had a button for a CD, it had only the radio and a cassette tape player. I had to put the changer in the trunk. It turned out to be an involved process. The following model year of my car had the wiring from the radio unit to the trunk already in place. Of course, mine did not. That meant I had to run a cable from the radio, through the cabin, to the trunk. I also had to drill holes in the metal frame of the car for the bracket that held the changer, also pre-drilled in the next year's model but not in mine.

Just as I had to examine and take steps to install that CD changer in my car that I would not have had to take in another model, so in presenting the gospel we want to examine what is already in place in the person's understanding and proceed from there. We may only be able to plug the cable in to the radio or drill one hole, leaving further work to others that God will raise up in that person's life. But we want to do it right and we do not want to just plug the cable into the changer of their mind without making sure the wire is run and connected to the message of the radio unit where the music of life is played. All the while, mindful that the power is all of God.

As a side note, let me mention that evangelism today often does great harm to people and great disservice to the cause of Christ by rushing to decision as though the gospel were a product to be sold. As a pastor, I have seen many people who have banked on a decision they made by walking an aisle or praying a prayer, with little awareness of the elements of the gospel and little fruitfulness in evidence of any sort of changed heart occupied by the Spirit of Christ. This can be nothing but presumption that holds a counterfeit ticket purchased from the evil one that offers no admission to heavenly glory.

Our God presents a beautiful picture of the gospel through the prophet Isaiah. That picture contrasts the genuine and the counterfeit, the real McCoy and the decoy.

'Come, all you who are thirsty, come to the waters; and you who have no money, come, buy and eat! Come, buy wine and milk without money and without cost. Why spend money on what is not bread, and your labor on what does not satisfy? Listen, listen to me, and eat what is good, and your soul will delight in the richest of fare. Give ear and come to me; hear me, that your soul may live. I will make an everlasting covenant with you, my faithful love promised to David.

Isaiah 55: 1–3

At stake is life. God is presented as the source of the authentic hope of life. His price for that hope is nothing. His source of life is the realization of his covenant promises, which are all yes and amen in Jesus Christ.[61] The call is to listen to God and come to him. We are reminded here that the kingdom of this age also has a message. That message is a false hope that will never satisfy. Its banner is only black, front and back.

What a magnificent banner we stand under as citizens of a heavenly kingdom! It is under this banner, displaying the colors of the cross so beautiful to us, that we march for the cause of Christ and the capture of others by his redeeming grace and purpose.

12

Battle Ready

Usually political cartoons are just that—cartoons, drawn in exaggerated fashion, in a contrived scenario to make a poignant point. I recently saw an actual photograph in my local paper that was every bit a political cartoon. The photo was of a slab of stone, half-buried in what looks like barren, burned-out ground, a sprig of grassy something poking out here and there. On the chipped and crooked slab jutting up from freshly dug soil was a single word written in capital letters. That word was 'MORALE.' It had been written by US troops about 50 miles west of Baghdad, after the war had been won but the battles waged on.

Morale has to do with fervor, with motivation for mission. Low morale cultivates a climate of despair. It fosters inactivity and half-hearted effort. It impedes mission.

Is it any wonder that our enemy the devil works in his devious ways to discourage and dissuade us from the mission given by our Lord for the sake of his kingdom? Satan looks to affect morale, to take the wind out of our sails, through his typical methods of temptation, accusation, and deception. His efforts prompt us to question the mission, to doubt ourselves, and even to impugn our King. He fuels the fires of unbelief that burn constantly as wildfires in our hearts. He entices us to withdraw into the cocoon of self-pity and the busyness of self-glory. He lures from the camaraderie and safety of fellow believers, with the goal of devouring us as we stray from the beaten path.

As long as we sojourn in this present age we will have to contend with the enemy's efforts to assault our morale and sideline us from mission. Yet our Lord knows that. He pre-empts the surprise of satanic oppression and prepares us for the hardships that we will surely face in this world: 'I have told you these things, so that in me you may have peace. In this world you will have trouble. But take heart! I have overcome the world' (John 16:33).

Jesus prays for our preservation, not as ones cryogenically frozen waiting for heaven, but for protection from spiritual opposition as we serve him in the world.

> I have given them your word and the world has hated them, for they are not of the world any more than I am of the world. My prayer is not that you take them out of the world but that you protect them from the evil one. They are not of the world, even as I am not of it. Sanctify them by the truth; your word is truth. As you sent me into the world, I have sent them into the world.
>
> John 17: 14–18

Our Lord wants us to remain engaged in the mission he gives us. He knows the enemy who opposes us and that he will be protective of his turf in the kingdom of this world. And so our God gives us his Spirit and provides all that we need to press on in service to him. In this final chapter, we want to spend time exploring those provisions given by our Lord to boost our morale and keep us motivated and mobilized in mission.

FAITH'S FOCUS

Ah, the genius of the video recorder. They allow us to watch television programming at our schedule. I enjoy football but am not always able to watch my favorite teams when they play. That's where the video recorder comes in. I record the game and tuck the tape safely away for future viewing. Most people who tape games don't seem to want to know the outcome of the game. They avoid listening to the radio or reading the sports section of the paper so as not to spoil the suspense of the contest. I, on the other hand, am just the opposite. I will try to find out who won the game at my earliest opportunity and before I view the tape. If my team won, I'll watch the tape. If they didn't, I put the tape back in circulation for family use.

Knowing the outcome encourages and sustains me when my team falls behind, when they fumble the ball and all those other things that lead you to yell at the TV screen. I am encouraged because I know they will win in the end.

That's how it is in the spiritual struggle we face in the work of evangelism. Knowing the kingdom of God wins in the end, despite appearances to the contrary in the meantime, provides great encouragement in the trenches.

I'm convinced that the primary purpose of Revelation is to paint the picture of Christ's victory for the encouragement of his people in the face of suffering and persecution in witness in the present age. It shows us not to be surprised by suffering or deterred by persecution. Apparent victory by the evil one through the political, educational and social establishments of this world is not to derail our faith. Rather, our faith is bolstered by focus on Christ and his redemptive realities even in the face of some pretty horrific assaults.

It's a matter of focus. Faith is not blind. Faith is spiritual sight. It is not wishful thinking but the assurance of things expected and the conviction of things not perceived with eyes of flesh. Faith can be likened to a spiritual muscle that must be used and strengthened. God gives us trials to strengthen our faith by its use. Trials add several extra pounds to the barbells of life's gym. Those extra pounds build our faith even more, preparing us for greater trials and faithful obedience.

The focus of our faith as we carry on in life and mission in this fallen world must be on Jesus Christ. He promises to be with us. We need to fix our gaze on him. In the battle of Manassas the southern troops were undergoing a tremendous barrage from the northern army. A southern officer trotted to the front, in view of the troops. He just sat there bolt upright on his horse, not cowering, not retreating. One of the soldiers remarked that he stood there as a stone wall. From that point on Brig. Gen. Thomas J. Jackson would bear that nickname and would gain a newfound respect from his troops. By his presence he would serve as an encouragement to them in the field of battle.

How much more should we find encouragement and courage to press on in the face of spiritual opposition as we lift our eyes of faith to our Commander, Jesus Christ, the rock of our salvation? The writer of the book of Hebrews ministers to believers undergoing severe persecution. He encourages them with the reality and outcome of faith as he walks them through the portrait gallery of God's saints of old who persevered in faith. The culmination of that encouragement gives the focal point that those saints saw only dimly, but which we on this side of the cross see clearly.

> Therefore, since we are surrounded by such a great cloud of witnesses, let us throw off everything that hinders and the sin that so easily entangles, and let us run with perseverance the race marked out for us. Let us fix our eyes on Jesus, the author and perfecter of our faith, who for the joy set before him endured the cross, scorning its shame, and sat down at the right hand of the throne of God. Consider him who endured such opposition from sinful men, so that you will not grow weary and lose heart.
>
> Heb. 12: 1–3

Actually the grammar of the original tells us to run the race (or in our case, to fight the fight) by continually fixing our eyes on Jesus. Christ is our model, our example of pressing on in the face of opposition and oppression. Notice though, that in view is not just Christ the exemplar, but Christ the Savior. He has sat down in finished, accomplished, unrepeated victory.

Our Lord Jesus is not now on the cross, but on the throne. He sits on the throne as one crucified. His victory is won. The scene to which the writer of Hebrews draws us in saying Christ 'sat down' is the Holy of Holies of the tabernacle of God. Into that inner sanctum the Old Testament high priests would enter once a year on the Day of Atonement, sacrificing first for their own sins and then for the sins of the people. The only piece of furniture in the Most Holy Place was the Ark of the Covenant. There was no chair because the sacrifice had to be repeated over and over, year by year, waiting, anticipating. Those sacrifices were not adequate. They were anticipatory. But this High Priest, sinless and with the righteousness of perfect obedience, entered the heavenly holy of holies, with his own blood, to be priest and sacrifice. And he sat down. Nothing more needed to be done, ever. The victory was his for his own.

We are to keep the bigger picture of glory in sight that will transform the sufferings now, as did Jesus. But our faith looks not only to Christ in battle but also to Christ in victory, victory for us, validation for our faith.

Our gaze as we fight the spiritual battles of the kingdom of God is on Jesus Christ. He has shown us the path to glory through the veil of suffering. He is our example. But he is also our encouragement in that he has won the war. We fight not for victory, but in victory. The battle is his and he has won. That knowledge encourages us to press on, not allowing the temptations, deceptions, and accusations of our enemy to slow us. The joy in adversity is not in the suffering, but in doing the will of God and knowing the outcome of the struggle.

PASSION FOR MISSION

What prompts patriotism? In the US, some of the most patriotic people are those who were not born Americans, but were inducted into citizenship. Their citizenship is new and fresh. The rights and privileges are novel and thrilling to them. They love their country.

For others events such as national tragedy or shared opposition engender love for their land and zeal for its protection. After the events of 9/11, recruitment surged as young men and women lined up to enter military service. Even discharged and retired military personnel wanted the opportunity to jump in the fray for the cause of their country. Patriotic zeal surged through their veins and animated their involvement.

Both elements are active in the kingdom of God. No one is born a citizen of heaven. Rather, we are born again as citizens of heaven. Citizenship in the kingdom of God is always bestowed by grace. In addition, we face constant threat and opposition from an enemy army. That enemy is the enemy of our King and ours by association. How can these realities for us as children of God stir up our spiritual passion for service in the corps of the kingdom?

The early new covenant church serves as an example to us. They carried the message of the gospel with extraordinary zeal. No cattails of guilt were applied to the backs of the servants of Jesus Christ in carrying out his mission mandate. What compelled the early New Testament church to the fever pitch of evangelism that it enjoyed? Above all else the early church was profoundly aware of the personal, gracious presence of the God of creation and redemption in their midst. He was their

God; they were his people. The wonders of his redeeming love were fresh to their taste.

Words like 'duty,' and concepts like 'obligation' could hardly describe the motive behind early church evangelism. The wind to their sails was a deep and profound awareness of the reality and promise of the gospel, and a compulsion in the power of God's Spirit to let the world know that Jesus is the Christ and that life could be had through faith in him. A sense of awe and appreciation propelled them to speak from the housetops and in the marketplace.

The drive from within, prompted by the realities from without, insured the propagation of the message. At the heart of it all was a love for God and heart-based devotion to the One who had loved them and given himself for them. He was their Father. Christ was risen; the hope was real. The kingdom was at hand.

FRESH GOSPEL, REFRESHED FAITH

Sometimes you can walk into a business and see something that at first seems a little odd. On the wall, in a frame, hangs something that should be in a wallet or in a cash register. It's money. You would think looking at the success of the business that the bill hanging on the wall would be a hundred or at least a fifty. But what hangs there is a one-dollar bill. What's that all about?

Ask the proprietor or the president and he will tell you that's the first dollar ever earned by the business. That dollar testifies to the business' lucrativeness. It also marks the beginning of something that has carried on to this day.

Why does he have it hanging up? Its display is not so much for the benefit of others as it is for himself. That dollar reminds him of a watershed point that changed the direction of his life and made him what he is today. It speaks of a before and an after, a past and a present with an eye to the future.

For our morale nothing is more vital for us to keep in view than the gospel of our salvation. It is the gospel that will revive us in our complacency, refresh us in our weariness, and restore us in our mission. Looking to the gospel will introduce us anew to the love of our God and the sacrifice of our Lord.

In other words, we want to see that the banner of the cross under which we want to see others fall in line is the banner under which we ourselves march. Sometimes you will see rabid football fans paint their faces with the colors of their team. We want the colors of the cross painted on the walls of our hearts. The things they represent have first come to us and transformed us and colored our lives henceforth.

Let's go back to pre-dollar days, those days when you were without God and without hope in this world, before the new life, the decree of pardon for your sin, and the deed to an inheritance in heaven. In those days, the light of God's truth and the reality of Christ's death for you shattered the darkness of your sin and unbelief. Never was your sin so offensive and heinous to you. Never was the beauty of Christ so desirable and necessary for you. You saw your tremendous need, your hopelessness and helplessness. The Spirit of God impressed on your heart the genius of the cross that God might be both just and the justifier of sinners. The river of God's love surged into your soul, welling up to eternal life. You had to squint at all the glories of the gospel shown with breathtaking brightness and beauty before your eyes. They captivated you. You fell to your face in adoration and awe of such a God and such a sacrifice. Such a salvation, full and free, was awesome in the fullest sense of the word.

What happened to that awe? What became of the adrenaline that animated us for service to our Lord? The answer is that we lose sight of life before Christ. The gospel can become encrusted with the dust of self-glory and the corrosion of self-righteousness. We forget the extent of our sin. We forget the degree of our despair. The cost of God's love and the sacrifice of our Savior are reduced to mere facts, dry doctrine. The grace of God becomes ordinary. It becomes something owed us as a right, instead of unexpected and undeserved as it really is.

Our hearts carry in them a chronic misalignment that will not be finally remedied until glory. We have that constant pull to the ditch of self-righteousness. We entertain the notion that God set his love upon us because we were not as bad as the other guy. Even though it's not our official position were we asked, we veer off into the notion that God continues his love of us because we do such a good job at this or that. In other words, we forget the gospel. We lose sight of the glory of grace. We become weary and worn out.

OXYGENATED BY GRACE

Jane was exhausted. Ordinarily a ball of energy, she felt like a wet dishrag. She used up her energy faster than fire burns newspaper. Jane's husband talked her into going to the doctor for a check up. It turned out that she was anemic. Her blood was deficient.

Our blood is amazing. It carries antibodies that fight disease. It transports nutrients throughout our body. If there's a problem with our blood, it shows up in our lives. The same is true spiritually. If our blood is deprived of the oxygen of grace, we grow weary, lethargic and inactive.

Blood carries two kinds of cells, white and red. The white fend off disease. The red ferry nutrients throughout our bodies. In our spiritual blood, the white corpuscles fight off the virus of self-righteousness. The red corpuscles infuse us with the nutrients of God's grace.

How do we go about oxygenating our blood with grace? The primary method of transfusion is repentance. Just as we come to Christ in repentance and faith, so we live in Christ in repentance and faith. One definition of repentance is: 'Repentance unto life is a saving grace, whereby a sinner, out of a true sense of his sin and apprehension of the mercy of God in Christ, does, with grief and hatred of his sin, turn from it unto God, with full purpose and endeavor after new obedience.'[62] Repentance maintains a view of sin and a view of grace. It also assumes a posture in regard to sin, to God, and to Christ.

But why would we want to look at our sin if we have been forgiven our sin? Because sin continues to exert its influence in our lives. We still sin and fail God. Our motives are mixed; our obedience flawed. We are often double-minded. Inclined to treason, we turn our backs on God to pursue sin and return to the feet of the idols of our hearts, serving them with the attitudes and pursuits of our lives. We see our sin that infects us in this life and affects the integrity of lives lived for Christ. We are no longer under its condemnation or mastery, but it's still there.

So we repent of it. We see it as vile. Satan draws our attention to our sin to drive us to despair. God directs our attention to our sin to drive us to Christ and to delight in his grace. The wonder of the gospel that embraces us is that no matter where we look in our lives and find sin, that sin has been accounted for and charged to the account of our Lord Jesus Christ, who paid for it in full. On the day of judgment, there will be no sin tucked away with which Satan will surprise us and find leverage to accuse us. In Christ, our sin is paid for fully and finally.

Reflection on these truths of the gospel oxygenates our blood with the amazing love and unfathomable grace of our God. We become animated for the activity of the kingdom of God in which we grow and serve. If repentance drives us to our knees in contrition, awareness of God's grace drives us to our faces in humility and submission—the posture of a soldier of the cross. It is repentance that will lead us forth, looking to our God for his strength to obey, empty of self, animated by grace.

The prophet Isaiah insisted, 'Here I am, send me.' He took a step forward to volunteer for the mission of God's message of redemption. What prompted his zeal and compelled his service? His eagerness issued from a meeting with God.

> In the year that King Uzziah died, I saw the Lord seated on a throne, high and exalted, and the train of his robe filled the temple. Above him were seraphs, each with six wings: With two wings they covered their faces, with two they covered their feet, and with two they were flying. And they were calling to one another: 'Holy, holy, holy is the Lord Almighty; the whole earth is full of his glory.' At the sound of their voices the doorposts and thresholds shook and the temple was filled with smoke. 'Woe to me!' I cried. 'I am ruined! For I am a man of unclean lips, and I live among a people of unclean lips, and my eyes have seen the King, the Lord Almighty.'
>
> Isa. 6: 1–5

Isaiah is escorted in a vision to the throne room of God himself. The picture is vivid, dynamic. God is depicted as enthroned, sovereign over all. He is God Most High, lofty and exalted. Angelic beings mentioned only in this text render to him the homage due his Name. Prominent in their proclamation and in their posture was the realization of the holiness of God. He is the glorious Lord over all the hosts of creation teeming with angels, stars, creatures, and the rest. The vastness and immanence of his transcendent presence is represented in a theophany of smoke. In other words, the prophet stood face to face with the God of glory. The first words out of Isaiah's mouth are not 'Wow,' but 'Woe.' The curse of the law loomed large before the judgment seat of God. Never was Isaiah more acutely and painfully aware of his sin and the sinfulness he shared with fallen humanity than when he stood before the holiness of God.

What could Isaiah do? Where could he hide? What defense could he make? He stood there exposed and empty of options. In that state, what does the holy God do?

> Then one of the seraphs flew to me with a live coal in his hand, which he had taken with tongs from the altar. With it he touched my mouth and said, 'See, this has touched your lips; your guilt is taken away and your sin atoned for.'
>
> Isa. 6: 6–7

God demonstrated his love and grace in that while Isaiah was still contaminated in sin, his righteousness nothing better than a menstrual rag, God himself acted to deal with that sin. From the altar a live coal is brought to remove Isaiah's guilt and to atone for his sin. That coal anticipates God's only provision for sin's remedy in his Son, taken from the altar of the cross, burning with the wrath of God poured out in the justice of his holiness. The burning coal touches Isaiah's confessing mouth but his mouth is unseared because the coal has taken all the heat of God's wrath.

The question then is put: 'Whom shall I send? Who will go for us?' Still reeling from the majesty of God's mercy and the glory of his grace, Isaiah takes the commission, willingly, eagerly, expectantly. The freshness of such truth in our lives is what will animate and invigorate us in like fashion.

G-RATIONS

How can we be motivated for mission in this way? It all comes down to the nourishment of the means of grace provided for us by God.

Prior to World War II, United States military scientists sought to develop rations of food that soldiers could carry with them to provide the nutrition and energy necessary for the rigors of the battlefield. Evidently, the 'food' was akin to fruitcake, never spoiling, rarely eaten, questionable ingredients, tasty to few. The result was C-rations, food so disgustingly greasy or tasteless that many soldiers preferred hunger. Even improvements in the C-rations by Vietnam could only bring the food up to the level of tolerable. Advances in preservation techniques eventually led to K-rations and then to the MRE, Meal Ready to Eat, offering the likes of pasta primavera.[63]

Recognizing our nutritional needs to sustain us in the battle, our God has provided for us G-rations, means of grace. These supplies are perfectly suited to our taste and perfectly sufficient to our needs. There are three staples to the nutritional supply of G-rations.

Prayer. The primary goal of prayer is drawing near to God in our relationship of redemption. In view here is not petition, not even praise, but intimacy. God is not some sort of abstract concept. He is the God who set his love upon us and sent his Son to redeem us and reconcile us to himself. Prayer is fellowship with the living God in the context of a reconciled relationship. We were his enemies. He had something against us in our rebellion and sinfulness. But now we are his children, adopted in love.

As we linger in communion with this God who rescued us, our hearts are refreshed in his love and renewed in his presence. Our souls are stirred and invigorated with the scent of his grace.

Moses would come down from the mountain with his face aglow with the reflective glory of the God before whose face he stood. From lingering with our majestic God in prayer, we leave with an afterglow of his presence, our hearts burning within us, enflamed with his glory, enamored with his grace.

The key to the nourishment of this means of grace is to linger, to delight in God, to bask in the light of his love. For most of my Christian life, my prayer life mainly consisted in checklist prayer. Certainly, there were prayers of praise and confession and thanksgiving and intercession. But they were like moving from one workstation to another. It was when God taught me to linger that I lifted my eyes from my list to look more fully in his face, to gaze upon his glory. I learned prayer as dialog where I genuinely communed with my Father, responding to what he brought to my mind. I would leave my time of prayer affected, changed, invigorated. Not that I would leave God where I had prayed, but the intensity and intimacy of the focus of faith seemed to give me a transfusion of grace.

The Word. I learned to pray God's Word. God's truth was fuel for my fellowship with him. It's so easy to read God's Word and walk away not remembering what you read. It was as if I took note in his Word of what God was telling me about himself, his glorious character, his remarkable dealings with people, that his revelation evoked response of praise, awe, confession and the like. My mind became the mouth and prayer in meditation and response the digestive juices that assimilated his Word in my heart and sent it coursing in my blood for the invigoration of my being.

God is the author of Scripture. It is his Word, penned by his human instruments. In his teaching and acts, we can learn of him. The Bible is a redemptive document. It is replete with reservoirs of grace from which to drink. We learn of Christ throughout. The triune God is the star of Scripture. In his battle with Goliath, David is not the hero. God is. In her stand with Naomi and her God, Ruth is not the hero. God is. God reveals himself in mercy and grace, goodness and faithfulness, holiness and wisdom. We want to take note, to take to heart and to give glory. And we want to bring to bear in our lives.

We are inclined to grow weary and lose heart. Those are problems of morale. Any portion of God's Word can be honey that brightens our eyes for battle. But look, for example, at God's approach in Isaiah 40: 27–31:

> Why do you say, O Jacob, and complain, O Israel, 'My way is hidden from the Lord; my cause is disregarded by my God'? Do you not know? Have you not heard? The Lord is the everlasting God, the Creator of the ends of the earth. He will not grow tired or weary, and his understanding no one can fathom. He gives strength to the weary and increases the power of the weak. Even youths grow tired and weary, and young men stumble and fall; but those who hope in the Lord will renew their strength. They will soar on wings like eagles; they will run and not grow weary, they will walk and not be faint.

The answer to weariness is not the best the world has to offer. Even youthfulness, so hallowed in our culture and expressive of vigor, fails. The answer is in God and the hope bound up in him, found in Jesus Christ. Prior to this passage God laid out his résumé. He is the Creator and he governs his creation. He is vastly different from us. His ways are inscrutable to us. So we are relegated to a position of trust and dependence. It may seem to us in our finiteness like he doesn't know or doesn't care as the opening complaint lays it out. But he is God. Our hope is in him. Renewal of strength and perseverance in mission will come from practical, personal knowledge of him.

Scripture is full of such sustenance, in implicit and explicit ways. The same God is at work in our day. The same God is your Father and at work in your life, honing you as his instrument. God wants us to grow to know him, to grow in the grace and knowledge of his Son. That means grow away from self-effort that will only disappoint, and self-will that will only frustrate, to trust and depend more upon him. And it means that he wants us to know more of the joy inherent in a personal relationship with him.

How many soldiers have access to the tent of the commanding officer on the field of battle? Not too many. In God's army, we all do and at all times.

Community. In God's infinite wisdom, he has enfolded each of us into a fighting unit. We share in mission. Every one of us, no matter how mature in the faith, no matter how experienced in the trenches of life, needs other believers. When I was in elementary school, teachers seemed extra-terrestrial to me. I couldn't fathom them having lives like I did. Sometimes pastors are put on that sort of pedestal. People think of them without temptations, knowing all the answers. But pastors are subject to the same spiritual struggles as every believer. As servants on the front lines, they can be filled with discouragement, prime targets for the enemy's efforts. I belong to a ministerial fellowship. Area pastors meet monthly to share our lives and burdens with one another. It seemed for a while there that each pastor took turns under the weight of severe personal and pastoral burdens, while the rest rallied around him.

That is a picture of community, of camaraderie in conflict. We desperately need one another. We place ourselves in great danger when we try to go it alone. All of us need to feel the weight of God's counsel, 'Let anyone who thinks he stands, take heed, lest he fall' (1 Cor. 10: 12 (ESV)). Listen again to the counsel of God in the book of Hebrews. 'See to it, brothers, that none of you has a sinful, unbelieving heart that turns away from the living God. But encourage one another daily, as long as it is called Today, so that none of you may be hardened by sin's deceitfulness' (Heb. 3: 12–13).

We need one another in light of the opposition of the world, the flesh and the devil we encounter in this fallen world. No one is sufficient to the task. We are all prone to wander, prone to act as deserters. We need the rebuke, exhortation, admonishment, encouragement, love and all the rest of 'one another' passages that describe the body life of the community of the kingdom.

How do we carry out this involvement in the lives of our fellow soldiers? Again, Hebrews gives us guidance: 'Let us consider how we may spur one another on toward love and good deeds. Let us not give up meeting together, as some are in the habit of doing, but let us encourage one another—and all the more as you see the Day approaching' (Heb. 10: 24–5).

We need to be with one another and not just socially, but ministerially in keeping with a common Father, a common Lord, and a common Spirit. The sense of the passage is that we are to give proactive thought to the needs of our brethren. We are to spur them on toward love and good deeds. The idea behind 'spur' is to nag, to irritate, like the irritation in an oyster's mouth produces a pearl. 'Let us not give up meeting together' is not a separate admonition, but a means. We spur by not forsaking community, but instead partaking of it. Community involves two or more, gathering for a purpose, under the colors of the kingdom, as companions and colleagues in Christ.

Worship. Perhaps the ultimate means of grace is worship. It is for worship that our God sought and saved us, to be worshippers in Spirit and truth. Worship gives us a taste of heaven and a renewed focus on God transcendent in glory, present in grace. When evangelism and discipleship have ceased, worship will continue.

When I was in college, my wife and I sold cookware. We would hold parties where people would invite their friends. All would be treated to an excellent meal prepared by yours truly and offered the opportunity to go and cook likewise with their own set of pots and pans.

Once a month the sales force would meet together to compare notes and celebrate results. In that meeting we were all on the same page, working for the same ends, working with the same means. There was a real sense of community. The sales manager would motivate us with a pep talk. We'd report on our activity. Awards would be given. Incentives held out.

At the beginning of the meeting we would all turn to our folders and together belt out songs in honor of our cookware and its merits. I could still give you the words of some of the songs. But I'd rather call you to a more worthy recipient of honor and a more noble activity of celebration. Worship celebrates the God of creation and redemption. Typical of victory under the mighty work of our King are songs. Look in Exodus 15 on the heels of the crossing of the Red Sea in the exodus from Egypt. God has fought for his people, delivering them from their enemies. Look also in Revelation 15: 3–4:

> [They] sang the song of Moses the servant of God and the song of the Lamb: 'Great and marvelous are your deeds, Lord God Almighty. Just and true are your ways, King of the ages. Who will not fear you, O Lord, and bring glory to your name? For you alone are holy. All nations will come and worship before you, for your righteous acts have been revealed.'

Worship centers on God and celebrates his victory. We belt out songs of deliverance with a common focus and a kindred spirit. This is battle song. Our hymnals are filled with such songs that exalt the name of our God, extol his mercies in salvation and engage his people in mission.

Just like with the cookware festivities, these songs can be boosters to morale. We recite God's praise. We recount his mighty works. We restore our wayward focus to the encouragement of his truth. Let me give you one of my favorite songs as an example of a battle song that can only boost morale in the face of spiritual opposition.

> Before the throne of God above
> I have a strong, a perfect plea,
> A great High Priest whose name is Love,
> Who ever lives and pleads for me.
> My name is graven on his hands,
> My name is written on his heart;
> I know that while in heaven he stands
> No tongue can bid me thence depart,
> No tongue can bid me thence depart.

When Satan tempts me to despair,
And tells me of the guilt within,
Upward I look and see him there
Who made an end to all my sin.
Because the sinless Savior died,
My sinful soul is counted free;
For God the just is satisfied
To look on him and pardon me,
To look on him and pardon me.

Behold him there! The risen Lamb,
My perfect, spotless righteousness;
The great unchangeable I AM,
The King of glory and of grace!
One with him I cannot die,
My soul is purchased with his blood;
My life is hid with Christ on high,
With Christ, my Savior and my God,
With Christ, my Savior and my God.[64]

No doubt you have your own songs that get your heart racing and your spiritual adrenaline pumping. Think of these songs as battle songs. Sing them to the glory of your King as you head out to engage in the skirmishes for the honor of his name and the sake of his kingdom.

FUELED BY FAITH, FORTIFIED BY TRUTH

The victory is won. The prize is ours. How mightily that affects our morale and motivates us in perseverance. The Apostle Paul expresses some of the frustrations in the mission given to us by our Lord: 'The god of this age has blinded the minds of unbelievers, so that they cannot see the light of the gospel of the glory of Christ, who is the image of God.' Yet that spiritual worldview is swallowed up in three things Paul expresses that bathe his weary soul in the refreshing springs of encouragement.[65]

Therefore we do not lose heart. Though outwardly we are wasting away, yet inwardly we are being renewed day by day. For our light and momentary troubles are achieving for us an eternal glory that far outweighs them all. So we fix our eyes not on what is seen, but on what is unseen. For what is seen is temporary, but what is unseen is eternal.

In the face of spiritual opposition and the frustration of sight that sees people rejecting the gospel, Paul finds: 1) the mercy of God in his own life, 2) the certain purpose of God that carries his power for his success, and 3) the smallness and temporary nature of the sufferings in light of the eternal glory to come.

We struggle against a spiritual foe, but we fight with weapons of a different kingdom, not deception or distortion. The God who created all that is, continues his new creating work in the hearts of his redeemed. Our struggle and pain are real. But though we are down, we are never out. His mission will not be frustrated. His purposes in salvation will be realized. For the joy set before us, we endure the light and momentary affliction, knowing that our present sufferings are not worth comparing to the glory in store for us.

And so our spirits are buoyed. Our morale is lifted. We are motivated for mission, even with the struggle against the evil forces of this dark world. Against Satan's tactic of accusation, we preach the gospel to ourselves, reminding ourselves of the grace in Jesus Christ that rose to bring the light of the new creation to dawn in our dark world and that will erupt in the brilliance of heavenly glory. There we will appear before God, without fault and with great joy, all because of the gospel that brings us forgiveness of sin and a perfect righteousness before a holy God. Our enemy's accusations are groundless in Christ.

Against Satan's tactic of temptation, grace leads us to walk by the Spirit so that we will not carry out the deeds of the flesh. The Spirit who turned our hearts from idols to know and serve the true and living God continues at work in our lives causing us to die more and more to sin and live more and more to righteousness. As children of the living God, we enjoy the full rights of sons and daughters. Our Father in heaven is disciplining us, directing and protecting us, working all things for our good that we might grow into the image of his Son in knowledge, righteousness, and holiness.

Against Satan's tactic of deception, God gives us his Word and Spirit that we might discern between truth and error. By the standard of that Word, which is truth, the devil's lies are exposed. Instead of being dispirited in the struggle and frustrations of the fight, we are filled with the Spirit, bringing the Word of God to dwell in us richly. We have solid ground on which to stand and firm footing from which to fight.

And so readied for battle by the energy of his grace, we move out in the valor of humility (Isa. 57: 15) that knows, trusts and depends on the God who is at work in and through us for his mission of salvation.

Epilogue

Barracks to Battlefield

The walls, thick and high, foreboding and impenetrable, rose before God's people camped outside the city of Jericho. The gates were closed and barred. Guards signaled an ever-watchful eye against intruders. The people of God held God's orders to lay siege to the city. They also held God's promises of a land. How could it possibly be accomplished?

The word of God came to them, 'See, I have delivered Jericho into your hands, along with its king and its fighting men' (Josh. 6: 2). How can that be? The city was still tightly secured and the people secure in their idolatry and fortifications. Then God lays out his battle plan, his way of attack, his way for victory.

The people of God gather in formation that defies conventional wisdom. They circle the city once in silence and take a seat. The next day they do the same. For six days the strange ritual is repeated. The seventh, they march around the city seven times. All the while, the priests lead the way, blowing rams' horns. With them is the Ark of the Covenant, the symbol of God's promised presence with them in mercy and grace. God is for them, not against them.

A long blast of the rams' horns interrupts the ritual. The war cry thunders from God's army. Immediately, according to plan, the wall collapses allowing entry and ability to carry out God's command. The entire city is given over to the Lord of lords and the King of kings. All feel the wrath of his justice and the penalty of destruction, except a prostitute and her family.

Rahab stands out as a trophy of God's grace. She deserved to die with the rest, but God set his love upon her. She would be numbered among the community of God's people.

The gates of hell loom large before us. The dark dominion looks ominous and menacing, impregnable, undesirable. Our orders are to lay siege to it, equipped with strategies that confound worldly wisdom, armed with weapons capable of bringing down strongholds. With our orders, we carry the word of our King that he has already delivered the kingdom into our hands.

With him going on before us, with him at our side, with him as our rear guard, we march on in confidence that the dark kingdom will not prevail. We enter the fallen kingdom at our doorstep in the name of our King, through whom he seeks to save the lost, those Rahabs of his electing love.

As you travel through the dark kingdom proclaiming the message of freedom to its subjects, beseeching your God and Father for his success, something catches your eye. It's a ledger. The cover indicates that it is a ledger of the subjects of the kingdom you have infiltrated at the command of your Lord. Beside each name stands a litany of offenses that ensure their condemnation. You scan down the list. You strain to see the faint impression of something that has been erased. You can barely make it out, but you squint to realize that name is yours. You follow it across the page to where the charges by which you would be accused are posted. Every one of them is gone. Over them is the notation: 'Paid in full. Citizenship transferred.'

> And tho' this world, with devils filled,
> Should threaten to undo us,
> We will not fear, for God hath willed
> his truth to triumph thro' us;
> The prince of Darkness grim,
> We tremble not for him;
> his rage we can endure,
> For lo, his doom is sure,
> One little word shall fell him.
>
> That word above all earthly pow'rs,
> No thanks to them, abideth;
> The Spirit and the gifts are ours
> Thro' him who with us sideth:
> Let goods and kindred go,

This mortal life also;
The body they may kill:
God's truth abideth still,
his kingdom is forever.

Soldiers of the cross, have you lost sight of the colors of the kingdom? Have you laid down the cause of him who laid down his life for you? Have you taken up weapons that are foreign to God's arsenal? Your Lord calls to you from the field of battle, saying 'About face. Present arms. Forward march.' He is with you to the very end of the age—he assures you.

AUTHOR'S NOTE

The perspective and principles outlined in this book are employed in *Community Houses of Prayer Ministry Manual* (Deo Volente, 2002) by the author. Community Houses of Prayer (CHOP) involves and trains Christ's disciples in strategic prayer outreach over a 12 to 16 week period. Participants commit themselves to weekly group meetings and daily private prayer, resulting in an increased awareness of their people environments, a heightened sense of personal involvement as witnesses, and a greater level of activity in verbal witness.

The ministry weaves together four areas for the work of outreach: lifestyle evangelism, strategic prayer, personal spiritual renewal and spiritual warfare. CHOP brings prayer to the foundation and heart of any training program for outreach. Although designed for groups of two or more, the CHOP Ministry Manual can be used on an individual basis as well.

CHOP is supported by a website that gives further information on the ministry and direction for implementation: www.CHOPministry.net. Manuals can be obtained through the website.

NOTES

1 Although there is a great deal of common ground in warfare evangelism among the writers of this popularized approach, there are differences. The description here is not simply a straw man but enfolds elements that are representative of the body of literature as a whole.

2 C. Peter Wagner. *Warfare Prayer: How to Seek God's Power and Protection in the Battle to Build his Kingdom.* Ventura, CA: Gospel Light Publications, 1992, 63.

3 Daniel 10 is appealed to in support of territoriality.

4 Kjell Sjöberg, 'Spiritual Mapping for Prophetic Prayer Actions,' in C. Peter Wagner, ed., *Breaking Strongholds in Your City: How to Use Spiritual Mapping to Make Your Prayers More Strategic, Effective and Targeted.* Ventura, CA: Gospel Light Publications, 1993, 114.

5 To say that I feel 'blue' does not mean that I am sad, off-color (i.e., blue movies), and turquoise all at the same time. The context shapes the meaning.

6 C. Peter Wagner, ed. *Engaging the Enemy: How to Fight and Defeat Territorial Spirits.* Ventura, CA: Gospel of Light Publications, 1995, 16.

7 *Breaking Strongholds*, 116.

8 Propositional revelation means that God communicates in his written Word in words and sentences and paragraphs which themselves are understood from the larger context in which they are found.

9 We'll return to this text later to see the practical direction it gives us for personal, everyday witness to Jesus Christ.

10 We will explore this authority in chapter 3 when we look at the redemptive kingdom of God.

11 In chapter 4, we'll study in greater detail the work of Christ as our basis and confidence for the mission he calls us to carry out.

12 The United Service Organization's mission is to provide morale, welfare and recreation-type services to United States men and women in uniform.

13 This quote and the quotes from Piper and Bunyon were part of an 'Armorbearer's Intercessory Ministry School of Prayer.'

14 Adapted from Stanley D. Gale, *Community Houses of Prayer Ministry Manual: Reaching People for Christ through Strategic Prayer*. Los Alamos, NM: Deo Volente Publications, 2002, 189.

15 Matthew 4:12-17. We'll have more to say about the kingdom of God as the dominion of life in the next chapter.

16 Biblical hope is not a 'hope so' hope, but a 'know so' hope. It is an assured conviction, a vibrant certainty, a confident expectation grounded on the triune God of salvation. This is why the hope Paul offers to the Thessalonians is a source of encouragement and comfort in 1 Thessalonians 4: 13–18. Its source and ground is given in 1 Thessalonians 5: 9–10: 'For God did not appoint us to suffer wrath but to receive salvation through our Lord Jesus Christ. He died for us so that, whether we are awake or asleep, we may live together with him.' Satan, too, offers a hope but that hope is empty, nothing but a counterfeit and a lie. A major purpose of the Book of Revelation is to expose the false hope found in Satan and to show its destination of destruction, while verifying the hope in Christ and its outcome, with the encouragement to persevere in faith.

17 For more thorough study, see Herman Ridderbos, *The Coming of the Kingdom*, trans. H. De Jongste, ed. Raymond O. Zorn, Phillipsburg, NJ: P&R, 1962, or T. Moore, *I Will Be Your God*, Phillipsburg, NJ: P&R, 2003.

18 The kingdom of God and the kingdom of heaven refer to the same kingdom. A comparison of the gospel accounts shows the kingdom of heaven and the kingdom of God being described in the same way. Matthew uses the expression kingdom of 'heaven' rather than kingdom of 'God' in deference to his Jewish target audience, who would be offended by the use of the name of God. This is a good reminder to us to try to communicate the truth of God in terms that avoid offense. We want the stumbling block to be the cross, not our words.

19 Compare Daniel 7: 13–14 with Revelation 5: 9–14. What Daniel was told to seal up (Dan. 12: 9), John was told to not to seal up (Rev. 22: 10). What Daniel was told was for a later time, John was told the time was at hand. Many of the visions of the book of Revelation use the same language as Daniel to draw his prophecy to John's day in terms of the start of fulfillment. The 'last days' looks to the coming of him who is the subject of God's prophetic word and deed. All of us who live on this side of the cross live in the 'last days' (see Heb. 1: 1–3). The outpouring

of the Spirit that Joel attributes to the last days, Peter explained as happening at Pentecost (see Acts 2: 14–21).

20 Not 'as if' slain as most translations render, but one who lives as one who was slain. Jesus is not merely the resurrected one. He is the resurrected one as the crucified one. His resurrection provides commentary and validation of the substitutionary, sacrificial work on the cross.

21 That's why the idea of embracing Christ as Savior but not as Lord is foreign to Scripture. To embrace a Christ who is not Lord is to embrace a different Christ. The Savior is the King, before whom the knee of faith is to bow.

22 Matthew 11: 3–12. John the Baptist represented the old covenant period of prophetic anticipation. The 'Law and the Prophets' is shorthand for the Old Testament scriptures. It is in that sense that the least in the kingdom of heaven is greater than John, because they live in the day of prophetic fulfillment.

23 The sense of Colossians 1: 24. It is not as though Christ's work of salvation were insufficient. The lack is not in Christ, but in that which remains of suffering for the cause of the gospel in the work of the Kingdom as we continue our labor in this present, evil age.

24 Often when people seek the will of God (e.g. for a spouse or job), they press in to know God's plan, those things he has said are secret. God holds us responsible for what he has told us in the revelation of his holy Word, which he says is sufficient for all of life and godliness, thoroughly equipping us to please him in decisions. Our goal in seeking God's will is the implementation of his revealed will, asking him for wisdom in its application and trust in his providential provision.

25 Some examples of God's sovereignty over Satan can be seen in the parallel involvement of both, but for cross-purposes. The Greek word for 'tempt' also means to 'try.' James 1: 13–15 uses this word and directs us to see the same circumstance given by God as a trial for the strengthening of our faith, yet used by Satan to tempt us and try to distance us from God. A comparison of 2 Samuel 24: 1 and 2 Chronicles 21: 1 shows the same event (i.e., the inciting of David to take a prideful census) ascribed to different subjects, the former to God and the latter Satan. In this God is the sovereign, Satan the tool. In the parable of the soils in Mark 4, the stealing of the seed of the gospel is ascribed to Satan in v. 15, yet we are reminded of the sovereign operation and saving purpose of God in v. 12.

26 Paul speaks in 1 Timothy 4: 1f. of deceiving spirits and the teaching of demons as coming through hypocritical liars.

27 Some of these observations are my own. Most, however, are derived from two excellent works on Revelation, which I heartily commend for further study. Poythress looks mainly at the forest while Beale ventures in to look at the trees. The references are: Verne S. Poythress, *The Returning King: A Guide to the Book of Revelation*, P & R Publishing, Phillipsburg, NJ, 2000. G. K. Beale. *The Book of Revelation: A Commentary on the Greek Text*, Wm. B. Eerdmans Publishing Company, Grand Rapids, 1999.

[28] See the counsel of God along these lines in Isaiah 55: 1–3. Psalm 1 also gives us this dividing line of truth and error, blessing or curse, as does the contrast in the book of Proverbs between wisdom that begins with the fear of the Lord and foolishness that is the way that seems right to a man. Understanding this tactic sets the stage for the spiritual weapon God gives us to counter Satan's efforts (see 2 Tim. 3: 16–4: 5, Col. 2: 6–8). The shepherding activity of Christ and the shepherding function of the church can be seen mainly in guiding and guarding, directing in truth and protecting from error (see Acts 20: 27–31).

[29] Wagner, *Warfare Prayer*, 63.

[30] Dr. Tremper Longman has written extensively on this topic and provides an overarching perspective on redemptive history from the vantage point of the Divine Warrior.

[31] *The Heidelberg Catechism*, Ecumenical Creeds & Reformed Confessions, Board of Publications of the CRC, Grand Rapids, 1979, 7.

[32] Edmund P. Clowney, *Living in Christ's Church* (Philadelphia, PA: Great Commission Publications, 1986), 71f.

[33] Some will hold up the rebuking of Satan by Michael in Jude 9 as giving license to address Satan. But Michael is an angelic being and carries out the capacity of angels as instruments of God, and is not held up as a model for our dealing with the devil.

[34] *The Westminster Standards* (Philadelphia, PA: Great Commission Publications, n.d.), 74.

[35] I believe this schematic was developed by Dr. Jay Adams.

[36] This whole discussion covers Colossians 1–2.

[37] Packer, *Evangelism and the Sovereignty of God*, 122.

[38] See Galatians 3: 16 as an example of an argument based on an appeal to the singular and plural of a word.

[39] See Numbers 23: 19; 1 Samuel 15: 29; Psalm 110: 4.

[40] I was first introduced to the gist of this thought in a training video for 'Neighborhood Houses of Prayer' by John DeVries and Alvin Vander Griend.

[41] Miller, *Evangelism & Your Church*, 38.

[42] Sinclair B. Ferguson and David F. Wright, eds., *New Dictionary of Theology* (Downers Grove, IL: InterVarsity Press, 1988), s.v. 'Prayer, theology of,' by Edmund P. Clowney.

[43] Packer, 124.

[44] see Isaiah 55: 10–11; 1 Peter 1: 23–5.

[45] see Luke 24:44–7.

[46] cf. John 15: 16; 16: 24.

[47] see Ephesians 2: 18; 1 Timothy 2:5; Hebrews 10: 19–22.

[48] Notice the various elements in view in James 1: 2-10.

[49] See the whole thrust and flow of Romans 8, especially v. 11, 26f.

[50] Matthew Henry, *A Method for Prayer* (London: W. Baynes, 1819; reprint, Greenville, SC: A Press, 1988), 191f.

[51] *Westminster Shorter Catechism*, 102.

[52] Water baptism is the sign of initiation into God's covenant community, an outward testimony to his objective promises to faith. The church is the incubator by which faith is nourished through the light of truth.

53 I am indebted to T. M. Moore for the concept and model of life-sphere mapping.

54 Of course, our suffering is not redemptive as was Christ's, but it is our lot in this life and our pattern for living. There is a vast chasm of difference between verses 21 and 24 of 1 Peter 2.

55 Nehemiah 4:9. The book of Nehemiah is a powerful book showcasing prayer, all sorts of prayer, against spiritual opposition for the work of the kingdom.

56 I am indebted to Rev. Stephen Smallman for conveying this metaphor.

57 I heard this at a seminar from Dr. Harry Reeder, although I don't know if it was original with him.

58 That's the sense of John's use of the word 'world,' saying that Christ gave his life not only for ethnic Jews but for non-Jews as well. Paul says that the gospel is the power of God unto salvation for all who will believe, both for Jew and Gentile. The book of Revelation depicts an ethnically diverse people gathered around the throne as the elect of God. The hallmark of the believer is not ethnicity but faith. The promises belong to believing Jews and believing Gentiles. Believers are the true seed of Abraham, the father of believers, and heirs of the promise. There will not be two wings in heaven, one for Jew and one for Gentile. There is but one promise, one people, one salvation.

59 This balance of perspective and flow is seen in Titus 3:3-8 and Titus 2:11-14. Grace teaches us in keeping with the new creation we are as part of the kingdom of God. Of course, grace will never teach us self-effort but always point us to Christ for reliance upon him apart from whom we can no nothing, but in whom we can do all things.

60 When John in his first epistle issues the promise of forgiveness of sin if we will confess our sin (1 John 1:9), he goes on to expose the ground of that forgiveness in the next chapter (an unfortunate chapter break). 'My dear children, I write this to you so that you will not sin. But if anybody does sin, we have one who speaks to the Father in our defense—Jesus Christ, the Righteous One. He is the atoning sacrifice for our sins, and not only for ours but also for the sins of the whole world.' (1 John 2:1-2) It is Christ in his priestly work as priest and sacrifice and his enduring intercession and advocacy that ensures forgiveness, the only basis for the whole world, i.e., Jew and Gentile alike.

61 The New Testament portrays Jesus as the bread and water of eternal life. See John 4:7ff., 6:32ff., 7:38f.

62 *Westminster Shorter Catechism*, question 47.

63 Steve Clark, 'A Moment in Time,' 2002. Resource: Moran, Barbara. 'Dinner goes to War,' *American Heritage of Invention and Technology* (Summer 1998): 10-19. Taken from World Wide Web.

64 'Before the Throne of God Above' by Charitie Lees Bancroft, 1893.

65 These passages come from 2 Corinthians 4, verses 1, 3 and 16-18. The whole of the chapter displays the victory and power in which we deal with the spiritual struggle of evangelism that leads to great encouragement and high morale.